Frommer's

Chicago
day BY day®

4th Edition

by Kate Silver

FrommerMedia LLC

Contents

Published by:

Frommer Media LLC

Frommer's is a trademark or registered trademark of Arthur Frommer.

ISBN: 978-1-628-87440-2 (paper); 978-1-628-87441-9 (ebk)

Editorial Director: Pauline Frommer
Editor: Lorraine Festa
Production Editor: Erin Geile
Photo Editor: Meghan Lamb
Assistant Photo Editor: Phil Vinke
Cartographer: Liz Puhl
Indexer: Maro Riofrancos

Front cover photos, left to right: Captain America competes in the Chicago Marathon (John Gress Media Inc. / Shutterstock.com); Cloud Gate, also called "the bean," in Millennium Park (Diego Mariottini / Shutterstock.com); Chicago at dawn (Rudy Balasko).

Back cover photo: Chicago skyline (Felix Mizioznikov).

For information on our other products and services, please go to Frommers.com.

Frommer's also publishes its books in a variety of electronic formats. Some content that appears in print may not be available in electronic formats.

5   4   3   2   1

About This Guide

Organizing your time. That's what this guide is all about.

Other guides give you long lists of things to see and do and then expect you to fit the pieces together. The Day by Day guides are different. These guides tell you the best of everything, and then they show you how to see it *in the smartest, most time-efficient way*. Our authors have designed detailed itineraries organized by time, neighborhood, or special interest. And each tour comes with a bulleted map that takes you from stop to stop.

Hoping to see the magnificent architecture of the Windy City, or to tour the highlights of the Museum of Science and Industry or the Art Institute of Chicago? Planning a walk through the Gold Coast, or a whirlwind tour of the very best that Chicago has to offer? Whatever your interest or schedule, the Day by Days give you the smartest routes to follow. Not only do we take you to the top attractions, hotels, and restaurants, but we also help you access those special moments that locals get to experience—those "finds" that turn tourists into travelers.

The Day by Days are also your top choice if you're looking for one complete guide for all your travel needs. The best hotels and restaurants for every budget, the greatest shopping values, the wildest nightlife—it's all here.

Why should you trust our judgment? Because our authors personally visit each place they write about. They're an independent lot who say what they think and would never include places they wouldn't recommend to their best friends. They're also open to suggestions from readers. If you'd like to contact them, please send your comments our way at feedback@frommers.com, and we'll pass them on.

Enjoy your Day by Day guide—the most helpful travel companion you can buy. And have the trip of a lifetime.

About the Author

As a travel journalist, **Kate Silver** is always on the lookout for her next adventure. She's waded in cranberry marshes in Wisconsin; jumped from rocky cliffs in Wales; toured Holland on two wheels; and walked a very slow and meandering DIY marathon through Chicago, where she lives with her husband, Neil, and cat, Lemmy. Silver also wrote *Frommer's EasyGuide to Chicago.*

An Additional Note

Please be advised that travel information is subject to change at any time—and this is especially true of prices. We therefore suggest that you write or call ahead for confirmation when making your travel plans. The authors, editors, and publisher cannot be held responsible for the experiences of readers while traveling. Your safety is important to us, however, so we encourage you to stay alert and be aware of your surroundings.

Star Ratings, Icons & Abbreviations

Every hotel, restaurant, and attraction listing in this guide has been ranked for quality, value, service, amenities, and special features using a **star-rating system.** Hotels, restaurants, attractions, shopping, and nightlife are rated on a scale of zero stars (recommended) to three stars (exceptional). In addition to the star-rating system, we also use a **kids icon** to point out the best bets for families. Within each tour, we recommend cafes, bars, or restaurants where you can take a break. Each of these stops appears in a shaded box marked with a coffee-cup-shaped bullet 🍵.

Travel Resources at Frommers.com

Frommer's travel resources don't end with this guide. Frommer's website, **www.frommers.com**, has travel information on more than 4,000 destinations. We update features regularly, giving you access to the most current trip-planning information and the best airfare, lodging, and car-rental bargains. You can also listen to podcasts, connect with other Frommers.com members through our active-reader forums, share your travel photos, read blogs from guidebook editors and fellow travelers, and much more.

A Note on Prices

In the "Take a Break" and "Best Bets" sections of this book, we have used a system of dollar signs to show a range of costs for 1 night in a hotel (the price of a double-occupancy room) or the cost of an entree at a restaurant. Use the following table to decipher the dollar signs:

Cost	Hotels	Restaurants
$	under $130	under $15
$$	$130–$200	$15–$30
$$$	$200–$300	$30–$40
$$$$	$300–$395	$40–$50
$$$$$	over $395	over $50

How to Contact Us

In researching this book, we discovered many wonderful places—hotels, restaurants, shops, and more. We're sure you'll find others. Please tell us about them, so we can share the information with your fellow travelers in upcoming editions. If you were disappointed with a recommendation, we'd love to know that, too. Please write to: Support@FrommerMedia.com.

16 Favorite
Moments

16 Favorite **Moments**

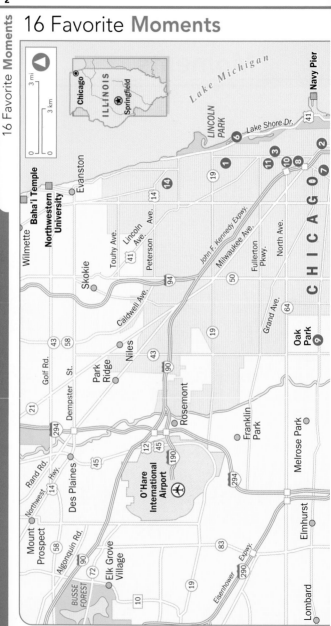

Lake Michigan

Navy Pier

Chicago
ILLINOIS
Springfield

LINCOLN
PARK

Lake Shore Dr.

CHICAGO

Baha'i Temple

Northwestern
University

Wilmette

Evanston

Skokie

Touhy Ave.

Lincoln Ave.

Peterson Ave.

John F. Kennedy Expwy.

Milwaukee Ave.

Fullerton Pkwy.

North Ave.

Grand Ave.

Oak
Park

Caldwell Ave.

Niles

Park Ridge

Golf Rd.

Dempster St.

Rosemont

Franklin
Park

Melrose Park

Mount Prospect

Rand Rd.

Northwest Hwy.

Des Plaines

O'Hare
International
Airport

Elk Grove
Village

Algonquin Rd.

BUSSE
FOREST

Elmhurst

Eisenhower Expwy.

Lombard

Previous page: The Chicago River and skyline.

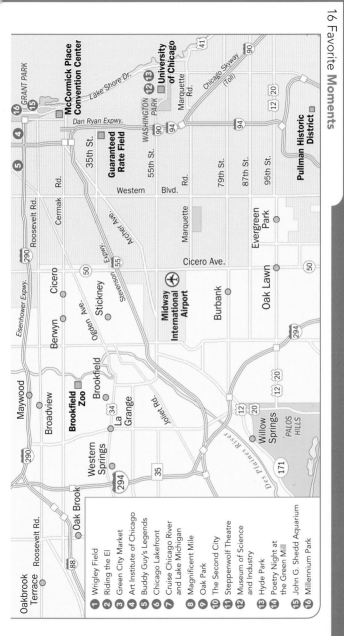

1 Wrigley Field
2 Riding the El
3 Green City Market
4 Art Institute of Chicago
5 Buddy Guy's Legends
6 Chicago Lakefront
7 Cruise Chicago River
and Lake Michigan
8 Magnificent Mile
9 Oak Park
10 The Second City
11 Steppenwolf Theatre
12 Museum of Science
and Industry
13 Hyde Park
14 Poetry Night at
the Green Mill
15 John G. Shedd Aquarium
16 Millennium Park

Frank Sinatra once proclaimed Chicago his kind of town. It will be yours as well. Awaiting you in the Windy City are new discoveries and favorite places you'll want to visit again and again, from riding the "El" to singing along with the crowds at Wrigley Field's seventh-inning stretch. In this section, I describe some quintessential Chicago experiences that just might become part of your family's vacation lore. They'll make Chicago your kind of town, too.

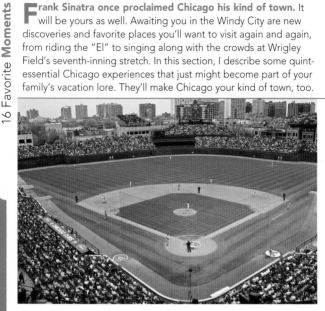

Chicago's beloved Wrigley Field.

❶ **Take yourself out to the ballgame at Wrigley Field.** Our historic ballpark approaches perfection with its ivy-covered walls, hand-operated scoreboard, and view of the jade-colored, glassy waters of Lake Michigan from the upper decks. The Cubs play night games, but Wrigley is best experienced on a summer afternoon, when you'll be surrounded by plenty of natives playing hooky from work—a Windy City tradition. *See p 26,* ❼.

❷ **Take a ride on our famous "El" train.** Our elevated train is not only the least expensive ride in town, but it's also a great way to get a birds-eye glimpse of Chicago. For the

Catch the El train for great city views.

The Art Institute of Chicago has one of the world's most notable collections of Impressionist and Post-Impressionist art.

best views, board the Brown Line at Washington/Wells, and ride it around the Loop through the canyons of office buildings (you'll be close enough to peer into some of them). It'll take less than 30 minutes of your touring time, it's inexpensive, and kids love it. *See p 11,* ❶.

❸ **Sample the Midwest's best farm-grown foods at the Chicago Green City Market.** Founded by prominent Chicago chefs, this

The Lincoln Park Zoo.

Lincoln Park market allows regular folks to buy the same organic and sustainably grown foods that will appear on plates in the best restaurants in town. There's music, live cooking demonstrations, and a chance to sample French-style crepes made to order with market ingredients. *See p 24,* ❷.

❹ **Marvel at the intricate pointillism of Seurat's *A Sunday on the Island of La Grande Jatte*** and other masterpieces at Chicago's grande dame of museums, the Art Institute. You'll find Seurat's work in the renowned Impressionist collection, which also features one of the world's largest displays of Monet paintings. Your second stop should be the collections of European and American contemporary art, home to works by Picasso, Matisse, Dalí, Pollock, and Warhol. *See p 14,* ❾.

❺ **Get the blues at one of the city's many great music joints.** At B.L.U.E.S., stellar female performers are the draw. At Buddy Guy's Legends, the Louisiana-style soul food and barbecue makes it worth arriving early and settling in for the evening. If you visit Chicago in January, don't miss out on a performance by

Chicago River cruise.

the legendary guitarist who owns this place; but book ahead—the shows sell out well in advance. *See p 116.*

6 Stroll the lakefront and ogle our inland ocean. Chicago's forefathers had the foresight to keep the city's 26 miles of lakefront free and clear of development. As a result, you can bike, rollerblade, jog, or walk along Lake Michigan and enjoy a chain of parks that includes Chicago's signature Lincoln Park and Grant Park. *See p 86.*

7 Admire our renowned skyline on a boat cruise along the Chicago River and Lake Michigan. The best way to get a perspective on Chicago's history and learn about the dramatic buildings that form the city's skyline is to take an architecture boat tour. Some of the best are run by the Chicago Architecture Center, covering some 40 buildings with entertaining and enlightening narrative from an army of well-versed docents. *See p 17, ❶.*

8 Check out the wares on the Magnificent Mile. Shopping is the thing on Michigan Avenue, and you can easily while away a day browsing and buying your way up the avenue. Other areas of the city offer chic boutiques and hard-to-find antiques and vintage clothing, but for a huge selection offering something for everyone, the Magnificent Mile is your best bet. *See p 71.*

9 Explore the outdoor architectural museum that is Oak Park. If you have a passion for architecture or literature, you'll find plenty of sights to see in this suburb on the western border of the city. Ernest Hemingway was born here, and his home offers insight into Oak Park's most famous native son. But most visitors are drawn to the Frank Lloyd Wright Home & Studio, and to the homes lining Oak Park's well-maintained streets that the famous architect designed. *See p 147.*

10 Share a laugh at The Second City. Training ground for the country's best comedians, The Second City excels in long-form improvisational comedy. Ensembles change frequently, so check the local newspapers for reviews of the latest offering. And, if you like your history mixed with humor (and who doesn't?), don't miss The Second City's Neighborhood Tour of Old

Shopping along the Magnificent Mile.

A Frank Lloyd Wright–designed house in Oak Park.

Town, which gives you a glimpse into the neighborhood's architecture and history, plus some insider info on Second City alumni and their legendary hangouts and real-life antics. *See p 126.*

⓫ **Grip the edge of your seat at a Chicago theater company performance.** Whether you choose a production by the Steppenwolf Theatre

Goodman Theatre.

Company, Goodman Theatre, or a smaller venue such as Victory Gardens Theater, don't miss a chance to see what might be the next big hit to move to Broadway. *See p 128.*

⓬ **Climb aboard a captured U-boat at the Museum of Science and Industry,** the granddaddy of interactive museums. The U-505, captured in 1944 and brought to the museum 10 years later, is only one of 2,000 exhibits. It's easy to spend a day here, especially if you take in an Omnimax movie, located in the Henry Crown Space Center, where you can also hop aboard a simulator to experience a space shuttle flight. *See p 46.*

⓭ **Explore Hyde Park's Gothic quadrangle and magnificent mansions.** Home to the University of Chicago, with its 90-plus Nobel laureates, intimidating buildings with Gothic spires, and hallowed academic halls, Hyde Park is sure to impress. Off campus, Hyde Park is an approachable, cosmopolitan neighborhood that's home to one of Frank Lloyd Wright's finest works, the Robie House. *See p 64.*

Baby belugas at John G. Shedd Aquarium.

⑭ Take in jazz or a poetry slam at Green Mill. This popular watering hole of the 1920s and 1930s still retains its speakeasy vibe. On Sunday night, Green Mill hosts the Uptown Poetry Slam, where poets vie for the open mic. Most nights, though, jazz is on the menu from about 9pm 'til the wee hours, so sink into a plush velvet booth and enjoy. *See p 130.*

⑮ Get snout-to-nose with the baby belugas at John G. Shedd Aquarium. The world's largest indoor aquarium is a city treasure. Don't miss the Aquatic Show at the Oceanarium, which re-creates a Pacific Northwest coastal environment and features a wall of windows that reveals the lake outside and creates the illusion of one uninterrupted expanse of sea (that's where you'll find those baby belugas and dolphins). Another all-time favorite is watching the diver feed the sea creatures in the Caribbean Reef during the free shows four times daily. *See p 20,* **④B**.

⑯ Interact with the sculpture at Millennium Park, the city's urban showpiece and one of its most popular tourist attractions. Pay a visit to *Cloud Gate,* the huge elliptical sculpture by British artist Anish Kapoor, in which you can examine your reflection in fun-house-like distortions. While you're here, make sure to catch a show at the stunning Frank Gehry–designed Pritzker Music Pavilion, home to free summer concerts performed by the Grant Park Symphony Orchestra. *See p 12,* **⑦**. ●

Cloud Gate, by Anish Kapoor.

1 The Best Full-Day Tours

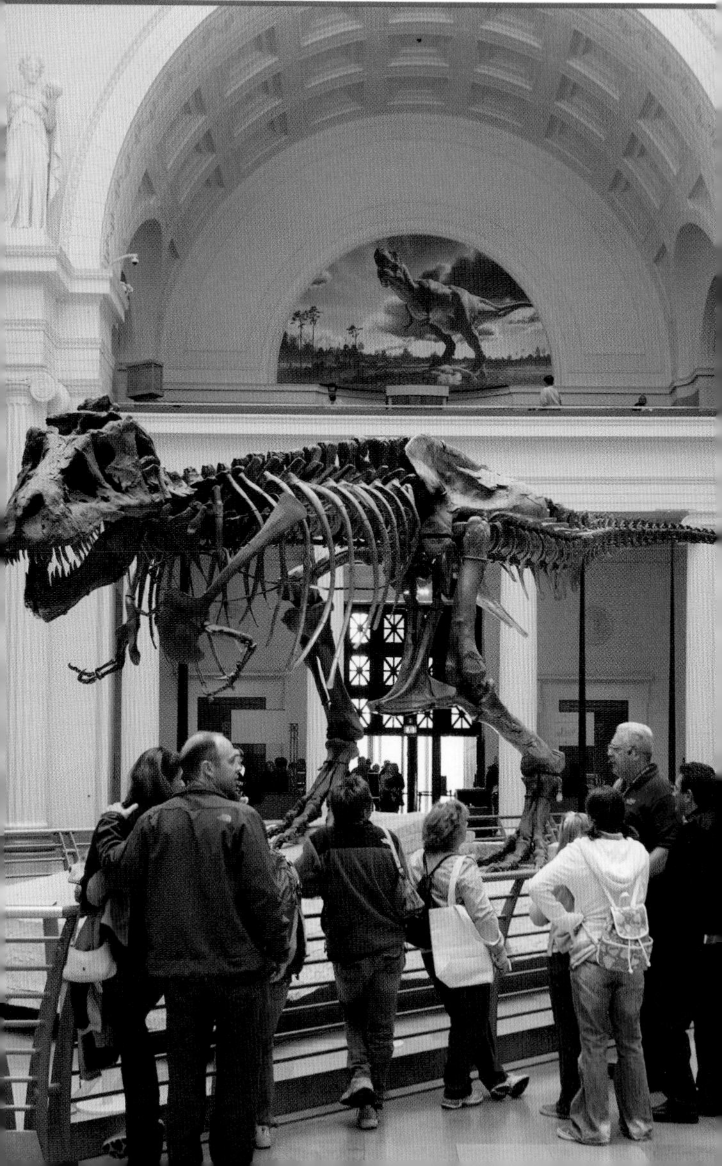

The Best **in One Day**

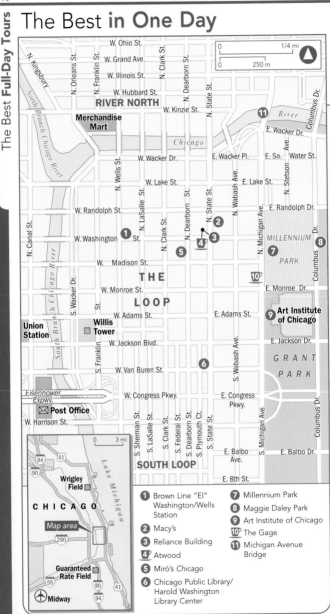

1 Brown Line "El" Washington/Wells Station
2 Macy's
3 Reliance Building
4 Atwood
5 Miró's *Chicago*
6 Chicago Public Library/ Harold Washington Library Center
7 Millennium Park
8 Maggie Daley Park
9 Art Institute of Chicago
10 The Gage
11 Michigan Avenue Bridge

Previous page: The family-friendly Field Museum is located on Lake Shore Drive, next to Lake Michigan.

With 1 day to spend in Chicago, focus on the heart of the city. The Loop is a collection of commercial, governmental, and cultural buildings contained within a corral of elevated train tracks. Here you'll find classic Chicago sights and experiences, plus the chance to relax in Chicago's beloved front yard, Millennium Park, and view Impressionist masterpieces at the city's world-class museum, the Art Institute. START: **Washington/Wells El Station.**

L-Line overground subway.

❶ ★★★ kids Ride the Brown Line "El" (Elevated Train) around the Loop. Board the Brown Line at Washington/Wells, and ride it around the Loop through the canyons of office buildings (you'll be close enough to peer into some of them). Stop off at Randolph/Wabash or, if you don't mind a longer walk, ride to Clark/Lake. ⏱ *30 min. Avoid rush-hour boarding before 9am and 3:30–6:30pm.* ☎ *888/YOURCTA (968-7282). www.transitchicago.com. Tickets $2.50 per ride, $1.25 kids 7–11 and seniors, free for kids 6 and under. El: Brown Line to Washington/Wells.*

❷ Macy's. In 2006, the former Marshall Field's became Macy's, much to locals' chagrin. This department store's clock is one of the city's most-recognized icons. Browse the store's famous windows, or stop in for Frango mints, a favorite Chicago souvenir. Head inside to check out the world's largest Tiffany glass mosaic dome above the ground-level sales floor. ⏱ *5 min.– 2 hrs. (if you want to shop). 111 N. State St., at Randolph St.* ☎ *312/ 781-1000. Hours vary seasonally; call ahead. El: Red Line to Washington.*

❸ Reliance Building. Now the Alise Chicago, this building, with a terracotta and glass exterior, was one of the world's first skyscrapers. Step inside to admire the terrazzo tile floors, white marble wainscoting, and mahogany door and window frames. Room numbers painted on the translucent doors recall the structure's days as an office building. Today, the Alise is a boutique hotel owned by Staypineapple, and its restaurant and bar, Atwood, is a favorite with the city's suits (p 32). ⏱ *15 min. 1 W. Washington St.* ☎ *312/940-7997. El: Red Line to Washington.*

❹ Atwood, located street-level in the Alise Chicago, offers views of State Street and an eclectic take on American comfort food, making it an ideal lunch stop. Make sure to leave room for the desserts, which are a high point of the menu, including seasonal fruit cobblers, decadent tarts, and boozy drinkable desserts. *1 W. Washington St.* ☎ *312/368-1900. www.atwoodcafe.com. $$.*

Miró's Chicago.

The Harold Washington Library Center.

5 Miró's Chicago. Head west a couple of blocks to see the sculpture originally called *The Sun, the Moon and One Star*. Joan Miró's *Chicago* was unveiled in 1981. This 40-foot-tall sculptural representation of a woman with outstretched arms sits in the Brunswick Plaza on Washington Street, and overlooks the Picasso sculpture at the Daley Center. ⓘ *5 min. On the plaza of 69 W. Washington St. El: Red Line to Washington.*

6 kids Chicago Public Library/ Harold Washington Library Center. When it opened, this hulking Italian Renaissance building was the world's largest public library. Named for the city's first and only African-American mayor, who died of a heart attack in 1987 while in office, the building fills an entire city block. On the second floor, the Thomas Hughes Children's Library makes an excellent resting spot for families traveling with kids. ⓘ *30 min. 400 S. State St. ☎ 312/747-4300. www.chipublib.org. Free admission. Mon–Thurs 9am–9pm; Fri–Sat 9am–5pm; Sun 1–5pm. Closed holidays. El: Brown or Purple line to Library.*

7 ★★★ kids Millennium Park. With its up-close-and-personal skyline views, this sprawling greenspace is universally loved for its gorgeous landscaping, classically inspired architecture, and public entertainment spaces. A tourist rite of passage is having a photo taken in the reflection of "The Bean," (officially *Cloud Gate*), which is Chicagoans' unofficial favorite sculpture. And the spectacular Frank Gehry–designed Jay Pritzker Pavilion is host to the nation's only free, outdoor, municipally supported classical music series, the Grant Park Music Festival.

Summer fun at Millennium Park.

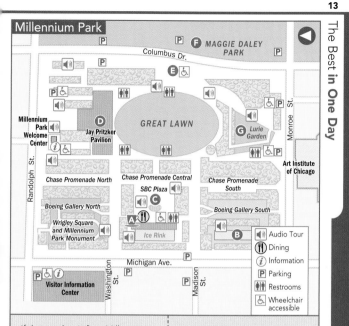

Millennium Park

🔊	Audio Tour
🍴	Dining
ⓘ	Information
P	Parking
🚻	Restrooms
♿	Wheelchair accessible

If the weather is fine, Millennium Park is an ideal spot for a picnic lunch, which you can buy at the **A Park Grill & Cafe** *(11 N. Michigan Ave.;* ☎ *312/521-7275; $).*
B The Crown Fountain, and its two towers of glass blocks with a shallow reflecting pool between them, is *the* place for kids to splash around in warm weather (late at night, you'll find revelers doing the same). Faces of Chicagoans are projected through the glass—and their mouths spew water when you least expect it. **C** *Cloud Gate* is an elliptical sculpture made of highly polished steel that reflects the nearby skyline, landscape, and lights. For the most mind-bending funhouse view, stand underneath the sculpture. The park's centerpiece is the

D Jay Pritzker Pavilion, an outdoor music venue designed by Frank Gehry; massive stainless steel ribbons top the stage. Another Gehry-designed standout, **E BP Pedestrian Bridge,** curves and winds its way over Columbus Drive to **F Maggie Daley Park,** providing changing views of the cityscape as you walk. Finally, stroll **G The Lurie Garden,** where 250 varieties of native perennial plants re-create a Midwestern prairie. ⏱ *2 hrs. Michigan Ave. from Randolph St. on the north end to Monroe St. on the south, and west to Columbus Dr.* ☎ *312/742-1168. www.millennium park.org. Free admission. Daily 6am–11pm. El: Blue Line to Washington; Red Line to Lake; or Brown, Green, Orange, or Purple line to Randolph.*

8 ★★★ kids **Maggie Daley Park.** This may well be the park to end all parks, with an elaborate playground, mini golf, tennis courts, a climbing wall, and, in the winter, a skating ribbon, all a pebble's toss from Millennium Park. ⏱ *1 hr. 337 E. Randolph St., northeast of Millennium Park.* ☎ *312/552-3000. www. maggiedaleypark.com. Free admission. Daily 6am–11pm. Bus: 4, 20, or 60.*

9 ★★★ **Art Institute of Chicago.** Even if you are hard-pressed for time, make sure to at least stop in to view the Impressionist collection on the second floor, a highlight of Chicago's grande dame of museums. With 33 paintings by Claude Monet, dancers by Degas, and Seurat's legendary *A Sunday Afternoon on the Island of La Grande Jatte,* this museum is a must for art lovers. ⏱ *3 hrs.* See p 42.

Summer Music Series at the Jay Pritzker Pavilion, Millennium Park.

The Art Institute of Chicago has one of the world's most notable collections of Impressionist and Post-Impressionist art.

Review the day's highlights over dinner at  **The Gage,** an Irish-inspired gastropub across the street from Millennium Park. It's located in a historic building that once housed a millinery factory; the menu includes everything from Scotch eggs to rack of elk. *24 S. Michigan Ave.* ☎ *312/372-4243. $$.*

⓫ ★ Michigan Avenue Bridge. Finish your day strolling up Michigan Avenue to the Chicago River, where you can gaze up at the Gothic splendor of the Tribune Tower and the white brilliance of the Wrigley Building from Chicago's most famous bridge, dating back to 1920. Views from every direction are stunning, but for one of the city's best photo ops, look west down the river. ⏱ *15 min. El: Green, Purple, Brown, or Orange line to State.*

The Gage.

The Best **in Two Days**

1 Chicago Architecture Center's Architecture River Cruise
2 Chicago Architecture Center
3 Nutella Café
4a Field Museum of Natural History
4b John G. Shedd Aquarium
4c Adler Planetarium
5 Buckingham Fountain
6 Chicago Hilton and Towers
7 Mercat a la Planxa
8 Spertus Institute for Jewish Learning and Leadership
9 The Fine Arts Building
10 Auditorium Building and Theatre
11 Chicago Cultural Center

M Subway/El stop

On your second day in Chicago, head to the water for a boat cruise, and take in stories of the spaces and faces that shaped the city's famous skyline. Then, head over to Museum Campus, a green expanse that's home to one of the most impressive collections of museums in the country, and choose from one of three museum stops. Finish your day with a stroll north along South Michigan Avenue, known as the "Michigan Avenue Cliff" because of its imposing wall of grand buildings. In warmer months, stop in Grant Park and stand in the refreshing spray of Buckingham Fountain. (In the off season, when there are no boat tours, walk the Michigan Avenue Cliff from north to south, and then head to Museum Campus.) START: **Southeast corner of the Michigan Ave. Bridge. Bus: 151 (Michigan Ave.) to Illinois St.**

❶ ★★★ Chicago Architecture Center's Architecture River Cruise. You'll see more than 50 buildings from a unique perspective as you glide along the north and south branches of the Chicago River. Narration is provided by docents, who do a remarkable job of making the cruise enjoyable for all visitors, no matter their level of architectural knowledge. If you have very young kids, you may prefer the shorter (and less expensive) tours by Wendella Sightseeing Boats. ⏱ *1½ hrs. Southeast corner of Michigan Ave. Bridge at Wacker Dr. Tickets $47 per person for daytime cruise, $52 for* twilight. *Daily June–Sept 10am–7:30pm weekdays, 9am–5:30pm Sat, 9am–7:30pm Sun; limited schedules in May, Oct, Nov. Purchase tickets in advance online through the Architecture Center's website, www.architecture.org, at the Chicago Architecture Center, 111 E. Wacker Dr., by phone* ☎ *312/922-TOUR (8687), or at the boat launch. Wendella Sightseeing Boats depart from Michigan Ave. Bridge (on the northwest side, near the Wrigley Building).* ☎ *312/337-1446. www.wendellaboats.com. Tickets $39 adults, $35 seniors, $18 children 3–11, free for children 2 and under. Daily Mar–Dec.*

You'll see more than 50 buildings on Chicago Architecture Center's Architecture River Cruise.

② ★★ **Chicago Architecture Center.** The intention of the Chicago Architecture Center's shop and tour center, new in 2018, is to help everyone appreciate the city's main claim to fame. Exhibits include a scale model of downtown Chicago; profiles of the people and buildings that shaped the city's look; a display that explores Chicago before and after the Great Chicago Fire of 1871; and a Skyscraper Gallery with looming models of some of the world's most impressive towers. The best gift shop in the city offers architecture-focused books, decorative accessories, and gifts. "Architecture ambassadors" provide information on a wide range of available tours. ⏱ *45 min. 111 E. Wacker Dr.* ☎ *312/922-TOUR (8687). www. architecture.org. Adults $12, students $8, kids 4 and under free. Daily 9am–5pm, open until 8pm Tues and Thurs. El: Red or Brown Line to State/Lake.*

③ **Nutella Café.** The chocolatey hazelnut spread has a cultlike following, and it comes in all forms at the world's first Nutella Café: croissants, crepes, gelato, and even dolloped on top of oatmeal. Nutella-free paninis, salads, and soups are also available. *189 N. Michigan Ave. (at Jackson).* ☎ *800/861-4888. $.*

④A ★★★ **kids Field Museum of Natural History.** My top pick at Museum Campus is the Field. It offers a wealth of interesting exhibits, from gems to dinosaurs, and always features a blockbuster special exhibit. The **Crown Family PlayLab** caters to the young set with hands-on digs for dinosaur bones; a dress-up station where kids can don a coyote costume to trot through a mock-up of the Illinois woodlands; and a science lab, where they can examine insects in amber, fossils, and animal skulls.

Field Museum of Natural History

Standing proudly at the north side of the grand **A Stanley Field Hall** is the largest dinosaur fossil ever unearthed. The titanosaur *Patagotitan mayorum* is named **B ★★ "Máximo,"** meaning "most" in Spanish, the language spoken in Patagonia, where it lived over 100 million years ago. Head downstairs to **C ★ Inside Ancient Egypt,** a spellbinding exhibit that realistically depicts scenes from Egyptian funeral, religious, and other social practices. **D Regenstein Halls of the Pacific** re-creates scenes of island life in the Pacific islands; there's even a rare, authentic Maori meeting house. **E Africa** is an assemblage of African artifacts and provocative, interactive multimedia presentations. Two other signature highlights: the taxidermied bodies of **F Bushman** (a legendary lowland gorilla from the city's Lincoln Park Zoo) and the **G Man-Eating Lions of Tsavo** (the pair of male lions who munched nearly 140 British railway workers constructing a bridge in East Africa in 1898). Upstairs, a 3D theater shows movies that bring natural history to life—most recently, a movie about Egypt that follows scientists unearthing mummies. ⏱ *3 hrs. 1400 S. Lake Shore Dr.* ☎ *312/922-9410. www.fieldmuseum.org. Admission $24 adults, $21 seniors and students with ID, $17 children 3–11, free for children 2 and under. Extra fee applies for special exhibits. Daily 9am–5pm. Closed Christmas. Bus: 146.*

48 ★★★ kids John G. Shedd Aquarium. If you love the sea and all its creatures, then choose the Shedd as your stop on Museum Campus. The first thing you'll see as you enter one of the world's largest indoor aquariums is the 90,000-gallon tank occupying the Beaux Arts–style central rotunda. The **Caribbean Coral Reef** exhibit features nurse sharks, barracudas, stingrays, and a hawksbill sea turtle. The next don't-miss exhibit is **Amazon Rising,** displaying piranhas, birds, sloths, insects, spiders, snakes, caiman lizards, and monkeys. **Wild Reef** features interconnected habitats that encompass a Philippine coral reef patrolled by sharks and other predators (they even swim over your head in certain spots). Another highlight is the 3-million-gallon saltwater **Oceanarium,** a sparkling indoor marine mammal pavilion that re-creates a Pacific Northwest coastal environment. During warmer months (June–Oct) Wednesday evenings draw an adult crowd to **Jazzin' at the Shedd** ($25) for cocktails and live music after hours, while fireworks light up the lakefront. ⏱ *3 hrs. 1200 S. Lake Shore Dr.* ☎ *312/939-2438. www. sheddaquarium.org. Shedd Pass (for all exhibits) $40 adults, $37 seniors, $30 children 3–11, free for children 2 and under. Memorial Day to Labor Day 9am–6pm; early Sept to late May Mon–Fri 9am–5pm, Sat–Sun 9am–6pm. Bus: 146.*

4C ★★★ kids Adler Planetarium. If you're a fan of the extraterrestrial, then choose the first planetarium in the Western Hemisphere for your visit to Museum Campus. Your initial stop should be the **Grainger Sky Theater**—one of three 3D theaters here—where the domed ceiling and 3D tech is so immersive, at times you feel like you're floating through the Milky Way to the distant galaxies in "Cosmic Wonder." As for the exhibits, if you're going to see only one, check out **Mission Moon,** an exhibit on lunar exploration that's full of interactive stations, including a stomp rocket. (It also showcases the personal collection of astronaut Jim Lovell, captain of the infamous Apollo 13 mission, who lives in the Chicago suburbs.) ⏱ *2 hrs., more if you want to see more than one show. 1300 S. Lake Shore Dr.* ☎ *312/922-STAR (7827). www.adlerplanetarium. org. Admission: $12 adults, $8 children 3–14, free for children 2 and under; admission including one sky show $25 adults, $20 children; admission including all shows $35 adults, $30 children. Memorial Day to Labor Day daily 9:30am–6pm; early May Mon–Fri 9:30am–4pm; Sky shows at three theaters run throughout the day; call main number or go online for times. Bus: 146.*

5 ★ Buckingham Fountain. On your way back toward Michigan Avenue, stop at Grant Park's immense baroque centerpiece— the starting point for the famous Route 66 to Los Angeles. April through October, the fountain spurts columns of water up to 150 feet in the air every hour on the hour; at dusk, a whirl of colored lights and music makes for quite a show (the fountain shuts down at 11pm). ⏱ *10 min. Inside Grant Park, at Columbus Dr. and Congress Pkwy. www.chicagoparkdistrict.com. Apr– Oct daily 9am–11pm. Bus: 6 or 146.*

6 Chicago Hilton and Towers. This massive brick-and-stone building was the largest hotel in the world when it opened in 1927. It's worth a stop to gaze at the Grand Stair lobby, done in a classical-rococo style, which is among the most magnificent in the city. ⏱ *15 min. 720 S. Michigan Ave. (at Balbo Dr.).* ☎ *312/922-4400. www.hilton. com. El: Red Line to Harrison/State.*

The Chicago skyline and Buckingham Fountain at dusk.

7 Mercat a la Planxa has breathed life into South Michigan Avenue with its bright, vivacious atmosphere and bi-level, loftlike space. The extensive menu offers traditional tapas as well as heartier options such as paellas, steaks, and a couple of different tasting menus. *638 S. Michigan Ave.* ☎ *312/765-0524. www.mercatchicago.com. $$.*

8 Spertus Institute for Jewish Learning and Leadership. The modern, glass, prism-like architecture of the Institute is among the most arresting on Michigan Avenue. Pop inside to peruse the collection of historic Jewish artifacts, sculptures, and rare books. ⏲ *20 min. 610 S. Michigan Ave. www.spertus.edu.* ☎ *312/322-1700. Free admission. El: Red Line to Harrison.*

9 The Fine Arts Building. This 1885 building was originally a showroom for Studebaker carriages. Converted into an arts center in 1898, the building provided offices and studios for the likes of *Wizard of Oz* author L. Frank Baum and Frank Lloyd Wright. Take a quick walk through the marble-and-wood lobby, and, if you like, ride the vintage elevators to the top floor to view walls of spectacular murals. ⏲ *30 min. 410 S. Michigan Ave.* ☎ *312/566-9800. Free admission. Daily 7am–10pm. El: Brown Line to Library.*

10 ★ Auditorium Building and Theatre. Designed and built in 1889 by Louis Sullivan and Dankmar Adler, with the help of a young Frank Lloyd Wright, the Auditorium was an architectural wonder of its time: the heaviest and most massive edifice on earth, the most fireproof building ever constructed, and the tallest building in Chicago. Today, the 4,000-seat theater hosts touring dance productions and concerts. Tours allow visitors to marvel at the gorgeous arched design, lit by thousands of bulbs. ⏲ *30 min. (1 hr. if you take a tour). 50 E. Congress Pkwy.* ☎ *312/341-2300. www.auditoriumtheatre.org. 1-hr. guided tour Mon at 10am and noon, Tues at 5:30pm, and Thurs at 10:30am. $12 per person. El: Brown Line to Library.*

11 ★ Chicago Cultural Center. Built in 1897 as the city's library, this National Historic Landmark's basic Beaux Arts exterior doesn't begin to hint at the building's sumptuous interior. Inside you'll find rare marble; fine hardwoods; stained glass; polished brass; and mosaics of Favrile glass, colored stone, and mother-of-pearl inlaid in white marble. The crowning centerpiece is the mind-blowing Louis Comfort Tiffany art glass dome in Preston Bradley Hall. The Center is the home base for the Chicago Greeter program, which offers free tours by local Chicagoans (☎ **312/744-8000;** www.chicagogreeter.com). ⏲ *30 min., longer with tour. 78 E. Washington St.* ☎ *312/744-3316. www.choosechicago.com. Free admission. Mon–Fri 10am–7pm; 10am–5pm Sat–Sun. Closed holidays. El: Brown, Green, Orange, or Purple line to Randolph, or Red Line to Washington/State.*

The Best **in Three Days**

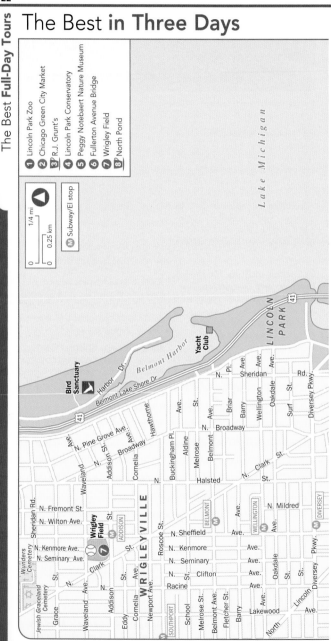

1 Lincoln Park Zoo
2 Chicago Green City Market
3 R.J. Grunt's
4 Lincoln Park Conservatory
5 Peggy Notebaert Nature Museum
6 Fullerton Avenue Bridge
7 Wrigley Field
8 North Pond

1/4 mi
0.25 km

Ⓜ Subway/El stop

Lake Michigan

LINCOLN PARK

Bird Sanctuary

Belmont Harbor

Yacht Club

Belmont Lake Shore Dr.

Harbor Dr.

Sheridan Rd.

N. Pine Grove Ave.
N. Broadway
Hawthorne
Addison
Broadway
Cornelia
Buckingham Pl.
Aldine
Melrose
Belmont
Pl.
Briar
Barry
Wellington
Oakdale
Surf St.
Diversey Pkwy.

Halsted St.

N. Clark St.

WRIGLEYVILLE

Wrigley Field

ADDISON

BELMONT

WELLINGTON

DIVERSEY

N. Fremont St.
N. Wilton Ave.
N. Kenmore Ave.
N. Seminary Ave.
N. Sheffield Ave.
N. Kenmore Ave.
N. Seminary Ave.
N. Clifton Ave.
Racine Ave.
N. Mildred Ave.
Oakdale Ave.
Lincoln Diversey Pkwy.

Wunders Cemetery
Jewish Graceland Cemetery

Sheridan Rd.
Waveland Ave.
Grace St.
Addison St.
Clark St.
Roscoe St.
Newport Ave.
Cornelia Ave.
Eddy
School
Melrose St.
Belmont Ave.
Fletcher St.
Barry
Lakewood Ave.
North

SOUTHPORT

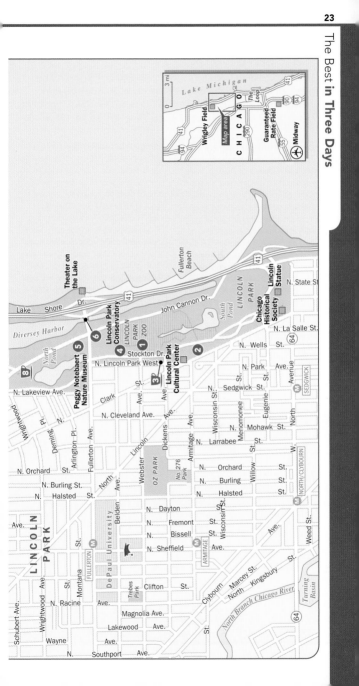

Lake Michigan

The Loop

Wrigley Field

Map area

CHICAGO

Guaranteed Rate Field

Midway

3 mi

Theater on the Lake

Lincoln Park Conservatory

Lincoln Statue

Chicago Historical Society

N. State St.

Lake Shore Dr.

John Cannon Dr.

LINCOLN PARK

Diversey Harbor

5 Peggy Notebaert Nature Museum

6

4 LINCOLN PARK ZOO **1**

Stockton Dr.

South Pond

N. La Salle St.

N. Wells St.

North Pond

8

N. Lincoln Park West

3 Lincoln Park Cultural Center

2

N. Park Ave.

Sedgwick St.

Wisconsin St.

Eugenie St.

SEDGWICK

N. Lakeview Ave.

Clark St.

Ave.

N. Cleveland Ave.

Dickens Ave.

Armitage Ave.

N. Menomonee St.

N. Mohawk St.

North Ave.

N. Orchard St.

Arlington Pl.

Deming Pl.

Fullerton Ave.

Lincoln Ave.

Webster Ave.

OZ PARK

No. 276 Park

N. Larrabee St.

N. Orchard St.

N. Burling St.

Willow St.

NORTH/CLYBOURN

Wrightwood

N. Orchard St.

N. Burling St.

N. Halsted St.

North Ave.

N. Dayton St.

N. Fremont St.

N. Bissell St.

N. Sheffield Ave.

Wisconsin St.

Weed St.

ARMITAGE

LINCOLN PARK

FULLERTON

Montana St.

DePaul University

Belden Ave.

Trebes Park

Clifton St.

Clybourn

Marcey St.

North Kingsbury

Turning Basin

Ave.

N. Racine Ave.

Magnolia Ave.

Lakewood Ave.

North Branch Chicago River

Schubert Ave.

Wrightwood Ave.

Wayne Ave.

N. Southport Ave.

On your third day in Chicago, head north to Lincoln Park to see how Chicagoans live, in one of the most graceful (and expensive) residential neighborhoods in the city. The east-west streets all run into Lincoln Park, a stunning stretch of lakefront greenery that includes a zoo, a nature museum, a conservatory, walking trails, and just plain glorious sightseeing and strolling. START: Lincoln Park Zoo, Cannon Dr. at Fullerton Pkwy. Bus: 22, 26, 151, or 156.

1 ★★★ kids **Lincoln Park Zoo.** The nation's oldest zoo, founded in 1868, is also one of the last free zoos in the country. You'll want to meander among the landmark Georgian revival buildings and modern structures set amid gently rolling pathways, verdant lawns, and a profusion of flower gardens. The star attraction is the **Regenstein Center for African Apes,** where you can watch chimpanzees and gorillas go about their days. Also worth a stop is the **Regenstein African Journey,** home to elephants, giraffes, rhinos, and other large mammals. Finish off your visit with a ride on the nostalgic **Endangered Species Carousel.** If you're looking for an extra special experience, book a **Malott Family**

Penguin Encounter ($60 per person; Apr–Oct; 10am and 3pm daily; ages 6 and up), and you'll get to go behind the scenes to learn about the birds as they waddle around you. ⏲ *3 hrs. 2001 N. Clark St.* ☎ *312/742-2000. www.lpzoo.com. Free admission. Buildings daily 10am–5pm; until 6:30pm Sat–Sun Memorial Day to Labor Day; until 4:30pm Nov–Mar; grounds 7am–6pm (until 7pm Memorial Day to Labor Day and until 5pm Nov 1–May 31). Parking $20–$35. Bus: 22, 36, 151, or 156.*

2 ★★ **Chicago Green City Market.** Chefs from Chicago's best restaurants load up their trucks with organic foods sold at this sprawling market, which takes place outdoors in Lincoln Park Wednesday and Saturday mornings June

Observing the polar bears at Lincoln Park Zoo.

Chicago's seasonal, sprawling Green City Market.

through October and indoors more sporadically (check for dates online) November through April. You might find fresh goat cheese, elk steaks, or (in season) freshly picked blueberries; if you're hungry, you can get a made-to-order French-style crepe and other on-the-go snacks, while listening to live music. ⏱ *1 hr. Outdoors: At the south end of Lincoln Park, between Clark St. and Stockton Dr. Indoors: at Peggy Notebaert Nature Museum, 2430 N. Cannon Dr.* ☎ *773/880-1266. www.chicagogreencitymarket.org. June–Oct Wed and Sat 7am–1pm; Nov–Apr on designated Sat 8am–1pm (check website). Bus: 151.*

There are a couple of restaurants inside the Lincoln Park Zoo, but I recommend taking a short walk west into the Lincoln Park neighborhood for more local fare. A spot that's great for kids is ③ **R.J. Grunt's,** which originated the concept of the salad bar in 1971, and it's still going strong. Grunt's is always crowded, but it's a classic. The restaurant gets busy around lunchtime, so prepare for a short wait. The good news is that once you get a seat, you can head immediately to the famous salad bar, which will stave off hunger and entertain the kids while you wait for your meal. *2056 N. Lincoln Park West.* ☎ *773/929-5363. www.rjgruntschicago.com. $.*

④ ★ **Lincoln Park Conservatory.** On days when Chicago's weather is uncooperative, a visit to this conservatory's climate-controlled environs can be a real mood-lifter. It comprises four greenhouses—the Palm House, the Fern Room, the Orchid House, and the Show House—that offer seasonal displays. Even on the coldest day of winter, the Spring Flower Show that begins in February is a bright reminder that warmer days will come. Outside the front doors of the conservatory is an expansive lawn with a French garden: Photo op! Don't miss the lovely Bates Fountain on the conservatory's south side, designed by famed sculptor Augustus Saint-Gaudens. ⏱ *30 min. 2391 N. Stockton Dr.* ☎ *312/742-7736. Free admission. Daily 9am–5pm. Bus: 151, or 156.*

⑤ kids ★ **Peggy Notebaert Nature Museum.** This environmental museum, built into the rise of an ancient sand dune that was once the shore of Lake Michigan, features rooftop-level walkways offering a view of birds and other urban wildlife below. Paths wind through gardens planted with native Midwestern wildflowers and grasses, and trace the shoreline of Lincoln Park's restored North Pond. The best exhibit is the **Judy Istock Butterfly Haven,** a greenhouse habitat you can walk through that's home to dozens of butterfly species. Another exhibit is, **Extreme Green House,** a bungalow where kids can play while learning how they can be environmentally friendly, and **Riverworks,** a water play exhibit that gives children an excuse to splash around while building dams and maneuvering boats along a mini river. ⏱ *1–2 hrs. 2430 N. Cannon Dr. www.naturemuseum.org.* ☎ *773/755-5100. Admission $9 adults, $7 seniors and students, $6 kids 3–12, free for kids 2* and under; free admission Thurs. Mon–Fri 9am–5pm; Sat–Sun 10am–5pm. Closed Thanksgiving and Dec 25. Bus: 22, 36, 151, or 156.

6 Fullerton Avenue Bridge. Take advantage of a social-media-ready photo opportunity at the bridge that runs over the lagoon, just before you get to Lake Shore Drive. Standing on the south side of Fullerton, you'll have a great view of the skyline and Lincoln Park. It's the perfect place to take a final snapshot to commemorate your day. ⏱ 5 min. Bus: 151 or 156.

7 ★★★ kids Wrigley Field. There's no better way to create a quintessential Chicago day than with a game at Wrigley, where you and your kids can stuff yourselves with hot dogs and nachos galore. Adults are fine in the inexpensive bleacher seats (if you don't mind the general rowdiness and over-zealous cheering and drinking), but I'd recommend standard seats if you're bringing the family. *For more on Wrigley Field, see p 128.*

Game day at Wrigley Field.

If it's not baseball season, finish the day at **8 North Pond,** a locals' fave for its romantic atmosphere. Tucked away behind a small pond in an idyllic location in the park, the restaurant has an arts and crafts feel. The menu relies on sustainable, locally grown ingredients, and features items like artisan cheeses, wine from boutique vintners, and seasonal fare such as sangria-marinated ribeye and seared duck breast. *2610 N. Cannon Dr. (south of Diversey Pkwy.).* ☎ 773/477-5845. $$$. ●

Taking Yourself Out to a Ball Game

Gone are the days when the Chicago Cubs were a punchline. Their comeback in 2016 as World Champions rewarded generations-long fans for their dedication while energizing new fans—and ratcheting up ticket prices in the process. It was, after all, the Cubbies' first time to make a World Series since 1945, and 108 years since their last World Championship win, in 1908. Catch 'em if you can. Each April, they show up for opening day at Wrigley Field in what is almost certainly inclement weather, ready to reign supreme yet again.

From the ivy-covered outfield walls to the hand-operated scoreboard and "W" or "L" flag announcing the outcome of the game to the unfortunates who couldn't attend, Wrigley Field is a pure slice of Americana. Buy a hot dog and some Cracker Jack, and join in the chorus of "Take Me Out to the Ball Game" during the seventh-inning stretch. *Wrigley Field, 1060 W. Addison St.* ☎ 800/THE-CUBS [843-2827]; www.cubs.mlb.com; *see p 128.*

The Loop: An Architectural Tour

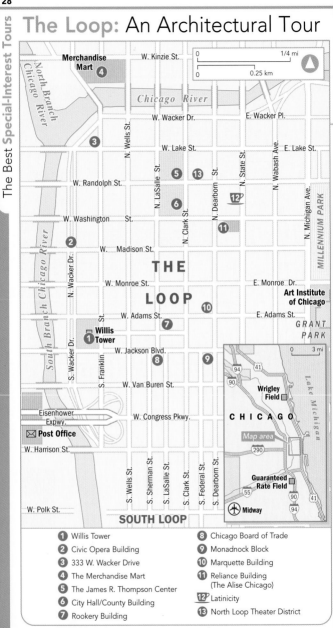

1. Willis Tower
2. Civic Opera Building
3. 333 W. Wacker Drive
4. The Merchandise Mart
5. The James R. Thompson Center
6. City Hall/County Building
7. Rookery Building
8. Chicago Board of Trade
9. Monadnock Block
10. Marquette Building
11. Reliance Building (The Alise Chicago)
12. Latinicity
13. North Loop Theater District

Previous page: The massive Merchandise Mart.

Architecture buffs and laypeople alike will revel in the design of the Loop's towering buildings. The structures found in this area represent a variety of important and influential historical styles, from the rounded arches and thick walls of Richardsonian Romanesque (1870–1900) to the stark simplicity and functionalism of International Style (1932–45). These buildings were the blueprints for many similar structures in North America. START: **Wacker Drive in front of the Civic Opera House. El: Brown Line to Washington Station.**

❶ ★★★ **Willis Tower.** The skyscraper formerly known as the Sears Tower (naming rights were sold to London-based insurance broker Willis Group in 2009) is 110 stories and was the tallest building in the world when it opened in 1973. Today, it proclaims itself the tallest building in the Western Hemisphere (One World Trade Center in New York City disagrees, and the technicality revolves around an antenna). Yet, more than 45 years since it was built, it's still a marvel of engineering, which you'll get a deeper understanding of as you wind your way through the building, passing a series of museum-style exhibits that put the height into context (like, how many of you need to be stacked to reach the top of Willis Tower?). The 60-second elevator ride to The Skydeck on the 103rd floor flies by, and then, lo and behold, breathtaking views of four states unfold. If you dare, step onto The Ledge, a series of observation boxes that jut out from the building. There's nothing between you and the ground but a layer of glass. Your best bet to beat the crowds is just after it opens or around 5pm. ⏱ 1½ hrs. 233 S. Wacker Dr. (enter on Jackson Blvd.). ☎ 312/875-9696. www.theskydeck.com. Admission $24 adults, $16 seniors and children 3–11, free for children 2 and under; Fast Pass $49 (allows you to bypass the line, which may be 2 hrs. during busiest times). Mar–Sept daily 9am–10pm; Oct–Feb daily 10am–8pm. El: Brown, Purple, or Orange line to Quincy, or Red or Blue line to Jackson; and then walk a few blocks west.

❷ ★ **Civic Opera Building.** Fronting the broad roadway of Wacker Drive (named after Charles Wacker, a civic-minded brewer and a director of the World's Columbian Exposition of 1893), this Art Deco/French Renaissance building was completed in 1929. Utility magnate Samuel Insull, the president of the Chicago Civic Opera Association in the '20s, installed a 3,500-seat opera house and a 900-seat theater in this 45-story office building so the property's commercial rents would subsidize the arts. The Grand Foyer of the opera house, with its 40-foot-high ceiling and gold leaf–topped marble columns, is worth a peek when the building is open, if you can swing it, or check the website of the Lyric Opera (p 127)—the resident of the

Willis Tower.

Civic Opera Building.

house—for backstage tours, which are offered throughout the year for $15. ⏰ *5 min. 20 N. Wacker Dr.* ☎ *312/827-5600. www.lyricopera. org. El: Brown Line to Washington.*

❸ 333 W. Wacker Dr. The green-hued facade of this 36-story building reflects the Chicago River like a massive looking glass. The postmodern structure was designed to blend with its surroundings, and the curved exterior artfully echoes the curve in the river. Indeed, the best way to view this building is from the river (you'll be able to experience this on an architectural river tour—see p 17, ❶). Designed by Kohn Pedersen Fox in 1983, the building was squeezed onto a triangular lot that was previously thought suitable only for a parking lot. Another good vantage point for viewing the edifice is from the Franklin Street Bridge. ⏰ *5 min. 333 W. Wacker Dr. (at Lake St.). El: Brown, Purple, or Orange line to Washington.*

❹ The Merchandise Mart. Staking its claim as the world's largest commercial building, this 2-city-block Art Deco structure was built by Marshall Field as a wholesale emporium and completed in 1931. If you view the building from across the river, you'll see a line of pillars upon which rest oversize busts of the icons of American merchandising, including Marshall Field, Edward A. Filene, Frank Winfield Woolworth, Julius Rosenwald (Sears), and Aaron

Montgomery Ward; the busts were commissioned by former owner Joseph Kennedy, of the politically famous Kennedy clan. Most of the Mart is open to designers and trade show goers, but the public can explore Luxe Home on the ground floor, with its eye-popping array of high-end home decorating shops. ⏰ *15 min. 222 W. Merchandise Mart Plaza. www.merchandisemart.com. El: Brown Line to Merchandise Mart.*

❺ The James R. Thompson Center. Chicagoans still refer to this cascading glass-and-steel building—the work of celebrated contemporary architect Helmut Jahn—by its original name, the State of Illinois building. That's fitting, as the 16-story structure houses the Chicago branches of the state government. The glass walls that enclose the offices are said to be a symbolic reference to "open government." For spectacular views, ride the glass elevator to the top, though this will not be a pleasant experience for anyone afraid of heights. ⏰ *10 min. 100 W. Randolph St. (at LaSalle St.). www2. illinois.gov.* ☎ *312/814-9600. El: Brown Line to Clark/Lake.*

❻ City Hall/County Building. This landmark Classical Revival

The James R. Thompson Center houses offices of the State of Illinois.

The Rookery Building's light court.

building, dating back to 1911, is composed of two sections: City Hall fronts LaSalle Street on the western side, and The County Building, the older and more classically inspired edifice, faces Clark Street on the east. The county section's exterior, with its 75-foot Corinthian columns, is the more notable of the two, designed in part by one of Chicago's legendary architectural firms, Holabird & Roche. The public meetings of the Chicago City Council, held in the council chambers of City Hall, are dramatic enough to be worth a visit for policy wonks. Call ahead to find out when the council is in session. ⏱ *10 min. 121 N. LaSalle St.* ☎ *312/742-5375. www.chicityclerk. com. El: Brown Line to Washington.*

❼ ★★★ Rookery Building.

This relic of Old Chicago, completed in 1888, was named for a demolished city hall building that once stood on this site—the roost of many pigeons and politicians. The rough granite base and turrets show the influence of the heavy Romanesque style of H. H. Richardson. Venetian and Moorish influences are evident on the exterior. I wholly recommend seeing the open interior court (designed by

Frank Lloyd Wright), which rises to the full height of the landmark building's 11 stories. The ornately decorated space was constructed from iron, copper, marble, glass, and terra-cotta. ⏱ *15 min. 209 S. LaSalle St. www.therookerybuilding. com. El: Brown Line to Quincy.*

❽ ★ Chicago Board of Trade.

It once housed the raucous economic free-for-all that was the world's largest commodities exchange, until open outcry trading started going the way of the ghost, replaced by computer screens (Chicago Board of Trade merged with Chicago Mercantile Exchange in 2007, forming CME Group, which is now headquartered about a mile north). Still, this streamlined Art Deco building is one of the best examples of that style in the city. Along the landmark building's rear wall, a postmodern addition by Helmut Jahn offers a repetition of the pyramid-shaped roof. The statue of the Roman goddess Ceres on the top of the 45-floor structure strikes a quirky architectural note—she was left faceless because the designers figured nobody would get close enough to see her features. Due to security restrictions, this one is best viewed from the sidewalk. ⏱ *5 min. 141 W. Jackson Blvd. www.141wjackson.com. El: Blue Line to Jackson/Dearborn.*

⑨ ★ Monadnock Block. This significant block actually consists of two buildings, built 2 years apart using two very different construction methods. **Monadnock I,** on the northern end, was built by Burnham and Root between 1889 and 1891, with deeply recessed windows at street level, encased by walls up to 8-feet thick. It was the last skyscraper in the United States to use this method of construction. **Monadnock II,** built by Holabird & Roche in 1893, is one of the country's first steel-framed buildings, but is noteworthy in that it maintains a continuity of style with Monadnock I. ⏱ *10 min. 53 W. Jackson Blvd. El: Blue Line to Jackson/Dearborn.*

⑩ ★ Marquette Building. Named for Jacques Marquette, a French Jesuit explorer who was one of the first Europeans to record the existence of the area now known as Chicago, this 1895 building was one of the country's first commercial skyscrapers. The marble lobby, which is worth seeing, commemorates the spirit of exploration with a series of explorer-themed relief sculptures and Tiffany windows. ⏱ *10 min. 56 W. Adams St. El: Blue Line to Jackson/Dearborn.*

⑪ ★★★ Reliance Building (The Alise Chicago). This

Cadillac Palace Theatre.

prototype of the modern skyscraper was made possible by the development of high-speed elevators and steel framing. The terra-cotta and glass facade gives the 1895 building a modern appearance. Its window design—a large central pane of glass flanked by two smaller, double-hung windows for ventilation—eventually became known as the Chicago Window. It's now home to a hotel called the Alise. The rooms all have doors that are a throwback to the days when this was an office building for the likes of Al Capone's dentist. Ask at the front desk if you can take a peek. ⏱ *5 min. 1 W. Washington St. (at State St.).* ☎ *312/940-7997. www.staypineapple.com. El: Red Line to Washington.*

⑫ Latinicity is a festive food hall by celeb Chef Richard Sandoval, where all the offerings, including tacos, soups, sandwiches, seafood, and more, have one thing in common: ties to the Latin world. *Block 37, 3rd floor, 108 N. State St.* ☎ *312/795-4444. www.latinicity.com. $–$$.*

⑬ ★ North Loop Theater District. This row of renovated historic theaters along Randolph Street was a longtime dream of city planners, and on this short tour you'll see why: Their colorful, glitzy facades and over-the-top decor give each a unique character.

North Loop Theater District

The Versailles-inspired **Ⓐ Cadillac Palace Theatre** is a former movie palace that now hosts touring musicals, dance performances, and concerts. Another former movie palace, the spectacular **Ⓑ Ford Center for the Performing Arts Oriental Theatre** opened in 1926 and was restored in the 1980s to its original, over-the-top Indian-inspired decor. Marked by a nostalgic orange-lettered marquee, the landmark **Ⓒ Chicago Theatre** is the oldest Beaux Arts building in the city. The 3,800-seat hall opened in 1928 and was restored in 1986 as a showplace for Broadway musicals, concerts, and dramas. All three theaters use a number run by **Broadway in Chicago** (☎ 312/977-1700). Home of the city's oldest resident theater company, the **Ⓓ Goodman**

Theatre opened in 2000, incorporating the landmark neo-Georgian and Palladian facades of the old Harris and Selwyn theaters. The facility includes 850- and 400-seat theaters (☎ 312/443-3800; www. goodmantheatre.org). The large bar at **Ⓔ Petterino's** (150 N. Dearborn St.; ☎ 312/422-0150; www. petterinos.com; $$) is an ideal place to dine at the end of a long day of walking or before a show. The menu is old school—wedge salad, chopped steak, salmon cakes—but done well. Some dishes are named after local celebrities. Take the Irv Kupcinet, for example, a popular salad of chopped minced greens and blue cheese named for the longtime *Sun-Times* columnist.
🕐 1 hr. El: Blue or Brown line to Clark/Lake.

Mag Mile: An Architectural Tour

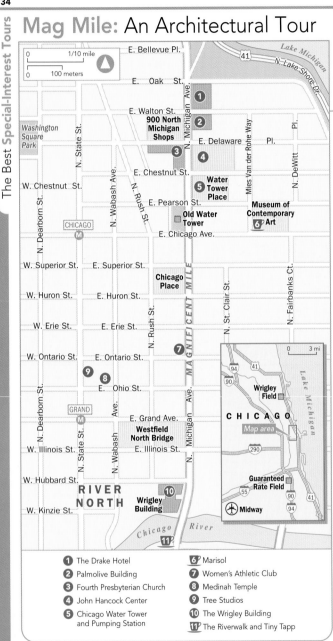

1 The Drake Hotel
2 Palmolive Building
3 Fourth Presbyterian Church
4 John Hancock Center
5 Chicago Water Tower
   and Pumping Station
6 Marisol
7 Women's Athletic Club
8 Medinah Temple
9 Tree Studios
10 The Wrigley Building
11 The Riverwalk and Tiny Tapp

Many of Chicago's signature buildings are found along the stretch of Michigan Avenue known as the Magnificent Mile. From private clubs to posh condominiums and historic churches, this entire area rose from the ashes after the Great Fire of 1871. Today, Michigan Avenue is one of the most architecturally significant avenues in the country. START: **Chicago/State El Station or Bus 151 (Michigan Ave.) to Walton St.**

① ★★ The Drake Hotel. This landmark 13-story building was constructed in 1920 of Bedford limestone in a design inspired by the Italian palazzos of the late Renaissance. You can stroll through the ornate lobby or stop in for finger fare at the serene Palm Court, one of the city's top spots for afternoon tea (call ☎ 312/787-2200 for reservations). ⏱ *20 min. 140 E. Walton Pl. www.thedrakehotel.com. El: Red Line to Chicago/State. See p 138.*

② ★ Palmolive Building. This "monument to cleanliness" was built in 1929 for Colgate-Palmolive, the world's leading soap manufacturer, but was known as the Playboy Building from 1965 to 1989, when it housed the famous skin mag (the publication moved to Los Angeles in 2012). The picturesque Art Deco landmark was Chicago's first commercial skyscraper built outside the Loop. It now houses luxury condos. ⏱ *5 min. 919 N. Michigan Ave. El: Red Line to Chicago/State.*

③ ★★★ Fourth Presbyterian Church. This church, built in 1914, was the creation of Ralph Adams Cram—America's leading Gothic Revival architect, best known for New York's Cathedral of St. John the Divine—and parishioner/architect Howard Van Doren Shaw. The church is an amalgam of English and French Gothic styles, while the parish buildings are Tudor in form. Check the website to see if a concert is playing while you're here.

The Drake Hotel's exquisite lobby recalls an era of grand hotels and elegant design.

The courtyard is a serene photo spot. ⏱ *15 min. 126 E. Chestnut St. (at N. Michigan Ave.). www.fourth church.org. El: Red Line to Chicago/ State.*

④ ★★ John Hancock Center.

The first giant on the Chicago skyline was erected in 1969 and featured several structural innovations, including crisscross steel framing and a tapering form that creates an illusion of super proportions, making the building look larger than it is. At 360 CHICAGO, the 94th-floor observatory, a fairly new attraction called TILT—glass boxes that tip toward the ground—will get your heart pumping. For a tamer experience, grab a drink at the Signature Lounge on the 96th floor and you can skip paying admission (although drinks aren't cheap). ⏱ *1 hr., if you visit 360 CHICAGO. 875 N. Michigan Ave.* ☎ *312/751-3681. www.360Chicago.com. Admission to observatory varies by time: $21–$23 adults, $14–$16 children 3–11, free for children 2 and under; TILT $8. Daily 8am–11pm. El: Red Line to Chicago/State.*

The John Hancock Center's observatory.

⑤ ★ Chicago Water Tower and Pumping Station.

Built in a castellated Gothic style, these two National Historic Landmarks, which sit across from each other on Michigan Avenue, were the only ones in the area to survive the Great Fire of 1871. Why the duo escaped unscathed when virtually every other building in the vicinity was wiped out remains a mystery. Made of a distinct yellow-tinted Illinois limestone, the buildings now house a city art gallery, the Lookingglass Theatre Company (p 129) and Water Works, a sweet little public library. ⏱ *30 min. Michigan Ave. at Chicago Ave. El: Red Line to Chicago/State.*

For a drink, snack, or something more elaborate, head to ⑥ ★ **Marisol,** at the Museum of Contemporary Art. The menu is seasonal and therefore always changing, but you can expect artfully plated pastas, seafood, salads, and inspired dips, like sunflower hummus. *205 E. Pearson, in MCA.* ☎ *312/799-3599. www.marisol chicago.com. $$–$$$.*

⑦ Woman's Athletic Club.

Modeled on elegant Parisian buildings, this 1929 creation of Philip B. Maher (1894–1981) is marked by French Second Empire influences. The nine-story structure houses a private club and the oldest women's athletic facility in the United States. ⏱ *5 min. 626 N. Michigan Ave. El: Red Line to Grand.*

⑧ ★★ Medinah Temple.

Built in 1912, this Moorish-style palace was the regional headquarters of the Shriners and site of their annual circus until 1998. The building, one of the finest examples of the Islamic Revival style in the country,

The historic Tree Studios.

nearly fell into ruin before it was declared a historic landmark and restored as a Bloomingdale's home furnishings store (p 82). ⏱ *10 min. 600 N. Wabash Ave. El: Red Line to Grand.*

⑨ Tree Studios. To encourage visiting artists working on the 1893 Columbian Exposition to stay in Chicago, this row of cottage-like buildings was built in 1894. The Queen Anne–style buildings feature retail stores on the street level and artists' studios upstairs (the latter are closed to the public). ⏱ *5 min. 601–623 N. State St. El: Red Line to Grand.*

⑩ ★★★ The Wrigley Building. The Wrigley family, of chewing gum fame, owns and operates this building, which was erected between 1919 and 1924. Its white, terra-cotta cladding (more than 250,000 tiles' worth) glitters in the sunlight and reflects the water of the nearby river. Six shades of white, darkest at the base and lightening up to the roofline, distinguish the exterior tiles. The shading is especially beautiful when the building is illuminated after dark. Another highlight is the south tower's immense, four-faced clock, which was inspired by the Giralda Tower in Seville, Spain. ⏱ *15 min. 400 and 410 N. Michigan Ave. www. thewrigleybuilding.com. El: Red Line to Grand.*

During Chicago's most glorious months (May–Sept), head down the steps at Dearborn Street and Wacker Drive to the Riverwalk. This beautifully landscaped 1.25-mile path takes you through floating gardens, under bridges, and past wine bars, restaurants, and patio cafes that burst at the seams with the happy-hour crowd. There's been a lot of turnover since the reformed Riverwalk opened in 2016, but one reliable stop, generally open May through October, is **⑪ Tiny Tapp & Cafe,** an excellent, locally owned spot for wine, cocktails, and creative gastropub fare. *55 W. Riverwalk South; no phone; www.tinytapp.com.*

To celebrate America's Independence Day, a nine-story-long American flag hangs from the Wrigley Building.

Navy Pier & Environs for Kids

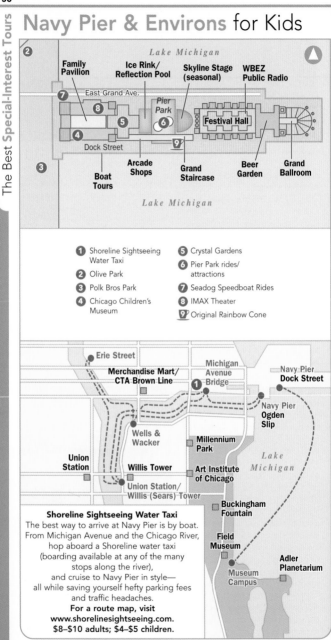

Lake Michigan

Family Pavilion

Ice Rink/ Reflection Pool

Skyline Stage (seasonal)

WBEZ Public Radio

East Grand Ave.

Pier Park

Festival Hall

Dock Street

Boat Tours

Arcade Shops

Grand Staircase

Beer Garden

Grand Ballroom

Lake Michigan

1 Shoreline Sightseeing Water Taxi

2 Olive Park

3 Polk Bros Park

4 Chicago Children's Museum

5 Crystal Gardens

6 Pier Park rides/ attractions

7 Seadog Speedboat Rides

8 IMAX Theater

9 Original Rainbow Cone

Erie Street

Merchandise Mart/ CTA Brown Line

Michigan Avenue Bridge

Navy Pier Dock Street

Navy Pier Ogden Slip

Wells & Wacker

Millennium Park

Lake Michigan

Union Station

Willis Tower

Art Institute of Chicago

Union Station/ Willis (Sears) Tower

Buckingham Fountain

Field Museum

Adler Planetarium

Museum Campus

Shoreline Sightseeing Water Taxi
The best way to arrive at Navy Pier is by boat. From Michigan Avenue and the Chicago River, hop aboard a Shoreline water taxi (boarding available at any of the many stops along the river), and cruise to Navy Pier in style— all while saving yourself hefty parking fees and traffic headaches.
For a route map, visit
www.shorelinesightseeing.com.
$8–$10 adults; $4–$5 children.

This 3,000-foot-long pier was built during World War I, and has served as a ballroom, a training center for navy pilots during World War II, and a satellite campus of the University of Illinois. Now, it's Chicago's top tourist draw (and it does feel touristy). The pier combines carnival rides (including a Ferris Wheel), climbing walls, food court, and restaurants, and the boat dock is a launching point for an array of lake tours. If you're not with kids, **Chicago Shakespeare Theater** (☎ 312/595-5600; www.chicagoshakes.com; p 128) on the pier puts on impressive shows, and the views of the lake are quite nice. But the truth is, locals without kids tend to stay away (unless visitors ask to go). START: **Red Line to Grand/State El Station, then Navy Pier's free trolley bus; or take Bus 29, 56, 65, or 66.**

Navy Pier Tip

Normal operating hours on Navy Pier change seasonally and vary with different holidays. It always opens at 10am and stays open until 10pm Sunday through Thursday and midnight Friday and Saturday in summer. In cooler months, it closes earlier, so be sure to call or check online for details (☎ *800/595 PIER [7437]; www.navypier.com*).

❶ ★★★ kids Shoreline Sightseeing Water Taxi. The best way to arrive at Navy Pier is by boat. For details, see the map.

❷ ★ kids Olive Park. Roam the most scenic sliver of parkland in the city. Fronted by a small beach, Olive Park is beloved by adults for its lovely city and lake vistas, and by kids, who have a perfect vantage point for spotting the various boats that ply the waters of our Great Lake. ⏱ *30 min. Just north and west of Navy Pier, 511 N. Columbus Dr.;* ☎ *312/742-PLAY (7529); www. chicagoparkdistrict.com.*

❸ ★ kids Polk Bros Park. Just south of Olive Park is another fantastic park, this one with two stages for movies and plays and an enormous fountain for frolicking. ⏱ *30 min. Just south and west of Navy Pier, 600 E. Grand Ave.* ☎ *312/742-PLAY (7529); www.chicagoparkdistrict.com.*

❹ ★★ kids Chicago Children's Museum. This three-story museum is a big draw, with areas designed especially for children up to age 11—including babies and toddlers. Don't miss **Dinosaur Expedition,** which re-creates an expedition to the Sahara, allowing kids to conduct scientific research and dig for the bones of an African dinosaur. **WaterWays** teaches about the uses and benefits of water resources, and a tri-level **Schooner** is open for kids to climb from the crow's nest

Olive Park.

The Chicago Children's Museum.

to the gangplank. ○ *2 hrs. On Navy Pier, 700 E. Grand Ave.* ☎ *312/527-1000. www.chicago childrensmuseum.org. Admission: $15; seniors $14; under age 1 free; free admission Thurs 5–8pm (for all) and first Sun of every month (for ages 15 and under). Daily 10am–5pm (Thurs until 8pm). Closed Thanksgiving and Christmas.*

⑤ Crystal Gardens. Rest your feet and soak up the tropical atmosphere in this relatively quiet six-story glass atrium, home to 70 full-size palm trees, dancing fountains, and other flora. ○ *10 min. Free admission.*

⑥ ★★★ kids Ferris Wheel. Year-round you can zip around 200 feet in the air in the enclosed gondolas of the Centennial Ferris Wheel. Chicago is, after all, where the first-ever Ferris Wheel debuted, and this modern version offers incredible views. ○ *15 min., longer at peak times. $18 adults, $13 kids 3–11, free under 3.*

⑥ kids Carousel and Light Tower. This colorful work of art features 36 hand-painted animals, and scenes from Navy Pier's history. (Riders must be 42 inches or taller.) Tickets include a ride on the Light Tower, which climbs up, up, up, and then drops to the sound of screams. ○ *25 min., longer at peak times. $9 (includes Light Tower). Operates May–Oct.*

⑥ kids Climbing Wall. Little monkeys (40 lb. and up), attached to a rope for safety, can scramble up this 24-foot outdoor climbing wall. ○ *15 min. $9. Operates May–Oct.*

⑥ kids Pepsi Wave Swinger. Go round and round in circles on this enormous mechanical swing—the kind you'd find at a carnival—and soak in the Lake Michigan blue views. ○ *15 min. $9 (includes Light Tower). Operates May–Oct.*

Navy Pier Revamp

If you haven't been to Navy Pier in a few years (or ever) now's a good time to revisit. There's been an impressive effort to bring more local restaurants and bars to the pier, so you can walk right past Bubba Gump and Jimmy Buffet's Margaritaville and opt for a "cheezborger" at Billy Goat or dive into deep dish at Giordano's. A good time to visit is on summer nights when fireworks are overhead (Wed at 9:30pm and Sat at 10:15pm). Grab a drink at the Miller Lite Beer Garden, where there's free, live music, and settle in for an alfresco evening. Find details at **www.navypier.com**.

The Navy Pier Carousel.

7 ★ Seadog Speedboat Rides. If your kids love speed, they'll love Seadog's 30-minute thrill ride on the lake. Racing south along the shoreline, you'll hear a bit about the city's skyline, but mostly the captain will crank the music and turbo-charged engines. Enjoy the spray from the lake! Find the bright yellow speedboats across from the Ferris wheel. Other Seadog cruises are also available, including a slower-moving 75-minute architectural cruise. ⏱ *30 min.* ☎ *866/636-7377. www.seadogcruises.com. $28 adults, $22 children 3–12, free for children 2 and under.*

8 ★ kids IMAX Theater. This updated 300-seat theater with its six-story screen is another big draw. You'll find everything from the latest Hollywood blockbusters to specially made 3-D films. Even better: the seats recline and you can grab a beer from the bar for the show. ⏱ *45–130 min., depending on the show. $17–$19 adults, $15–$18 seniors, $15–$16 children 2–12.*

Get your camera ready and head to **9 Original Rainbow Cone** for a treat of the same name: a cone stacked sky-high with chocolate, strawberry, Palmer House (vanilla with cherries and walnuts), pistachio, and orange sherbet. It's a classic South Side treat that dates back to 1926, but this outpost is much more recent to Navy Pier. *Kiosk is on the south side of Navy Pier, across from Riva Restaurant. $.*

Seadog speedboats.

The Art Institute of Chicago

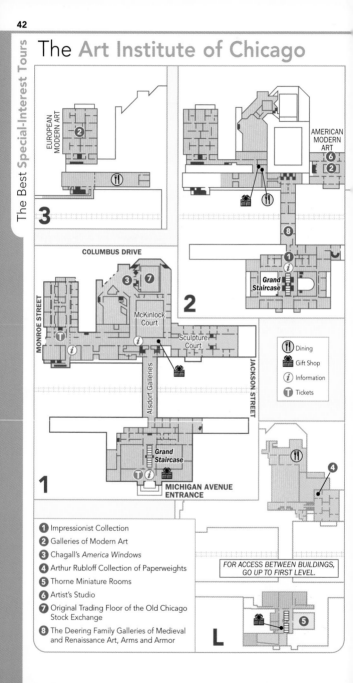

EUROPEAN MODERN ART

2

3

AMERICAN MODERN ART

6
2

8

COLUMBUS DRIVE

3
7

MONROE STREET

McKinlock Court

Sculpture Court

2

Grand Staircase

1

Grand Staircase

JACKSON STREET

Alsdorf Galleries

🍴 Dining
🎁 Gift Shop
ⓘ Information
🎫 Tickets

MICHIGAN AVENUE ENTRANCE

4

FOR ACCESS BETWEEN BUILDINGS, GO UP TO FIRST LEVEL.

5

L

1 Impressionist Collection
2 Galleries of Modern Art
3 Chagall's *America Windows*
4 Arthur Rubloff Collection of Paperweights
5 Thorne Miniature Rooms
6 Artist's Studio
7 Original Trading Floor of the Old Chicago Stock Exchange
8 The Deering Family Galleries of Medieval and Renaissance Art, Arms and Armor

Chicago's pride and joy is a gargantuan and welcoming museum that's surprisingly unstuffy (during the holidays, the famous lion sculptures that guard its entrance sport wreaths around their necks). Founded in 1879 as the Chicago Academy of Fine Arts, the institute contains one of the world's great collections (more than 5,000 years' worth) of antiquities, paintings, and sculptures. Its current Beaux Arts home was constructed as a conference venue for the 1893 World's Columbian Exposition. The Modern Wing houses works by more contemporary masters. For a dramatic entrance, access it from the floating pedestrian bridge that begins in Millennium Park. START: **Monroe/State or Jackson/State El stations.**

The Art Institute's Modern Wing.

❶ ★★★ **Impressionist Collection.** This is one of the more renowned, and therefore highly trafficked, areas of the museum. It includes one of the world's largest collections of Monet paintings (the museum's *Arrival of the Normandy Train, Gare Saint-Lazare* is a rare urban scene by the painter). Other artists represented include Renoir, van Gogh, Manet, and Degas. Among the many treasures here is Seurat's pointillist masterpiece *Sunday Afternoon on the Island of La Grande Jatte.* ⏱ *45 min. Second floor.*

❷ ★ **Modern Wing.** This stunning newer wing of the museum houses works by modern masters like Picasso, Matisse, de Kooning, and Pollock, as well as rotating exhibits of contemporary art. Confusingly, American modern art from before the 1950s is tucked into a separate gallery on the second floor of the main building, so head there to see two of the museum's biggest draws, Grant Wood's *American Gothic* and Edward Hopper's *Nighthawks.*

❸ ★★ **Marc Chagall's America Windows.** These rich, blue, stained-glass windows pay homage to artistic freedom of expression. It's easy to lose yourself in the panels and their thought-provoking symbols, which are on the first floor of the museum. ⏱ *10 min. First floor.*

❹ **Arthur Rubloff Collection of Paperweights.** Don't miss this quirky collection, donated to the museum by Chicago real estate magnate Arthur Rubloff (1902–83) in 1978. You'll find nearly 1,400 of these charming and useful objects (most made of multicolored glass), which became popular in the mid–19th century, when the establishment of a mail service made letter writing, and letter-writing accessories, highly fashionable. ⏱ *15 min. Lower level.*

❺ ★★★ kids **Thorne Miniature Rooms.** Particularly entrancing to children and dollhouse

Chagall's America Windows.

fanatics, this must-see gallery features 68 miniature rooms (the scale ranges from about 1 in. to 1 ft.) designed from 1937 to 1940 by Narcissa Ward Thorne, a miniaturist and the daughter-in-law of the founder of Montgomery Ward & Co. Each room is filled with tiny reproductions of furnished interiors from periods in European and American history. Styles run the gamut from the medieval 1300s to the modern 1930s. Especially noteworthy are the Louis XVI salon (inspired by Versailles's Petit Trianon) and the Georgian English Drawing Room (the keys on that tiny harpsichord actually move). The level of detail and masterful craftsmanship is extraordinary. ⏱ *20 min. Lower level.*

Art Institute Tips

Some tips for avoiding the rush hour: Many people don't realize the museum is open on Monday; keep this secret to yourself and visit when the galleries are relatively subdued. Also, many visitors aren't aware that the museum stays open late on Thursdays, so consider stopping by after an early dinner.

⑥ **kids Artist's Studio.** Feeling inspired by *American Gothic*? Try your hand at your own painting. The Ryan Learning Center in the Modern Wing is home to an interactive studio where kids and their families can drop in and work on their own art projects. Open to all ages; children must be accompanied by an adult. ⏱ *30 min. Lower level of the Modern Wing.*

⑦ ★ **Original Trading Floor of the Old Chicago Stock Exchange.** This room, originally built between 1893 and 1894, was salvaged and then reconstructed here when the Stock Exchange building was demolished in 1972. The room's elaborate stenciled decorations, molded plaster capitals, and art glass illustrate the work of Dankmar Adler and Louis Sullivan, two of Chicago's most important early architects. ⏱ *15 min. First level.*

⑧ **The Deering Family Galleries of Medieval and Renaissance Art, Arms, and Armor.** If you're a fan of *Game of Thrones*, you'll want to spend time in this gallery, which opened in 2017 and

Practical Matters

The Art Institute of Chicago (☎ **312/443-3566;** www.artic.edu) is located at 111 S. Michigan Ave. (at Adams St.). Take Bus 3, 4, 6, 145, 147, or 151 to Michigan Avenue and Jackson Street or the Red Line El to the Jackson/State or Monroe/State stations.

Admission is $25 for adults and $19 for seniors, children, and students with ID. Children 14 and under are free. Chicago residents receive a $5 discount on admission and Illinois residents receive a $3 discount. For an additional $10, you can bypass lines with a fast pass. Admission is free to Illinois residents Thursday evenings from 5 to 8pm. The museum is open Friday through Wednesday 10:30am to 5pm, Thursday 10:30am to 8pm. It's closed on Thanksgiving, December 25, and January 1.

is home to an enormous collection of nearly 700 items from around the Middle Ages, dating back to 1200 to 1600. The space paints a colorful portrait of life in Medieval Europe, and houses an elaborate wooden altar, crucifixes, and art from that time. And then there's the armor. Displays feature horse models in complete armor, and swords, daggers, maces, and more. Some of the full suits of armor are elaborate, shiny—and quite spooky. ⓧ *30 min.*

The Thorne Miniature Rooms.

Museum of Science & Industry

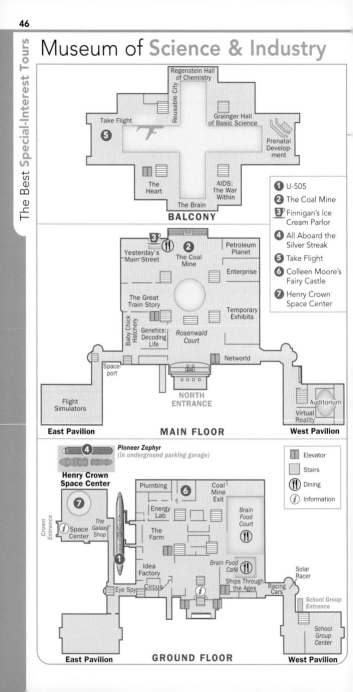

BALCONY

- Regenstein Hall of Chemistry
- Reusable City
- Take Flight
- Grainger Hall of Basic Science
- Prenatal Development
- The Heart
- The Brain
- AIDS: The War Within

1. U-505
2. The Coal Mine
3. Finnigan's Ice Cream Parlor
4. All Aboard the Silver Streak
5. Take Flight
6. Colleen Moore's Fairy Castle
7. Henry Crown Space Center

MAIN FLOOR

- Yesterday's Main Street
- The Coal Mine
- Petroleum Planet
- Enterprise
- The Great Train Story
- Baby Chick Hatchery
- Genetics: Decoding Life
- Rosenwald Court
- Temporary Exhibits
- Spaceport
- Networld
- NORTH ENTRANCE
- Flight Simulators
- Auditorium
- Virtual Reality
- **East Pavilion**
- **West Pavilion**

GROUND FLOOR

- Pioneer Zephyr (in underground parking garage)
- Henry Crown Space Center
- Space Center
- The Galaxy Shop
- Plumbing
- Energy Lab
- The Farm
- Coal Mine Exit
- Brain Food Court
- Idea Factory
- Eye Spy
- Circus
- Brain Food Café
- Ships Through the Ages
- Racing Cars
- Solar Racer
- School Group Entrance
- School Group Center
- Crown Entrance
- **East Pavilion**
- **West Pavilion**

Legend:
- Elevator
- Stairs
- Dining
- (i) Information

Built as the only permanent structure for the 1893 World Columbian Exposition, the classical-style Palace of Fine Arts building is now home to 14 acres of scientific wonders. Generations of children recount fond memories of this world-famous museum—the granddaddy of interactive museums, with some 2,000 exhibits. The good news: It still thrills kids (and adults too). START: **Bus 6 or Metra Electric train to 57th St. and Lake Park Ave.**

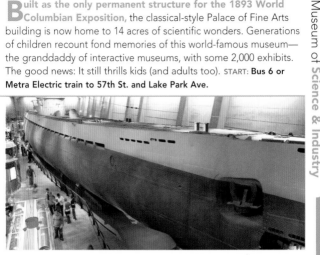

The U-505.

1 ★★★ U-505. The highlight of this 35,000-square-foot exhibit is a German submarine (known as a U-boat) that sank a number of Allied ships during World War II before it was captured by the U.S. Navy in 1944. It was installed here in 1954 and remains the only German submarine on display in North America. You have to pay extra for a guided tour of the sub's interior, but it's worth your time even if you don't go inside the actual submarine; there are interesting photos and exhibits surrounding it.

🕐 *30 min. To avoid serious crowds, come at museum opening. Ground floor. Optional 15-min. tour requires an additional experience ticket.*

2 ★★ The Coal Mine. This exhibit, which dates back to 1934, incorporates modern mining techniques—but the best part is a simulated trip down into a dark, mysterious re-created mine that's not for the claustrophobic. A stop here is worth the inevitable theme park–like lines you'll face. 🕐 *30 min. First floor. Requires an additional experience ticket.*

Exploring the Coal Mine.

3 **Finnigan's Ice Cream Parlor** is modeled on a real Hyde Park ice-cream shop that opened in 1917. Soak up the turn-of-the-20th-century atmosphere and indulge in awesome sundaes and shakes. For heartier appetites, there are sandwiches and chips, and great coffee. *Main floor, near the Coal Mine. $.*

4 ★ **kids** **All Aboard the Silver Streak.** The Burlington Pioneer Zephyr—the world's first streamlined, diesel-electric train—was built in the 1930s and revolutionized train design. The 197-foot train, nicknamed the Silver Streak, is installed (along with a simulated train station) in the museum's three-story underground parking garage. This is a must for train buffs. ○ *15 min. Great Hall.*

5 **kids** **Take Flight.** This aviation-themed exhibit features a full-size Boeing 727 airplane that revs up its engines and replays voice recordings from a San Francisco–Chicago flight periodically throughout the day. ○ *15 min. Balcony.*

6 ★★ **kids** **Colleen Moore's Fairy Castle.** Colleen Moore, a popular silent film actress and miniatures fan, set out in 1928 to create her version of a dream dollhouse. It took more than 7 years and 700 craftsmen to create this lavishly decorated miniature palace, filled with more than 2,000 miniatures. ○ *20 min. Ground floor.*

7 ★★★ **Henry Crown Space Center.** The story of space exploration is documented in copious detail inside this 35,000-square-foot addition to the museum—a must for space buffs. A highlight is the **Apollo 8 Command Module,** the first manned craft to orbit the moon. Other items of interest include astronaut training gear and a moon rock. You can even control a Mars rover using a remote control. The movie, *The Story of Earth,* which is about the birth of our planet and is shown via laser projection in a giant, domed theater, is a good complement. ○ *40 min. (more if you see a film, which requires an additional fee). Off ground level.* ●

Practical Information

The Museum of Science and Industry (☎ **773/684-1414;** www.msichicago.org) is located at 5700 S. Lake Shore Drive. Take Bus 2, 6 or the Metra Rail to 57th Street and Lake Park Avenue.

Admission to the museum only is $22 adults, $13 kids 3 to 11, and free for children 2 and under ($17 and $10, respectively, for Chicago residents). Admission plus one experience is $34 for adults and $22 for kids; tickets are also available that include two and three experiences. Admission is free during various times of the year, so check the website under "admission prices" for a full listing.

From Memorial Day to Labor Day, the museum is open daily 9:30am to 5:30pm. From early September to late May, it's open daily from 9:30am to 4pm. Closed Thanksgiving and Christmas.

The Gold Coast

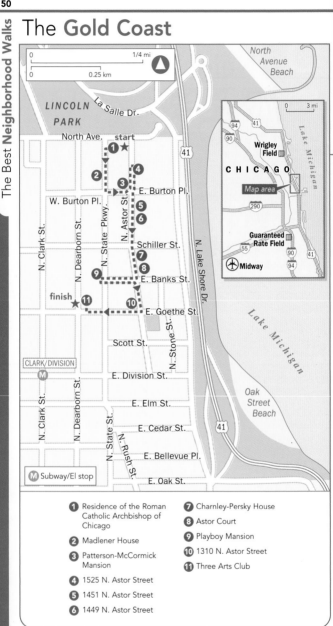

1. Residence of the Roman Catholic Archbishop of Chicago
2. Madlener House
3. Patterson-McCormick Mansion
4. 1525 N. Astor Street
5. 1451 N. Astor Street
6. 1449 N. Astor Street
7. Charnley-Persky House
8. Astor Court
9. Playboy Mansion
10. 1310 N. Astor Street
11. Three Arts Club

Previous page: A stroll through iconic Old Town.

This scenic and exclusive neighborhood of leafy streets and historic mansions fronts Lake Michigan and is home to some of Chicago's most famous and moneyed families. It dates back to the 1880s, when retailing wizard Potter Palmer built a lakeshore castle in the midst of what was then wild marshland (his spectacular home, at what is now 1450 N. Lake Shore Dr., was eventually torn down and a high-rise complex built in its place). After buying up the neighboring land, Palmer watched the city's most prominent social families follow his lead, turning his marshland into real estate gold.

START: **Oak St. Beach, Lake Shore Dr. just south of Oak St. Bus: 151.**

❶ Residence of the Roman Catholic Archbishop of Chicago. This 2½-story Queen Anne–style mansion dates back to 1880 and stands on the grounds of a former cemetery. One of the oldest and most notable residences on the Gold Coast, it's also one of the best preserved. Note the elaborate chimneys—there are 19 of them. The red-brick structure is the current home of Cardinal Blase Cupich. *1555 N. State Pkwy. (at North Ave.).*

❷ Madlener House. Designed as a private residence by Richard E. Schmidt in 1902, this National Historic Landmark foreshadowed the Art Deco style that would not emerge in Chicago for another 20 years. The brick-and-limestone structure's clean lines and its doorways ornamented with delicate bronze grillwork offer hints of both the Prairie and Chicago schools of design. It's currently home to the Graham Foundation for Advanced Studies in the Fine Arts, which has installed a collection of fragments from famous Chicago buildings in the courtyard. It's a must for architecture buffs and historic home fans. ⏱ *30 min. 4 W. Burton Place.* ☎ *312/787-4071. www.grahamfoundation.org. Gallery/bookshop open Wed–Sat 11am–6pm.*

❸ Patterson-McCormick Mansion. Designed by New York architect Stanford White, this palazzo-style mansion was commissioned in 1893 by Joseph Medill, owner of the *Chicago Tribune,* as a wedding present for his daughter. The Georgian structure is faced with Roman bricks of burnt yellow and terra-cotta trim, and marked the beginning of an

Patterson-McCormick Mansion.

architectural movement toward classical exteriors. The home was purchased in 1914 by Cyrus McCormick, Jr., son of the inventor of the reaper and the first president of International Harvester. McCormick had it enlarged to its current size in 1927. The building now houses condominiums. *20 E. Burton Place.*

④ ★★ **1525 N. Astor St.** This attractive town house (on a block full of multimillon-dollar homes) is the former home of Robert Todd Lincoln (1843–1926), the son of Abraham and Mary Todd Lincoln. Lincoln operated a private law practice in Chicago before moving on to serve as secretary of war to Presidents Garfield and Arthur. Upon the death of George Pullman, one of his clients, Lincoln became president of the Palace Car Company in 1897.

⑤ ★★ **1451 N. Astor St.** Designed by Howard Van Doren Shaw, who built several of the mansions on ritzy Astor Street, this mansion showcases the unique "Jacobethan" style (a mixture of 16th- and 17th-c. features of Elizabethan and Jacobean architecture). It was originally built for brewer Peter Fortune in 1912.

⑥ ★★ **1449 N. Astor St.** The origins of this grandiose château remain a mystery, though it was definitely built around 1890. The exterior features, including an intimidating stone porch, decorative friezes, and a large front bay, make for worthwhile viewing.

⑦ ★★ **Charnley-Persky House.** This 1892 National Historic Landmark was built by the firm of Adler and Sullivan, back when a 19-year-old draftsman named Frank Lloyd Wright was laboring there in obscurity. Wright's role in designing the building (he called it "the first modern house in America") is evident in its progressive shape, especially

when compared to its fanciful neighbors, homes that drew on styles based on antiquity. Even today, this home is an excellent illustration of the timelessness of Wright's ideas. Charles Persky donated the building to the Society of Architectural Historians in 1995, and the society runs public tours on Wednesdays (45 min.) and Saturdays (60 min.). Call for information. ① *1 hr. 1365 N. Astor St.* ☎ *312/573-1365. www.sah.org. Apr–Oct, tours are free Wed at noon; Sat tours at 10am and noon include other historic neighborhood residences and cost $10 adults, $8 seniors, and $5 kids 5–13.*

⑧ **Astor Court.** If this building evokes images of England when you look at it, that's because of its Georgian formality, typical of the architecture you'd find in London. It was designed in 1914 by Howard Van Doren Shaw. Look up at the ornament over the central drive, which leads to a formal inner court surrounded by residential units: The ornament is the source of the structure's nickname, "The Court of the Golden Hands." *1355 N. Astor St.*

⑨ **Playboy Mansion.** Built in 1899, this very traditional-looking mansion was home to *Playboy's* Hugh Hefner during his Chicago heyday in the 1960s. The building has been converted into very expensive private condos, so you'll need your imagination to envision Hugh romping here with his bunnies and hosting legendary parties. (Playboy Enterprises no longer has a presence in Chicago; it's now in Los Angeles.) *1340 N. State Pkwy.*

⑩ **1310 N. Astor St.** John Wellborn Root (1850–91), one of the founders of the Chicago School of Architecture and a former director of the American Institute of Architects, is best known for his work on skyscrapers with Daniel Burnham (their collaborations include the

The original Playboy Mansion.

Monadnock and Rookery buildings). But this lovely brick town house, built by Root in 1887, must have struck a chord with the architect—he moved in and lived here with his family (including his son, John Root, Jr., a renowned architect in his own right) until he died of pneumonia at the young age of 41.

⓫ ★★ **Three Arts Club.** This four-story Chicago landmark, which is now a Restoration Hardware retail store (p 83), was built in 1914 by architect John Holabird to house a club dedicated to providing women with a suitable environment for the study of painting, music, and drama. Many of the club's founders were prominent women of the time, including social reformer Jane Addams and socialite Edith Rockefeller McCormick. The club's residential units were arranged around a central courtyard, in the style of a Tuscan villa (a lot of the exterior ornamentation is also Byzantine in nature). The ornamental mosaics over the terra-cotta entrance salute the three branches of the arts that the club is named for. *1300 N. Dearborn St.*

The landmark Three Arts Club.

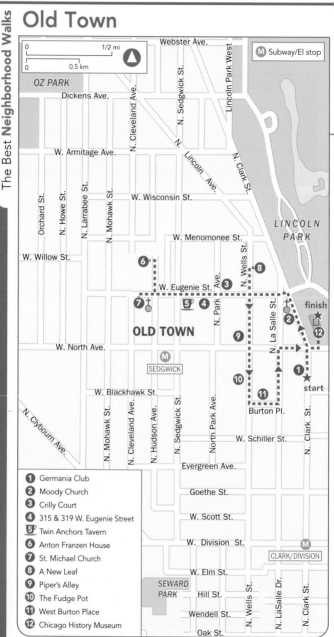

Old Town

0		1/2 mi
0	0.5 km	

M Subway/El stop

Webster Ave.

OZ PARK

Dickens Ave.

W. Armitage Ave.

W. Wisconsin St.

LINCOLN PARK

W. Menomonee St.

W. Willow St.

6

W. Eugenie St. **3**

8

7 † **5** **4**

finish

2

OLD TOWN

9

12

W. North Ave.

M SEDGWICK

10

1

start

W. Blackhawk St.

11

Burton Pl.

N. Clybourn Ave.

W. Schiller St.

Evergreen Ave.

1 Germania Club
2 Moody Church
3 Crilly Court
4 315 & 319 W. Eugenie Street
5 Twin Anchors Tavern
6 Anton Franzen House
7 St. Michael Church
8 A New Leaf
9 Piper's Alley
10 The Fudge Pot
11 West Burton Place
12 Chicago History Museum

Goethe St.

W. Scott St.

W. Division St.

M CLARK/DIVISION

W. Elm St.

SEWARD PARK

Hill St.

Wendell St.

Oak St.

Old Town is an eclectic residential neighborhood that mixes frame cottages, brick town houses, historic taverns, and churches. Home to the city's German immigrant population at the turn of the 20th century, Old Town became famous in the '60s as a hippie haven (a time that saw the birth of the area's most famous landmark, The Second City comedy theater). After falling down on its luck in the '70s, the area has reinvigorated and is now a top destination for boutique shopping, dining, and theater. START: **Intersection of Clark St. and North Ave. Bus: 22 (Clark).**

❶ Germania Club. This lovely red-brick building, built in 1889, was the original home of a German-American *Sangverein* (singing society), a social outlet for immigrants in Chicago. Today, it's home to a Starbucks. Note the elaborate terra-cotta ornamentation on the exterior and the oversize, arched windows on the second floor. *1536 N. Clark St.*

❷ The Moody Church. Dwight L. Moody came to Chicago from Massachusetts in 1856 to work as a shoe salesman, but eventually became one of the city's most colorful evangelists. He worked as a missionary mostly in the city's poorer sections, notably the area that later became known as Cabrini Green, one of the nation's most notorious housing projects (once located at Clybourn St., Cabrini Green is disassembled, and its residents have moved to low-rise, mixed-income housing). The church he founded was originally at Chicago Avenue and LaSalle Drive, where the Moody Bible Institute is now located. This

The Moody Church.

building, dating from 1925, incorporates Byzantine (the decorative exterior) and Romanesque (the arched stained-glass windows) designs. Visitors are welcome to attend services. Free campus tours are offered Monday through Friday at 11am. *1635 N. LaSalle St.* ☎ *312/327-8600. www.moodychurch.org.*

❸ Crilly Court. Resembling homes in an old quarter of New Orleans (complete with wrought-iron balconies in the back), these well-maintained row houses sit on one of Chicago's oldest streets. The

The Germania Club.

houses (and the apartment buildings opposite them) were built by contractor Daniel F. Crilly around 1885, when he cut a lane, named it for himself, and offered cottages to working families on the lower end of the economic scale. The owl-eyed among you might spot the names of the Crillys' children carved into the entrances to the Queen Anne–style buildings. *Block of Eugenie St., just west of Wells St.*

④ 315 & 319 W. Eugenie St.

These privately owned homes are excellent examples of the wooden dwellings built outside the city limits in the years immediately following the Great Fire of 1871 (wooden buildings were outlawed in the city proper following the conflagration). They are noteworthy for their fanciful exterior trim work, not a rare sight in this immigrant neighborhood, where so many skilled artisans once made their homes.

Stop in for the famous ribs at ⑤ ★ **Twin Anchors Tavern,** a neighborhood watering hole. This down-home spot, decorated with memorabilia dating back to the days when Frank Sinatra was a frequent visitor, is a favorite of locals. *1655 N. Sedgwick St.* ☎ *312/266-1616. www.twinanchorsribs.com. $–$$.*

⑥ Anton Franzen House. This

classic Chicago cottage measures a story and a half and features a broad gabled facade. Built in 1880 of brick (as opposed to the prevailing wood), it is not so different in appearance from Frank Lloyd Wright's original Oak Park cottage (p 146). If you want to see a prime example of the typical late-19th-century Chicago house, this is it. *1726 N. Hudson Ave.*

⑦ ★★ St. Michael Church. It's

said that if you can hear the bells of St. Michael Church, you know that you're in Old Town. Historically a German parish (as opposed to the Irish parishes found elsewhere in the city during the early 1900s), St. Michael is a massive Romanesque church that reveals a strong Southern European influence. The latter is especially evident in the stained-glass windows, embellished with Catholic iconography, that were imported from Munich at the turn of the 20th century. *1633 N. Cleveland Ave. (btw. North Ave. and Eugenie St.).* ☎ *312/642-2498. www.st-mikes.org.*

⑧ ★★ A New Leaf. North Wells

Street offers great window-shopping, and this store is a standout. The loft-style space is filled with cut flowers, vintage plant varieties, tropical foliage, succulents, and everything else you need to make a house a home, including candles in a rainbow of colors, ribbons to match, votive holders, and other tabletop necessities. *1818 N. Wells St.* ☎ *312/642-1676. www.anewleafchicago.com.*

⑨ Piper's Alley. This entertain-

ment space was the site of a bakery

A bike tour stops outside St. Michael Church.

A mural in Piper's Alley.

owned by Henry Piper in 1880. During the 1960s, it was Old Town's most popular tourist zone, filled with boutiques and bead shops. Today it's home to an art film cinema, several theaters and shops, and, since the 1950s, The Second City comedy club (p 126). *1616 N. Wells St.*

10 **The Fudge Pot.** Walking down the steps to this chocoholic's dream shop is a little like stepping back in time. It's been here since the '60s, and the Wonka-like treats are made in house. The chocolate artists can create just about anything you dream up in cacao form, including the face of Abraham Lincoln. *1532 N. Wells St.* ☎ *312/943-1777. www. thefudgepotchicago.com. $.*

11 **West Burton Place.** What was once a short block of cookie-cutter Victorian homes was remodeled in 1927 into inspired apartment buildings by Sol Kogen and Edgar Miller, two Old Town artists who had studied together at the Art Institute in 1917. The heavily embellished structures were rehabbed with an assortment of salvaged materials

(glass, marble, terra-cotta, etc.) from various demolished buildings in the area. Miller's masterpiece is 155 W. Burton Place (observe the bounty of transparent stained glass—Miller's favorite medium). At the time of writing, a unit here was for sale for a cool $1.5 million, if you're interested in moving in.

12 **★★★ Chicago History Museum.** Founded in 1856, the History Museum is one of Chicago's oldest cultural institutions, and, somewhat secretly, one of the best. Its handsome Georgian red-brick headquarters underwent a massive renovation in 2006. The galleries feature interactive exhibits, including a re-creation of an 1890s El station; an exhibit on "Facing Freedom in America" (covering everything from women's suffrage to Japanese internment); and a section on Illinois's most famous native son, Abraham Lincoln. There's a special gallery just for kids, where you can dress up like a giant Chicago hot dog with all the fixings and admire yourself, hot peppers and all, in the mirror. *1601 N. Clark St. (at North Ave.).* ☎ *312/642-4600. www.chicagohistory.org.*

Chicago History Museum's "Crossroads of America" exhibit.

Bucktown & Wicker Park

0   1/4 mi
0   0.25 km

W. Dickens Ave.

W. Armitage Ave.

W. Armitage Ave.

W. Homer St.

BUCKTOWN

finish
19

W. Cortland St.

W. Cortland St.

W. Moffat St.

W. Churchill St.

W. Bloomingdale Ave.

W. Willow St.

W. St. Paul Ave.

W. St. Paul Ave.

W. Wabansia Ave.

W. Wabansia Ave.

12

W. Concord Pl.

15

17

W. North Ave. (64)

13

16

11

9

W. North Ave.

M DAMEN

10

8

W. Pierce Ave.

W. Pierce Ave.

W. Le Moyne St.

W. Le Moyne St.

M Subway/El stop

W. Le Moyne St.

1 start

W. Julian St.

7

WICKER PARK

W. Beach Ave.

W. Schiller St.

6 2 3 4 5

W. Schiller St.

WICKER PARK

W. Ellen St.

1 Wicker Park
2 1959–1961 W. Schiller Street
3 1951 W. Schiller Street
4 Harris Cohn House
5 Nelson Algren House
6 Pritzker School
7 1407 N. Hoyne Avenue
8 1521 N. Hoyne Avenue
9 1558 N. Hoyne Avenue
10 Hermann Weinhardt House
11 Hans D. Runge House
12 2156 W. Caton Street
13 Flat Iron Bulding
14 Luxor Baths
15 Northwest Tower Building
16 1934 W. North Avenue
17 Window-shop along Damen Avenue
18 Mindy's Hot Chocolate
19 St. Mary of the Angels

W. Potomac Ave.

W. Crystal St.

W. Division St.

W. Haddon St.

W. Thomas St.

0   3 mi

Wrigley Field

Map area

CHICAGO

The Loop

W. Augusta Blvd.

Guaranteed Rate Field

W. Walton St.

Midway

W. Iowa St.

Wicker Park is an artists' community filled with trendy shops, funky restaurants, and side streets lined with pricey mansions and other examples of Victorian architecture. Bucktown, traditionally working-class, is alive with new development. Both are favorite nighttime destinations of Chicagoans in search of the latest and greatest clubs and bars, but many don't get to see the neighborhoods' historic architecture, which is best viewed during the day. START: **Take El's Blue Line to Damen station, then go 1 block south to Wicker Park.**

Wicker Park neighborhood.

1 Wicker Park. One the smaller parks in the city (a mere 4 acres) gave its name to one of Chicago's most famous neighborhoods. The park was donated to the city around 1870 by siblings Charles (an alderman who made his money building railroads) and Joel Wicker. The brothers had extensive real estate holdings in the area and figured the park could only enhance the value of their property. *At the intersection of N. Damen Ave. and Schiller St.*

2 1959–1961 W. Schiller St. This double home was built in 1886 in the fashionable Second Empire style (note the large mansard roof and decorative sawtooth pattern in the brickwork). Its owner was a ship's captain and medical doctor. In the 1920s it became a rooming house. It has thankfully been restored with lively Victorian colors.

3 1951 W. Schiller St. Built as the residence of Dr. Nels T. Quales, a Norwegian immigrant and humanitarian who founded Chicago's Lutheran Deaconess Hospital, this house dates from 1873 and features Italianate styling and a Romanesque exterior noted for its use of arches and truncated columns. The addition of Moorish windows on the first and second stories altered the facade around 1890, and the house is currently being restored to its original condition.

4 Harris Cohn House. This mansion (built in 1890–91) was the home of a partner in the Cohn Brothers Clothing Company. The Italian Romanesque facade features square columns of granite (polished to resemble marble) and a turret resting on a shell-shaped base. Stonework on the second-floor balcony follows a checkerboard pattern, and handrails are scrolled with a motif of oak leaves. The residence was reconverted from a boarding house into a single-family home after a fire damaged it around 1980, and underwent extensive interior restoration and beautification in the 1990s. *1941 W. Schiller St.*

⑤ Nelson Algren House. The exterior stonework on this three-story home is worth a look, but more interesting than the facade is the fact that novelist Nelson Algren (1909–81) lived in one of the building's third-floor apartments from 1959 to 1975. The National Book Award winner (for his landmark *The Man with the Golden Arm*) and journalist drew inspiration for his writing from the surrounding neighborhood. A sidewalk marker provides info about Algren's life and writings. *1958 W. Evergreen St.*

⑥ Pritzker School. This Chicago public school is named for its most famous alumnus. A. N. Pritzker, the son of a Russian immigrant, grew up in the neighborhood and graduated from this school when it was known as Wicker Park School (Pritzker's family went on to found the Hyatt hotel chain). *2009 W. Schiller St.*

⑦ 1407 N. Hoyne Ave. In the late 19th century, so many brewers built mansions along the stretch of Hoyne running from Evergreen Avenue to North Avenue that it became known as **Beer Baron Row.** This mansion, built in 1880 by German wine merchant John Rapp, was the largest single-family estate in Wicker Park at the time (the estate's Coach House is now a separate residence at 2044 W. Schiller St.). The mansard roof and wrought-iron

fence are characteristic of the Second Empire style of the estate. For all of its grandeur, however, this was not a happy home: Rapp was murdered here by his bookkeeper, his wife went insane, and their son was convicted of embezzlement. Note that locals refer to this place as either the Goldblatt or Wieboldt Mansion, though no member of these two prominent Chicago mercantile families (both Wicker Park fixtures) ever resided here.

⑧ 1521 N. Hoyne Ave. German manufacturing executive Adolph Borgmeier was definitely behind the design of this fetching mansion, built in 1890 (though some claim it was actually built by a war profiteer who scammed the federal government for millions during the Civil War). The design is a brilliant mix of Romanesque and Queen Anne elements; look closely at the metal trim, and you'll spot a host of decorative symbols (flowers, scrolls, and so on). The likeness of a woman carved into the exterior is a typical embellishment on German-built houses.

⑨ 1558 N. Hoyne Ave. Ever fearful of another conflagration after the events of the Great Fire of 1871, the designers of this 1877 mansion stuck to ornamental pressed metal when creating its decorative trim. The Queen Anne–style home was originally built for Hermann Plautz, the president of the Northwestern Brewing Company. From 1927 to 1972, it served as the headquarters for the local American Legion (which is why that seemingly out-of-place cannon is still in the front yard).

⑩ Hermann Weinhardt House. When furniture company exec Hermann Weinhardt commissioned a home that would remind him of his German roots, this must-see mix of fairy-tale Victorian and Bavarian gingerbread was the result. The

The Flat Iron Building.

1888 mansion features three stories of extraordinary detailing, including an elaborately carved balcony and an unusual juxtaposition of green stone and red-brick limestone. *2135 W. Pierce Ave. (btw. N. Hoyne Ave. and N. Leavitt St.).*

⓫ **Hans D. Runge House.** This 1884 home, built by the treasurer of the Wolf Brothers Milling Company, is considered a prime example of the intricate Eastlake style (named for 19th-c. English designer Charles Eastlake) of ornamentation, and it features lots of elaborate woodwork. Architecture aside, the house is best known for a 1930 concert given by the great Polish pianist and statesman Ignacy Paderewski from the upper level of the building's two-story porch, when the home functioned as the Polish consulate. *2138 W. Pierce Ave. (btw. N. Hoyne Ave. and N. Leavitt St.).*

⓬ **2156 W. Caton St.** Import-export entrepreneur Ole Thorpe built this German-influenced Romanesque mansion in 1892. The most obvious feature is the round, domed turret rising from the flared and rough-surfaced foundations. Other highlights include a host of stained-glass windows and a notable sunburst design over the door on the second-story porch.

⓭ **Flat Iron Building.** Wicker Park is known for its artistic bent, and this office building, designed in 1929 by the firm of Holabird & Root, is best known as the home of many artists' lofts and galleries (most are open to the public, so feel free to wander around inside). *1569 N. Milwaukee Ave. (at W. North Ave.).*

⓮ **Luxor Baths.** Also known as the North Avenue Baths, this

The historic Luxor Baths building.

Rooftop of the Northwest Tower Building.

building dates back to the 1920s, when public baths were all the rage. The baths were a popular meeting spot for wheelers and dealers back in the day, and, according to legend, were also a mob hangout. The gleaming terracotta exterior is all that remains of the past; the interior has been transformed into a bunch of private yuppie apartments. *2041 W. North Ave.*

⓯ ★★ **Northwest Tower Building.** One of the finest examples of Art Deco architecture in Chicago, this handsome 12-story building, which is now a trendy hotel called The Robey, was built in 1929 and was the tallest structure outside of the downtown area at the time. During the Prohibition era, the building was the terminus for a secret underground tunnel (now closed) that allowed patrons to escape a speak-easy across the

street during raids. *2018 W. North Ave. www.therobey.com.*

⓰ **1934 W. North Ave.** The coolness quotient of the Wicker Park/Bucktown area may have soared in 2001, when MTV selected it as the site of that season's hit reality soap opera, *The Real World*, but quite a number of locals were anything but thrilled by the accompanying publicity. This Wicker Park loft apartment will be familiar to viewers as the spot where the young and the restless lived during filming (several of the seven cast members worked a few doors down, at the hip pizzeria Piece [p 105]).

⓱ ★★★ **Window-shop along Damen Avenue.** The best way to travel from Wicker Park into Bucktown is to window-shop along Damen Avenue, the street that marks the heart of the

A festival along Damen Avenue.

A decadent option at Mindy's Hot Chocolate.

neighborhood. Start at its intersection with North Avenue and work your way up. The busy thoroughfare is loaded with vintage and designer clothing stores, cozy coffee shops, and trendy bars. Good shopping bets include **p 45** (p 78), and **Scotch and Soda** (p 79). It's also fabulous for people-watching.

Refresh and refuel at **18** ★ **Mindy's Hot Chocolate,** a sophisticated sit-down restaurant where you can go sweet (the namesake hot chocolate and ridiculous desserts, like hot fudge cream puffs) or savory (an awesome burger as well as fancier fare, ranging from seafood to roast duck). And you can't go wrong with a boozy hot chocolate. *1747 N. Damen Ave.* ☎ *773/489-1747. www. hotchocolatechicago.com. $–$$.*

19 ★ **St. Mary of the Angels.** The dome on this Renaissance-style Roman Catholic church dominates the neighborhood's skyline, and was modeled on the Vatican's St. Peter's Basilica. The immense building—it takes up an entire block—opened in 1920 to serve Bucktown's Polish parish, but by the 1980s had deteriorated to the point that it had been slated for demolition. A massive outcry from the local community led instead to a huge restoration campaign (the repairs cost more than the price of the original construction). Today, the dome of the church has been renovated, and the rest, from the carved angels on its rooftop to its stained-glass windows, is in picture-perfect shape. *1850 N. Hermitage Ave. (at W. Cordlandt St.).* ☎ *773/ 278-2644. www.sma-church.org.*

St. Mary of the Angels Catholic church.

The Best Neighborhood Walks

Hyde Park

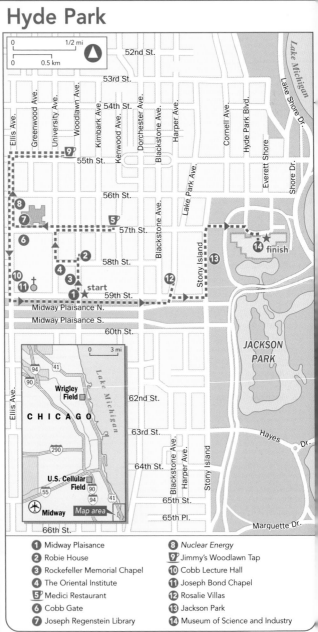

0 1/2 mi
0 0.5 km

52nd St.

53rd St.

54th St.

55th St.

56th St.

57th St.

58th St.

start

59th St.

Midway Plaisance N.

Midway Plaisance S.

60th St.

Ellis Ave.
Greenwood Ave.
University Ave.
Woodlawn Ave.
Kimbark Ave.
Kenwood Ave.
Dorchester Ave.
Blackstone Ave.
Harper Ave.
Cornell Ave.
Hyde Park Blvd.
Everett Shore
Shore Dr.
Lake Shore Dr.
Lake Michigan
Lake Park Ave.
Stony Island

finish

JACKSON
PARK

62nd St.

63rd St.

64th St.

65th St.

65th Pl.

66th St.

Hayes Dr.

Marquette Dr.

Wrigley
Field

CHICAGO

Lake Michigan

94
90
41
290

U.S. Cellular
Field
90
94
41

55

Midway   Map area

Ellis Ave.

Blackstone Ave.
Harper Ave.
Stony Island

0 3 mi

1 Midway Plaisance
2 Robie House
3 Rockefeller Memorial Chapel
4 The Oriental Institute
5 Medici Restaurant
6 Cobb Gate
7 Joseph Regenstein Library

8 *Nuclear Energy*
9 Jimmy's Woodlawn Tap
10 Cobb Lecture Hall
11 Joseph Bond Chapel
12 Rosalie Villas
13 Jackson Park
14 Museum of Science and Industry

Hyde Park combines a top attraction for kids—The Museum of Science and Industry—with the University of Chicago's 175 acres of gorgeous Gothic buildings and some of the city's most distinctive residential architecture. It's a truly racially integrated neighborhood and well worth visiting, but be aware that some of the neighboring areas have experienced crime and blight. START: Take the Metra to 56th St. and walk 4 blocks south to 60th St.

Stroll along the Midway Plaisance.

❶ Midway Plaisance. The heart of the University of Chicago campus is a broad (1-block-wide), grassy thoroughfare designed by Frederick Law Olmsted, the famous landscape architect behind New York City's Central Park. The mile-long stretch was the site of the 1893 World Columbian Exposition's Bazaar of Nations, which featured the world's first Ferris wheel and carnival sideshow attractions. The term "midway" has been used ever since to refer to the heart of a carnival. *At 60th St. and Stony Island Ave., west to Cottage Grove Ave.*

❷ ★★★ Frederick C. Robie House. Considered a masterpiece of 20th-century American architecture, this National Historic Landmark features the open layout,

linear geometry of form, and craftsmanship that are typical of Frank Lloyd Wright's Prairie School design. Completed in 1909 for inventor Frederick Robie, a bicycle and motorcycle manufacturer, the home is also notable for its exquisite leaded- and stained-glass doors and windows. It's also among the last of Wright's Prairie School–style homes: During its construction, Wright abandoned both his family and his Oak Park practice to follow other pursuits, most prominently the realization of his Taliesin home and studio in Spring Green, Wisconsin. Docents from Oak Park's Frank Lloyd Wright Home & Studio Foundation (p 147, ❷) lead tours here. After a massive, 10-year restoration in honor of the house's 100th anniversary, it looks better than ever. A

The Robie House, a 20th-century masterpiece.

Wright specialty bookshop is located in the building's former three-car garage—a structure that was highly unusual for the time in which it was built. ⏱ *1 hr. 5757 S. Woodlawn Ave. (at 58th St.).* ☎ *312/994-4000. www.wrightplus.org. Admission $18 adults, $15 seniors, students and military, free for children 3 and under. Thurs–Mon tours 10am–3pm. Museum shop Thurs–Mon 9:30am–4:30pm. Bus: 6 or Metra Electric train to 57th St. and Lake Park Ave.*

③ ★★★ **Rockefeller Memorial Chapel.** John D. Rockefeller founded the University of Chicago in cooperation with the American Baptist Society, and his bequest to the university included funds for this magnificent Gothic minicathedral (a mere chapel, it isn't). The building was designed by Bertram Goodhue (who was also the architect behind Cal Tech's campus) and dedicated in 1928; it was renamed for its benefactor upon his death in 1937. Outstanding features include the circular stained-glass window high above the main altar, a series

University of Chicago's Oriental Institute.

of statues depicting important figures in religion, and the world's second-largest carillon (72 bells). *5850 S. Woodlawn Ave.* ☎ *773/702-2100. http://rockefeller.uchicago.edu. Free admission. Tues–Fri when school is in session, 11am–6pm. Bus: 6.*

④ ★★ **The Oriental Institute.** The Oriental Institute houses one of the world's major collections of Near Eastern art (some of the exhibits here date back to 9000 B.C.). Many of the galleries have been renovated since the Institute's opening in 1931, but this is still a traditional museum: lots of glass cases, very few interactive exhibits. The must-see Egyptian Gallery includes a monumental 17-foot solid-quartzite statue of King Tutankhamen (the boy king who ruled Egypt about 1335–24 B.C.), the largest Egyptian sculpture in the Western Hemisphere (tipping the scales at 6 tons). The highlight of the Mesopotamian Gallery is a massive, 16-foot-tall sculpture of a winged bull with a human head, which once stood in the palace of Assyrian King Sargon II. Many of the gallery's other works have become one-of-a-kind since the looting of the National Museum in Baghdad in 2003. ⏱ *1 hr. 1155 E. 58th St. (at University Ave.).* ☎ *773/702-9514. www.oi.uchicago.edu. Free admission; suggested donation $10 adults, $5 children. Tues–Sun 10am–5pm (Wed until 8pm). Bus: 6 or Metra Electric train to 57th St. and Lake Park Ave.*

The main aisle and altar of Rockefeller Memorial Chapel.

Cobb Gate.

The casual **5 Medici Restaurant,** near the university campus, has fed generations of students, who've carved their names into the tables while chowing down on the house specialty—pizza. Also great for salads and insanely delish apple pie. *1327 E. 57th St.* ☎ *773/667-7394. www.medici57.com. $.*

6 Cobb Gate. Enter the campus of the world-renowned University of Chicago (more than 90 Nobel Laureates have graced its halls) through Cobb Gate (movie buffs might recognize it as the place where Harry met Sally in *When Harry Met Sally*), which features lots of Gothic detailing. The mythic figures climbing to the tip of the gate's pointed gable are said to represent the admissions counselor and college examiner, defying students an easy passage into the university. You, however, can pass through without problem, and can stroll around the campus's dramatic stone buildings (most of them designed by renowned Gothic architect Henry Ives Cobb), patterned after England's Oxford University. *57th St. between Ellis and University aves.*

7 Joseph Regenstein Library. This building is a behemoth that was ostensibly designed to blend in with its neighbors, but does nothing of the sort. The building's brutalist textured limestone looks like slab concrete and is not beloved by critics. In contrast, on the west lawn is the glass-domed Joe and Rika Mansueto library. Made of steel, aluminum, and glass, it's a functional modern work of art. The library is generally closed to the public, but out-of-state visitors with a valid photo ID and research needs can get a day pass at the library's Privileges Office (worth it if you're a bookworm or a map fan). *1100 E. 57th St. (btw. S. University and S. Ellis aves.).* ☎ *773/702-8782. www.lib.uchicago.edu.*

8 Nuclear Energy. This abstract sculpture (representing a skull and a mushroom cloud) by Henry Moore was installed in 1967 to commemorate the site of the world's first controlled nuclear chain reaction. In 1942, Nobel Laureate Enrico Fermi supervised that historic event in a makeshift underground laboratory beneath what was then the grandstand of the university's Stagg Field sports stadium. *Ellis Ave. between 56th and 57th sts.*

Henry Moore's Nuclear Energy.

9 **Jimmy's Woodlawn Tap** is the University of Chicago's most famous watering hole. Founded in 1948, Jimmy's doesn't offer much in the way of atmosphere (it's famously rough around the edges), but it's a great place to grab a drink, a burger, or a Reuben sandwich. *1172 E. 55th St.* ☎ *773/643-5516. $.*

10 **Cobb Lecture Hall.** This distinctive Gothic building, the first of 19 that Henry I. Cobb (1859–1931) designed for the campus, was all there was to the University of Chicago when it opened for business in 1892. Classes are still held here today (the interior was revamped in 1963), and the building is also home to the Renaissance Society, Chicago's oldest contemporary art museum (founded in 1915). The Society holds frequent exhibitions that are open to the public in the Bregman Gallery on the fourth floor. *5811 S. Ellis Ave.* ☎ *773/702-8670. www.renaissance society.org. Free admission. Gallery Tues–Fri 10am–5pm (until 8pm on Thurs); Sat–Sun noon–5pm.*

11 **★★ Joseph Bond Chapel.** Even nonbelievers applaud the exquisite interiors of this showcase for ecclesiastical architecture. The 300-seat chapel was donated to the university in 1926 in honor of the memory of Joseph Bond, a former trustee of the Baptist Theological Union. The structure is richly decorated with detailed carvings, etchings, sculptures, stained glass, and detailed woodwork. The picturesque chapel is a very popular venue for weddings. *1050 E. 59th St.* ☎ *773/702-8200. https://divinity. uchicago.edu/bond-chapel.*

12 **Rosalie Villas.** In 1883, a developer named Rosalie Buckingham purchased this land and planned to build a subdivision of 42 houses on spacious lots to recreate a semi-rural environment. She hired George Pullman's architect, Solon S. Berman, who had recently completed building the Pullman planned community, just to the south. Today, many of the cottages they constructed remain, in various states of repair, and line both sides of the block. Their eclectic color schemes and overgrown gardens give the street a distinctive countercultural flavor. *Harper Ave., between 59th and 57th sts.*

13 **★★ Jackson Park.** This 1,055-acre park was laid out in 1871 by Olmsted and Vaux, the team that designed New York City's Central Park. The full plan for the park, however, wasn't carried out until 1890, when Olmsted returned to Chicago to work with Daniel Burnham on the World's Columbian Exposition. Together, the two architects mapped out broad boulevards and built fountains and temporary, ornate, white buildings (the park was nicknamed The White City during the fair). Today, few of the Beaux Arts structures and gardens erected for the Exposition remain (an exception is the Fine Arts Palace, which now houses the Museum of Science and Industry; see p 46), though the park has aged gracefully and is a popular spot for strolling, tennis, golf, and birding. It's also the future home of the Obama Presidential Center. *6401 S. Stony Island Ave. Bus: 1 or 6.*

14 **★★★ kids Museum of Science and Industry.** Cap your walking tour with a stop at this museum's stellar Henry Crown Space Center. If time allows, rest your legs while taking in a movie at the center's giant dome theater. See p 48, **7**. ●

Shopping Best Bets

Best Place for **Take-Home Gifts**
★★★ Chicago Architecture Center Store, *111 E. Wacker Dr.* (p 82)

Best **Store for Kids**
★★★ LEGO Store, *835 N. Michigan Ave.* (p 84)

Best **Stationery Store**
★★ Paper Source, *232 W. Chicago Ave.* (p 76)

Best **Home Furnishings**
★★★ Restoration Hardware, *1300 N. Dearborn St.* (p 83)

Best **Boutique for Women + Men**
★★★ Hazel, *1926 W. Montrose Ave.* (p 78)

Best **Place for a Treasure Hunt**
★★★ Architectural Artifacts, *4325 N. Ravenswood Ave.* (p 75)

Best **Shop for Custom Hats**
★★ Optimo, *51 W. Jackson Blvd.* (p 78)

Best **Bargain Beauty Supplies**
★ Bravco, *43 E. Oak St.* (p 75)

Best **Pop Culture Collectibles**
★★ Rotofugi, *2780 N. Lincoln Ave.* (p 84)

Best **Children's Books**
★★ Women & Children First, *5233 N. Clark St.* (p 77)

Best Place for **Women's High Fashion**
★★ Swaby, *750 N. Franklin St.* (p 79)

Best **Hip and Wearable Women's Fashion**
★ Florodora, *330 S. Dearborn St.* (p 78)

Best **Wine Store**
★★ House of Glunz, *1206 N. Wells St.* (p 81)

Best **Museum Shop**
★★ MCA Store, *220 E. Chicago Ave.* (p 82)

Best **Designer Vintage**
★★ McShane's Exchange, *815 W. Armitage Ave.* (p 78)

Best **Place for Antiques**
★★ Randolph Street Market, *1341 W. Randolph St.* (p 75)

Best **Gourmet Picnic Shopping**
★★★ Eataly, *43 E. Ohio St.* (p 81)

Best **Place for Handmade Crafts**
★★★ Andersonville Galleria, *5247 N. Clark St.* (p 82)

Previous page: Shopping at Merz Apothecary.
Below: The food court at French Market has more than a dozen gourmet food stalls.

Magnificent Mile Shopping

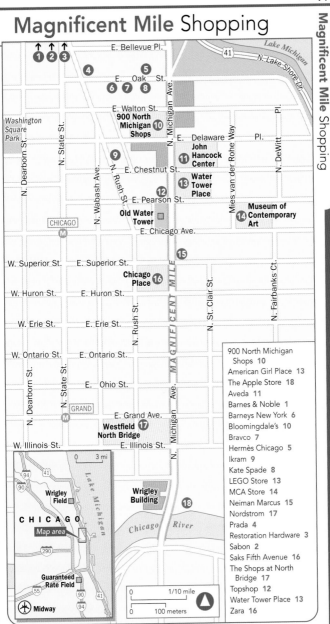

900 North Michigan
  Shops **10**
American Girl Place **13**
The Apple Store **18**
Aveda **11**
Barnes & Noble **1**
Barneys New York **6**
Bloomingdale's **10**
Bravco **7**
Hermès Chicago **5**
Ikram **9**
Kate Spade **8**
LEGO Store **13**
MCA Store **14**
Neiman Marcus **15**
Nordstrom **17**
Prada **4**
Restoration Hardware **3**
Sabon **2**
Saks Fifth Avenue **16**
The Shops at North
  Bridge **17**
Topshop **12**
Water Tower Place **13**
Zara **16**

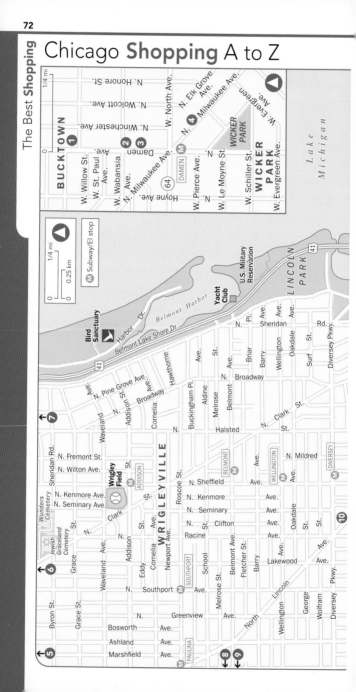

BUCKTOWN ❶

N. Honore St.

N. Wolcott Ave.

N. North Ave.

N. Winchester Ave.

N. Elk Grove Ave.

Milwaukee Ave.

N. Evergreen Ave.

W. Willow St.

W. St. Paul Ave.

W. Wabansia Ave.

Ave.

❷ ❸

Damen Ave.

N. Milwaukee Ave.

Ⓜ DAMEN

W. 64

❹ Ⓜ

WICKER PARK

WICKER PARK

Hoyne Ave.

W. Pierce Ave.

W. Le Moyne St.

W. Schiller St.

W. Evergreen Ave.

▲ 1/4 mi

0

◀

▲ 0 1/4 mi

0 0.25 km

Ⓜ Subway/El stop

Lake Michigan

LINCOLN PARK

41

U.S. Military Reservation

Yacht Club

Bird Sanctuary ▲

Belmont Harbor

Harbor Dr.

Belmont Lake Shore Dr.

41

N. Sheridan

N. Pl.

Ave.

Ave.

Briar

Barry

Wellington

Oakdale

Surf St.

Diversey Pkwy.

Rd.

N. Pine Grove Ave.

Hawthorne

Ave.

St.

Ave.

N. Addison St.

Broadway

Ave.

Cornelia

N. Broadway

❼ ←

Waveland

Buckingham Pl.

Aldine

Melrose

Belmont

N. Clark St.

Sheridan Rd.

N. Fremont St.

N. Wilton Ave.

Halsted

N.

St.

BELMONT Ⓜ

Ave.

WELLINGTON Ⓜ

N. Mildred

DIVERSEY

Wrigley Field

Ⓜ ADDISON

Roscoe St.

N. Sheffield Ave.

WELLINGTON

Ave.

DIVERSEY Ⓜ

Wunders Cemetery

Jewish Graceland Cemetery

N. Kenmore Ave.

N. Seminary Ave.

Clark

St.

WRIGLEYVILLE

St.

N. Kenmore

N. Seminary

N. Clifton

Racine

Ave.

Ave.

Ave.

Oakdale St.

❻ ←

Grace St.

Waveland Ave.

Addison

Eddy

Cornelia

Newport Ave.

School

Melrose

Belmont Ave.

Fletcher St.

Barry

Lakewood Ave.

Lincoln

❿

Byron St.

Grace St.

N.

Southport

N. Southport Ⓜ SOUTHPORT Ave.

Greenview Ave.

Ave.

North

Wellington

George

Wolfram

Diversey Pkwy.

❺ ←

Bosworth Ave.

Ashland Ave.

Marshfield Ave.

PAULINA Ⓜ

❽ ↓ ❾ ↓

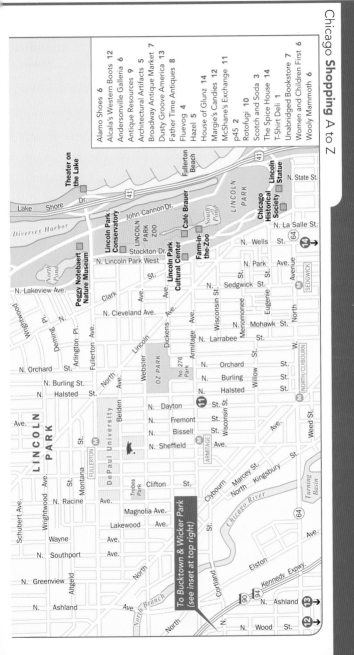

Alamo Shoes 6
Alcala's Western Boots 12
Andersonville Galleria 6
Antique Resources 9
Architectural Artifacts 5
Broadway Antique Market 7
Dusty Groove America 13
Father Time Antiques 8
Fluevog 4
Hazel 5
House of Glunz 14
Margie's Candies 12
McShane's Exchange 11
p45 2
Rotofugi 10
Scotch and Soda 3
The Spice House 14
T-Shirt Deli 1
Unabridged Bookstore 7
Women and Children First 6
Wooly Mammoth 6

To Bucktown & Wicker Park
(see inset at top right)

Loop & River North Shopping

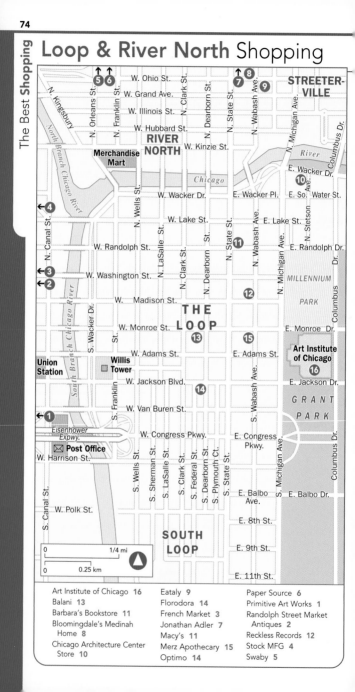

Shopping A to Z

There's much to explore at Antique Resources.

Antiques

Antique Resources WEST LAKEVIEW   This spot specializes in antique lighting fixtures, especially French chandeliers, and also features a good array of Georgian furniture. *1741 W. Belmont Ave. ☎ 773/871-4242. www.antique resourcesinc.com. El: Red or Brown line to Belmont. Map p 72.*

★★★ Architectural Artifacts RAVENSWOOD   The sprawling showrooms are a treasure hunt. You may see a 12th-century bathtub from Italy, fretwork by Frank Lloyd Wright, and hefty terra-cotta gargoyles from a Midwestern bank—all for sale. *4325 N. Ravenswood Ave. ☎ 773/348-0622. www. architecturalartifacts.com. El: Brown Line to Damen. Map p 72.*

★ Broadway Antique Market EDGEWATER   Two floors of funky, fun 20th-century antiques and collectibles. *6130 N. Broadway. ☎ 773/743-5444. www.bamchicago.com. El: Red Line to Granville. Map p 72.*

Father Time Antiques WEST LAKEVIEW   This family-owned shop, in business since 1979, sells the Midwest's largest variety of antique timepieces. *2108 W. Belmont Ave. ☎ 773/880-5599. www. fathertimeantiques.com. El: Red or Brown line to Belmont. Map p 72.*

★★ Randolph Street Market Antiques WEST LOOP   It's a little bit swap meet, a little bit street fest. Hundreds of vendors are onsite, peddling vintage clothing, antique furniture, art, and plenty of weird trinkets. Held indoors the last weekend of the month throughout the year, and outdoors in warmer months. Entry $10 online, $12 at gate. *1341 W. Randolph St. ☎ 312/666-1200. www.randolphstreet market.com. El: Green or Pink line to Ashland. Map p 74.*

Beauty Products & Cosmetics

Aveda MAGNIFICENT MILE   This branch of the eco-friendly Minnesota-based cosmetics company sells all-natural scents, lotions, haircare products, and makeup. Come here and breathe in the aromatherapy. *835 N. Michigan Ave., in Water Tower Place. ☎ 312/664-0417. www.aveda.com. El: Red Line to Chicago. Map p 71.*

★ Bravco GOLD COAST   A bargain hunter's beauty-supply paradise

Architectural Artifacts.

Shopping in Chicago: Just the Facts

Chicago stores usually open for business at 9 or 10am. Smaller stores usually close by 5 or 6pm. Traditionally, larger stores stay open latest—until 8pm or so—on Thursday night. On all other nights, except Sunday, when they open around 11am and close around 6pm, department stores stay open until about 7pm.

The biggest sales of the year take place in January, when retailers slash prices on winter clothing to make room for spring offerings. This is the best time to shop (if you didn't blow all your bucks over the holidays), especially because Chicago has the highest total sales tax of any major city in the country at 10.25%. Car rentals are taxed at about 21%, hotel rooms at 17.4%, and soft drinks 13.25%. Ouch. Grocery items and medications are much less, at about 2%.

on a very pricey street, this crowded, narrow drugstore is a popular spot among Chicago's hairstylists and makeup artists. You'll find an excellent selection of professional hair and beauty products, including Aveda, Sebastian, and Bumble and bumble. And it all costs much less than at the salon. *43 E. Oak St.* ☎ *312/943-4305. www.bravco.com. El: Red Line to Chicago. Map p 71.*

★★★ **Merz Apothecary** LOOP Potions, salves, tonics—they're all here at this European-style pharmacy that dates back to 1875. The savvy staff can point you to natural remedies from around the world. *17 E. Monroe St. (at Wabash Ave.).* ☎ *312/781-6900. www.merz apothecary.com. El: Brown Line to Adams. Map p 74.*

Sabon GOLD COAST Known for its body scrubs and minimalist packaging, this is the place to pop into for a free Dead Sea hand scrub. You'll also find home scents, facial bars, and—perfect for those long Chicago winters—deep moisturizing body butter. *1152–1154 N. State St.* ☎ *312/981-1234.*

www.sabonchicago.com. El: Red Line to Chicago. Map p 71.

Books & Stationery

Barbara's Bookstore LOOP This local chain feels a bit like an airport bookstore, meaning it has a decent variety but isn't especially cozy. *Inside Macy's, 111 N. State St.* ☎ *312/781-5257. www.barbaras bookstore.com. El: Brown or Red Line to Lake. Map p 74.*

kids **Barnes & Noble** GOLD COAST Buy a book and sip coffee at the ground-level cafe in this well-situated store, just steps away from the hustle and bustle of Michigan Avenue. *1130 N. State St.* ☎ *312/ 280-8155. El: Red Line to Clark/ Division. Map p 74.*

★★ **Paper Source** RIVER NORTH The acknowledged leader of stationery stores in Chicago since 1983 is now a national chain. Make your own scrapbooks, buy cards and small gifts, choose among reams of exotic papers, or add to your collection of rubber stamps. *232 W. Chicago Ave.* ☎ *312/337-0798. www.papersource.com. El: Red or Brown Line to Chicago. Map p 74.*

The independent Unabridged Bookstore.

★ kids Unabridged Bookstore
LAKEVIEW This independent bookseller is known for its gay and lesbian specialty section, and also its award-winning range of children's books. The knowledgeable staff handwrites recommendations and customers can be a tight-knit bunch. Check out the online schedule to see what authors and poetry readings are scheduled during your visit. *3251 N. Broadway Ave.* ☎ *773/883-9119. www.unabridgedbookstore.com. El: Red Line to Addison. Map p 72.*

★★ kids Women & Children
First ANDERSONVILLE Located in the neighborhood of Andersonville, this bookstore is known for having the best selection of titles for, by, and about women. But the shop is

far from a male-free zone. The owners promote great independent fiction by authors of both genders, making this a place to discover books that have been overlooked by the bestseller lists. *5233 N. Clark St.* ☎ *773/769-9299. www.women andchildrenfirst.com. El: Red Line to Berwyn. Map p 72.*

Clothing & Shoes
★ kids **Alamo Shoes** ANDERSON-VILLE This old-school shoe store (clerks help you try them on) is a little bit granola and only sells shoes that are actually comfortable. Expect an array of Keens, Birkenstocks, and Clarks. *5321 N. Clark St.* ☎ *773/784-8936. www.alamoshoes.com. El: Red Line to Berwyn. Map p 72.*

★★ Alcala's Western Boots
WEST TOWN Texas ain't got nothin' on Alcala's, Chicago's go-to shop for pearl-button shirts, 10-gallon hats, and more leather boots than you can swing a cat at. *1733 W. Chicago Ave.* ☎ *312/226-0152. www.alcalas.com. El: Blue Line to Chicago. Map p 72.*

★ **Balani** THE LOOP If a custom suit is your idea of a souvenir, then Balani is your spot. You'll be treated like a king as measurements are taken and then the suit is created just for you. The shirts, jackets, and pants will draw compliments from fashionistas, but aren't too showy. *55 W. Monroe St. (at Dearborn St.).*

Co-owners Sarah Hollenbeck and Lynn Mooney give a reading at Women & Children First.

☎ 312/263-9003. www.balani custom.com. El: Red Line to Monroe. Map p 74.

★★★ **Barneys New York** MAGNIFICENT MILE A mini version of New York's Barneys, this is the place in town for buying top-of-the-line men's suits, spotting trends, and people-watching. (For bargains, head to Barneys Warehouse at the Fashion Outlets of Chicago, near O'Hare in Rosemont at 5220 Fashion Outlets Way; ☎ 847/678-9127.) 15 E. Oak St. ☎ 312/587-1700. www.barneys.com. El: Red Line to Chicago/State. Map p 71.

★ **Florodora** THE LOOP Old-meets-new at this women's boutique, which sells contemporary clothing based on vintage looks. The shop is in an historic building, which adds to the vibe. 330 S. Dearborn St. (at Van Buren St.). www.florodora.com. ☎ 312/212-8860. El: Blue Line to Monroe. Map p 74.

★★ **Fluevog** WICKER PARK The styles at this shoe store are a little bit elfin, a little bit rockabilly, and a lot intriguing. The Wicker Park shop has options for women and men, and runs decent sales. 1539 N. Milwaukee Ave. (near North Ave.). ☎ 773/772-1983. www.fluevog.com. El: Blue Line to Damen. Map p 72.

★★★ **Hazel** RAVENSWOOD The women's selections are a bit flirty and men's are quite dapper at this reasonably priced boutique. Talented buyers bring in fun finds from around the world. For accessories, there's a shop by the same name about a block east. 1926 W. Montrose Ave. ☎ 773/904-7779. www.hazelchicago.com. Brown line to Montrose. Map p 72.

★★★ **Hermès Chicago** MAGNIFICENT MILE Hermès makes the world's most sought-after scarves and ties. Don't be intimidated; even if you're not buying, it's fun to walk through and gaze at the colorful designs that earned these silk accessories a cult following. 25 E. Oak St. ☎ 312/787-8175. www.hermes.com. El: Red Line to Chicago. Map p 71.

Ikram MAGNIFICENT MILE This exclusive boutique, which outfitted Michelle Obama, stocks all the big names, from Alexander McQueen to Valentino. The store's out-there, bright red architecture is as high fashion as the wares it carries. 15 E. Huron St. www.ikram.com. ☎ 312/587-1000. El: Red Line to Chicago. Map p 71.

★★ **Kate Spade** MAGNIFICENT MILE Head here for designer handbags, ranging in style from plaid and gingham to snakeskin and basic black. The shoes and stationery goods are adorable, too. 56 E. Oak St. ☎ 312/654-8853. www.katespade.com. El: Red Line to Chicago. Map p 71.

★★ **McShane's Exchange** LINCOLN PARK This consignment shop sells designer clothes at real-person prices. Sorry guys: They carry only women's clothing. 815 W. Armitage Ave. ☎ 773/525-0282. www.mcshanesexchange.com. El: Brown Line to Armitage. Map p 72.

★★ **Optimo** THE LOOP "Dashing" is an understatement for the hats made at this shop, the name of which is uttered with reverence by fashion hounds. Those purchasing custom felt and straw hats are interviewed and measured, and hats are created for their noggin alone. 51 W. Jackson Blvd. (at Dearborn St.). ☎ 312/922-2999. www.optimo.com. El: Blue Line to Monroe. Map p 74.

★ **p45** BUCKTOWN Of the cool boutiques aimed at the well-heeled crowd clustered along Damen Avenue in Bucktown, this is among the more daring. The urbane women's fashion is funky rather than girly,

The showroom at Stock MFG.

and carries a mix of new and known designers, with clothing, shoes, and accessories. *1643 N. Damen Ave.* ☎ *773/862-4523. www.P45.com. El: Blue Line to Damen. Map p 72.*

Prada MAGNIFICENT MILE A boutique so chic it's almost painful. Chicago's top spot for buying the famous Italian designer's signature bags. *30 E. Oak St.* ☎ *312/951-1113. www.prada.com. El: Red Line to Chicago. Map p 71.*

★ Scotch and Soda WICKER PARK This Amsterdam-based brand brings Euro fashion to town for men and women. Styles range from simple and conservative to bright, pattern-filled conversation pieces. *1639 N. Damen Ave.* ☎ *773/687-8980. www.scotch-soda.com. El: Blue Line to Damen. Map p 72.*

Stock MFG WEST LOOP No more baggy khaki's and puffy shirts. This men's store sells quality, locally made clothes that fit. *2136 W. Fulton St.* ☎ *312/371-1555. www. stockmfgco.com. El: Green Line to Ashland. Map p 74.*

★★ Swaby RIVER NORTH Shernett Swaby, a finalist on Project Runway, sells her boundary-pushing designs at her River North shop. It's not cheap, but you know you'll never run into someone else dressed alike. *750 N. Franklin St. (at Chicago Ave.).* ☎ *312/285-2810. www.shernettswaby.com. El: Red Line to Chicago. Map p 74.*

Topshop MAGNIFICENT MILE Fashion ranges from playful elegance to comfy T-shirts for cheap. Usually sold in Nordstrom, Chicago is home to one of a handful of U.S. retail store locations for the U.K.-based brand. Topman, the masculine counterpart, is a few doors down. *830 N. Michigan Ave. (at Pearson St.).* ☎ *312/280-6834. www.topshop.com. El: Red Line to Chicago. Map p 71.*

★★ kids T-Shirt Deli BUCK-TOWN The staff here serves up customized T-shirts while you wait. Come up with your own message, or browse the pre-made offerings, rich in Chicago themes. Just like at a real deli, your purchase is wrapped in white paper and served with a bag of potato chips. There's also a location in Andersonville. *1739 N. Damen Ave.* ☎ *773/276-6266; Andersonville: 1482 W. Berwyn Ave.* ☎ *773/561-7410. www.tshirt deli.com. El: Blue Line to Damen; Red Line to Berwyn. Map p 72.*

Zara MAGNIFICENT MILE Euro chic clothing, shoes, and accessories from the Spanish mass merchandiser have taken Michigan Avenue by storm at this Chicago flagship. You'll find three floors of classic pieces with an edge, as well as the trendiest items from across the Atlantic, all at extremely reasonable prices. *700 N. Michigan Ave.* ☎ *312/255-8123. www.zara.com. El: Red Line to Chicago. Map p 71.*

Consumer Electronics
The Apple Store MAGNIFICENT MILE The riverfront flagship store is home to all gadgets beginning with "i": iPhone, iPad, and more.

Farmers' Markets

From mid-May to late October, Chicago's downtown plazas and neighborhoods overflow with fruits, vegetables, flowers, and food from nearby farms. Markets in residential neighborhoods, such as the can't-miss Green City Market that packs Lincoln Park on Saturdays (1817 N. Clark St.; www.greencitymarket.org), usually take place on weekends. The farmers' markets downtown—including those listed here—take place during the week. Schedules may vary, so contact the city's Department of Cultural Affairs and Special Events (☎ 312/744-3316) for details.

- Daley Plaza, 50 W. Washington St., on Thursdays
- Federal Plaza, Adams Street and Dearborn Street, on Tuesdays
- SOAR, 220 E. Chicago, on Tuesdays
- South Loop, 1936 S. Michigan Ave. on Thursdays

The prices are retail, but the store offers in-house workshops (Macs only, of course) and an extremely knowledgeable sales staff. *401 N. Michigan Ave.* ☎ *312/529-9500. www.apple.com. El: Red Line to Grand. Map p 71.*

Department Stores
Bloomingdale's MAGNIFICENT MILE The first Midwestern branch of the famed upscale New York department store features six manageably sized floors of shopping. The store carries its own in-house brands as well as the full range of designers that you'd expect, with especially good shoe and jewelry selections. *900 N. Michigan Ave. (at Walton St.).* ☎ *312/440-4460. www. bloomingdales.com. El: Red Line to Chicago. Map p 71.*

Macy's THE LOOP Federated Department Stores changed the legendary Marshall Field's flagship store into a Macy's in 2006 (many locals still refuse to use any name but the original). The name may be different, but this landmark (opened in 1852) still offers 73 acres

of shopping. Chicago traditions include meeting under the store's clock and viewing the famous animated holiday window displays. Take afternoon tea in the gracious Walnut Room. *111 N. State St.* ☎ *312/781-1000. www.macys.com. El: Red Line to Lake. Map p 74.*

Neiman Marcus MAGNIFICENT MILE Yes, you'll pay top dollar for designer names here, but Neiman's has a broader price range than many of its critics care to admit. It also has some great sales. Once you've shopped 'til you've dropped, get your blood sugar back up with a soufflé at Mariposa. *737 N. Michigan Ave. (at Superior St.).* ☎ *312/642-5900. www.neimanmarcus.com. El: Red Line to Chicago. Map p 71.*

Nordstrom MAGNIFICENT MILE A spacious, airy design and trendy touches complement this store's famed focus on service. Cafe Nordstrom offers a shopping break, with salads and sandwiches. *The Shops at North Bridge, 55 E. Grand Ave. (at Rush St.).* ☎ *312/464-1515. www.nordstrom.com. El: Red Line to Grand. Map p 71.*

Saks Fifth Avenue MAGNIFICENT MILE   For my money, the first-floor cosmetics and fragrance counters are the best on the Magnificent Mile. The first floor, filled with fragrances and skincare brands, such as Kiehl's, is worth a stop. The other floors are packed with your usual high-end department store offerings from Diane von Furstenberg and Stuart Weitzman, among many others. The men's offerings, on the 6th and 7th floors, hit all the fashion highs—Fendi, Del Toro, Versace, and beyond—and the excellent sales staff make getting dressed a snap. Style advisors are available to help with all your fashion needs, online, in store, or even at your hotel. *700 N. Michigan Ave.* ☎ *312/944-6500. www.saksfifthavenue.com. El: Red Line to Chicago. Map p 71.*

Food, Chocolates & Wine
★★★ **Eataly** RIVER NORTH   At this two-story market—one of just five in the U.S.—you can fill your picnic basket or your belly. Grab a glass of wine at one of the many bars and peruse the pasta counter, butcher shop, seafood shop, and pantry. Or, have a progressive dinner at one of the six restaurants, and cap it off with dessert at the Nutella bar. *43 E. Ohio St. (at Wabash Ave.).* ☎ *312/521-8700. www.eataly.com. El: Red Line to Grand. Map p 74.*

★ **French Market** NEAR WEST   Conveniently located within the Metra commuter train station, this darling, European-style market is filled with nearly three dozen stalls, from restaurants serving grab-and-go meals, like poke bowls and lobster rolls, to bakeries creating addictive mini doughnuts and brightly colored French macarons. Open year-round, it gets busy at lunchtime with locals grabbing a quick bite. *131 N. Clinton St. (at Randolph St.).* ☎ *312/575-0306. www.frenchmarketchicago.com. El: Brown Line to Washington/Wells. Map p 74.*

★★ **House of Glunz** OLD TOWN   Chicago's oldest wine shop carries an inventory of some 1,500 wines, some of which date back to 1811. Ask the knowledgeable owners to steer you to the right bottle for your budget. *1206 N. Wells St.* ☎ *312/642-3000. www.thehouseofglunz.com. El: Red Line to Clark/Division. Map p 72.*

★★ **Margie's Candies** WICKER PARK   This family-run candy and ice-cream shop hasn't changed much since it opened in 1921. It still offers some of the city's finest handmade fudge, whether it comes in a box or melted over a banana split. The store is known for its turtles—chocolate-covered pecan and caramel clusters. *1960 N. Western Ave.* ☎ *773/384-1035. www.margiesfinecandies.com. El: Blue Line to Western. Map p 72.*

★ **The Spice House** OLD TOWN   This charming shop blends and grinds its spices in small batches, and the resulting smell is, of course, amazing. The packaging is lovely, making the spices a great gift or souvenir option. *1512 N. Wells St.* ☎ *312/676-2414. www.thespicehouse.com. El: Brown Line to Sedgwick. Map p 72.*

Gift Shops
★★ **Art Institute of Chicago** THE LOOP   Jewelry, glassware, classic reproductions, Frank Lloyd Wright socks—it's all here at this museum's bustling gift shop. *111 S. Michigan Ave.* ☎ *800/518-4214. www.artinstituteshop.org. El: Brown Line to Adams or Red Line to Monroe. Map p 74.*

★★★ **Chicago Architecture Center Store** THE LOOP   The

Andersonville Galleria features the work of more than 100 local artisans.

best gift shop in the city offers architecture-focused books, decorative accessories, and gifts. Frank Lloyd Wright bookmarks, puzzles of the Chicago skyline, picture frames with patterns designed by Louis Sullivan, and a huge selection of Chicago history books mean you'll find a souvenir for everyone on your list. *111 E. Wacker Dr.* ☎ *312/922-3432. www.architecture.org. El: Brown or Red Line to Lake. Map p 74.*

★★ **MCA Store** MAGNIFICENT MILE   Inkblot tests, metallic balloon dogs, and intriguing jewelry make for great modern-art souvies and gifts at this fantastic museum store at the MCA. *220 E. Chicago Ave.* ☎ *312/397-4000. www.mca chicagostore.org. El: Red Line to Chicago. Map p 71.*

Housewares, Furnishings & Art
★★★ **Andersonville Galleria**
ANDERSONVILLE   It's like a year-round craft fair, with all wheat, no chaff. More than 100 vendors sell hats, jewelry, clothing, soaps, and more at this North Side favorite.

5247 N. Clark St. ☎ *773/878-8570. www.andersonvillegalleria.com. El: Red Line to Berwyn. Map p 72.*

Bloomingdale's Medinah Home
RIVER NORTH   Even if you're not interested in perusing the artfully displayed, high-end kitchen accessories and bathroom necessities, go for the architecture. This intriguing, Moorish building, topped with an onion dome, was once a temple for the Shriners. *600 N. Wabash Ave. (at Ohio St.).* ☎ *312/324-7500. www.bloomingdales.com. El: Red Line to Grand. Map p 74.*

★★ **Jonathan Adler** RIVER NORTH   Known for his groovy needlepoint throw pillows; you can find all of those "homemade" touches you need to make a house a happening home. *676 N. Wabash St.* ☎ *312/274-9920. www.jonathan adler.com. El: Red Line to Grand. Map p 74.*

★★★ **Primitive Art Works**
WEST LOOP   Winding your way through this 31,000-square-foot store, you'll feel as if you're on

shopping with Indiana Jones. Packed with furniture, artifacts, rugs, and jewels from various cultures, on one day this store might yield a giant Buddha head acquired from a Korean temple that was being destroyed; on another, you might discover an exquisite embroidered rug from Turkmenistan. *130 N. Jefferson St.* ☎ *312/575-9600. www.beprimitive.com. El: Red Line to Chicago. Map p 74.*

★★★ Restoration Hardware
GOLD COAST This RH store sits within a gorgeous, 19th-century building that was once an arts school for women (see p 53). Shoppers can wander the six floors, sit in the posh rooms and behold a glorious rooftop, complete with foliage (I bring guests here to take a peek and have a sit), all while imagining the furniture in their own home. Sustenance is within reach, thanks to a first-floor bar and skylight-lined restaurant, Three Arts Club, that looks like it's been filtered on Instagram, it's so beautiful. *1300 N. Dearborn St.* ☎ *312/475-9116. www.restorationhardware.com. El: Red Line to Clark/Division. Map p 71.*

★ Wooly Mammoth
ANDERSONVILLE This bizarro store is a mix between a curiosity shop, an art gallery, and a weird acid trip. You might find a stuffed two-headed cow, various and sundry skulls, taxidermy tools, and more. Heaven for freakshow fans. *1513 W. Foster Ave.* ☎ *773/989-3294. www.woollymammothchicago.com. El: Red Line to Berwyn. Map p 72.*

Michigan Avenue's Vertical Shopping Malls
900 North Michigan Shops
MAGNIFICENT MILE The most upscale of the Magnificent Mile malls is often called the "Bloomingdale's building" for its most

prominent tenant. There are about 70 stores, a few good restaurants, and a chic salon named for well-known local hairdresser Mario Tricoci—book well in advance, as it's always bustling. *900 N. Michigan Ave.* ☎ *312/915-3916. www.shop900.com. El: Red Line to Chicago. Map p 71.*

kids The Shops at North Bridge
MAGNIFICENT MILE More tranquil than its retail-rich neighbors, this four-level shopping center is anchored by Nordstrom; specialty shops such as Eloquii and Clark Street Sports offer diverse options. *520 N. Michigan Ave.* ☎ *312/327-2300. www.theshopsatnorthbridge.com. El: Red Line to Grand/State. Map p 71.*

kids Water Tower Place
MAGNIFICENT MILE Chicago's first—and busiest—vertical mall, this seven-floor building has about 100 mostly upscale stores, including American Girl Store. It connects to The Ritz-Carlton, should you want to shop 'til you drop. *835 N. Michigan Ave.* ☎ *312/440-3580. www.shopwatertower.com. El: Red Line to Chicago. Map p 71.*

Music
Dusty Groove America
WEST TOWN Soul, funk, jazz, Brazilian, lounge, Latin, and hip-hop music on new and used vinyl. All the new CDs are rare or imported—or both. *1120 N. Ashland Ave.* ☎ *773/342-5800. www.dustygroove.com. El: Blue Line to Division. Map p 72.*

Reckless Records
THE LOOP This new-and-used record shop has been a grungy favorite since opening in '89. There are larger outposts in Wicker Park and Lake View, but this location is notable for bringing vinyl and CDs downtown. *26 E. Madison St. (at Wabash Ave.).* ☎ *312/795-0878. www.reckless.com. El: Red Line to Monroe. Map p 74.*

Art Fairs and Festivals

Throughout the year, the art scene gets more colorful, as fests, fairs, and shows set up shop:

One of a Kind Show, at Merchandise Mart (☎ **312/527-4141;** http://oneofakindshowchicago.com), draws hundreds of talented artists, jewelry makers, clothing producers, and other crafty entrepreneurs twice a year in early December and late April.

The **57th Street Art Fair,** 57th Street in downtown Hyde Park (☎ **773/234-3247;** www.57thstreetartfair.org), is a long-standing fair in early June that's a natural outgrowth of the intellectual and artsy enclave of Hyde Park.

Old Town Art Fair, Lincoln Avenue and Wisconsin Street (☎ **312/337-1938;** www.oldtownartfair.org), in early June, is the most high-end of Chicago's art-fair offerings, boasting art prices to match.

Toys

kids American Girl Place MAGNIFICENT MILE The "in" place for the preteen set, this store has everything a doll could possibly need, with ear piercing, hair styling, a doctor's office to repair injured dolls, and, of course, an enormous selection of dolls and accessories. Call ahead to book a lunch or afternoon tea in the cafe. *835 N. Michigan Ave. (Water Tower Place).* ☎ *877/247-5223. www.americangirl.com. El: Red Line to Chicago. Map p 71.*

A plant-based Lego display at the Lego Store.

★★★ **kids LEGO Store** MAGNIFICENT MILE This Water Tower Place shop is a brick-loving kid's dream. Build your own mini figures and cities, and then choose individual bricks from the "pick and build" wall. Even adults will find something to love here, including architecture kits of iconic edifices. Plan to spend some time building and creating. *835 N. Michigan Ave. (Water Tower Place).* ☎ *312/202-0946. www.lego.com. El: Red Line to Chicago. Map p 71.*

★★ **kids Rotofugi** LINCOLN PARK This art gallery and design store doubles as a toy shop, with figurines, plushies, and Japanese vinyl toys that are adorable, if a bit weird. Don't be surprised if you see, say, a *Bob's Burgers* figurine next to a plush that looks like soft serve. The gallery shows and sells works by local and international artists. *2780 N Lincoln Ave.* ☎ *773/868-3308. www.rotofugi.com. El: Brown Line to Diversey. Map p 73.* ●

5 The Best of the **Outdoors**

Chicago **Lakeshore**

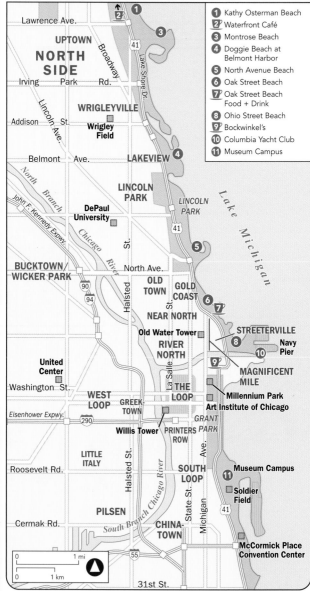

1 Kathy Osterman Beach
2 Waterfront Café
3 Montrose Beach
4 Doggie Beach at Belmont Harbor
5 North Avenue Beach
6 Oak Street Beach
7 Oak Street Beach Food + Drink
8 Ohio Street Beach
9 Bockwinkel's
10 Columbia Yacht Club
11 Museum Campus

Lawrence Ave.

UPTOWN

NORTH SIDE

Irving   Park   Rd.

Broadway

41

Lake Shore Dr.

WRIGLEYVILLE

Addison   St.

Lincoln Ave.

Wrigley Field

Belmont   Ave.

LAKEVIEW

North Branch

John F. Kennedy Expwy.

LINCOLN PARK

DePaul University

Chicago River

Halsted   St.

LINCOLN PARK

41

Lake Michigan

BUCKTOWN/ WICKER PARK

90 94

North Ave.

OLD TOWN

GOLD COAST

NEAR NORTH

Old Water Tower

RIVER NORTH

La Salle   St.

STREETERVILLE

Navy Pier

MAGNIFICENT MILE

United Center

Washington St.

WEST LOOP

GREEK TOWN

THE LOOP

Eisenhower Expwy.

290

Willis Tower

PRINTERS ROW

GRANT PARK

Michigan   Ave.

Millennium Park

Art Institute of Chicago

LITTLE ITALY

Roosevelt Rd.

Halsted   St.

SOUTH LOOP

State   St.

Museum Campus

Soldier Field

41

PILSEN

Cermak Rd.

South Branch Chicago River

CHINA TOWN

McCormick Place Convention Center

0   1 mi

0   1 km

55

31st St.

Previous page: North Avenue Beach.

Chicago is a beach town. That's something that comes as a surprise to visitors, but locals all have their favorite spot of sand among the 26 miles of beaches hugging the chilly rim of Lake Michigan. A path called the Lakefront Trail extends along the shore, and it's perfect for biking, jogging, and strolling. Or bring a towel to spread on the sand or grass and watch the world go by. A quick note about safety: Beach season runs from Memorial Day to Labor Day, and beaches are open from 6am to 11pm. Swimming is allowed when lifeguards are on duty, from 11am to 7pm daily. The beaches are overseen by the Chicago Park District; learn more about individual beaches and swimming conditions at www.chicagopark district.com. START: **Hollywood-Ardmore Beach, Berwyn El Station.**

❶ Kathy Osterman Beach.
Known to locals as Hollywood-Ardmore Beach, this lovely crescent of sand is less congested than many of the city's beaches. If you're looking for relative quiet and seclusion (relative because this is a big city, after all), you'll find a like-minded crowd here, sunning themselves. The beach is gay-friendly but the south end is especially popular with the LGBTQ crowd. Facilities include bathrooms and drinking fountains. This is one of the city's 16 wheelchair-accessible beaches. ⏱ *30 min. 5800 N. Lake Shore Dr. (at*

Hollywood St.). ☎ 312/742-PLAY (7529). www.chicagoparkdistrict.com.

One of my favorite summer spots is **❷ Waterfront Café,** about a mile north of Kathy Osterman Beach. The alfresco restaurant overlooks the lake, making it the perfect summer spot for beer, wine, pub grub, and live music (Wed–Sun night). *6219 N. Sheridan. ☎ 773/761-3294. www.waterfrontcafechicago.com. $.*

❸ Montrose Beach. This unsung treasure is midway between

Montrose Beach.

Hollywood-Ardmore and North Avenue beaches. Long popular with the city's Hispanic community, it offers an expanse of sand mostly uninterrupted by jetties or piers (unlike North Ave. Beach), a large dog beach where pups dart into the lake, a huge adjacent park with soccer fields, and one big hill that's great for kite flying. If you're interested in having some green space for tossing a baseball, or want to watch a soccer game, this beach is your best choice—no other beach in the area boasts such proximity to a park. Also worth checking out is Montrose Beach Dunes; its 11 acres of sandy, hilly terrain dip into wooded areas before guiding you to a large pier. The area is also home to a bird sanctuary, so keep your eyes peeled for sparrows, plovers, sandpipers, and more. You'll find bathrooms, drinking fountains, bike racks, and concession stands. It's also a popular spot for fishing. ⏱ *30 min. 4400 N. Lake Shore Dr. (at Montrose Ave.).* ☎ *312/742-PLAY (7529). www.chicagoparkdistrict.com.*

④ Doggie Beach at Belmont Harbor. Chicago is a town of dog lovers, many of whom bring their pooches here for a dip. Nestled in a small corner of a harbor near Hawthorne and Lake Shore Drive,

this is not so much a beach as an enclosed strip of sand where locals take their dogs to fetch sticks and play in the water. Facilities are minimal. ⏱ *10 min. 3200 N. Lake Shore Dr. (just south of Addison St.).* ☎ *312/742-PLAY (7529). www.chicagoparkdistrict.com.*

⑤ North Avenue Beach. I'm one of many Chicagoans who can't get enough of the view from the lakefront bike path here, looking south to the John Hancock Center—a view so famous it's often featured on the cover of guide books. To get a snapshot of the picture-perfect scene, walk north, parallel to Lake Shore Drive to North Avenue, and take the tunnel to North Avenue Beach. Once on the lakefront path, turn south toward the city, and you will have your Kodak moment. (Just watch out for all the cyclists, skaters, runners, and dog walkers if it's a nice summer day.) Accessible to both those with mobility impairments and families toting strollers, the beach also offers an array of facilities, including restrooms, concession stands, drinking fountains, bike racks, volleyball courts, and a chess pavilion. One of the most iconic beachfront sites resides here: Castaways, an enormous, blue-and-white

Getting Out Onto the Water

Where there's water, there are water sports, and you can take a stand-up paddleboard class near North Avenue Beach at **Chicago SUP** (☎ 773/575-4787; www.chicagosup.com) for about $65 for up to 30 minutes of lesson time, plus an hour of paddle time. **Urban Kayaks** (☎ 312/965-0035; www.urbankayaks.com) rents kayaks by the hour ($30 per person per hour) and offers guided tours (starting at $45). You can choose to take in the skyline from Lake Michigan or paddle along the Chicago River. Urban Kayaks has two locations—at Columbia Yacht Club, 111 N. Lake Shore Dr., and the Chicago Riverwalk, 435 E. Chicago Riverwalk.

Volleyball at Oak Street Beach.

The warm-weather-only beachfront cafe **7** **Oak Street Beach Food + Drink** is set right on the sands of Oak Street Beach. It serves decent beach fare, including tacos, sandwiches, and nachos. Beer and wine are also available. *1001 N. Lake Shore Dr. at Oak St. Beach.* ☎ *312/988-4650. www.oakstreet beach.com. $.*

8 **Ohio Street Beach.** If it's a workout you're seeking, you'll enjoy Ohio Street Beach, an intimate slice of sand just west of Navy Pier. Thanks to buoys marking a 1-mile swimming course and a location in a protected harbor (making for calmer waters than you'll find elsewhere on the lake), Ohio Street Beach is also the place for serious open-water swimming. On most summer mornings, you'll see athletes (often in wet suits) training in the water, many of them preparing for the annual Chicago Triathlon in August. ⏱ *20 min. 600 N. Lake Shore Dr.* ☎ *312/742-PLAY (7529). www.chicagoparkdistrict.com.*

boat-shaped bar and restaurant. It's a spot that everyone must go, at least once. ⏱ *30 min. 1600 Lake Shore Dr. (at North Ave.).* ☎ *312/ 742-PLAY (7529). www.chicagopark district.com.*

6 **Oak Street Beach.** The city's best-known beach, which is oh so accessible from downtown, is a pristine place to relax. Its location, at the northern tip of the Magnificent Mile, creates some interesting people-watching moments: In season, check out the local sun worshipers wearing flip-flops and carrying coolers as they make their way up tony Michigan Avenue toward this curving slice of sand. The beach is accessible to families with strollers and those with mobility impairments, but this trendy spot can get crowded on summer afternoons. Facilities include volleyball courts and bathrooms. ⏱ *30 min. 1000 Lake Shore Dr. (at Oak St.).* ☎ *312/742-PLAY (7529). www. chicagoparkdistrict.com.*

For picnic supplies, do as the locals do and head to **9** **Bockwinkel's.** Known for its lunch specials (sandwiches, a superior salad bar, and good fruit), you'll find it on the ground floor of the Park Millennium building, located 1 block north of Millennium Park and 1 block east of Michigan Avenue. *222 N. Columbus Dr.* ☎ *312/228-9920. www.bockwinkels.com. $.*

10 **Columbia Yacht Club.** Farther south along the lakefront, you'll find this yacht club, housed in a 372-foot Canadian icebreaker and ferry named *Abegweit* (often called *Abby* by locals). This private club

The original ferry Abegweit *is now owned by the Columbia Yacht Club.*

dates back to 1892, and is now the premier spot for sailing lessons on Lake Michigan. Even if you're not a yachting fan, the harbor area offers lovely views. ⓘ *5 min., unless you're taking a lesson. In Monroe Harbor, at the foot of Randolph Dr. and Lake Shore Dr.* ☎ *312/938-3625. www. columbiayachtclub.org. Sailing school rates vary; contact the club or check the website.*

⓫ **Museum Campus.** Created by the relocation of Lake Shore Drive, this beautiful park was opened in 1998 with the goal of being recognized as one of the most innovative cultural playgrounds in the country. The Campus connects three Chicago cultural

institutions: the Adler Planetarium, p 20, ⓬, Field Museum of Natural History (p 18, ⓭), and John G. Shedd Aquarium (p 20, ⓮). Today, broad walkways make it easier for pedestrians to visit the museums, and the reclaimed parkland and terraced gardens offer space for picnicking, theater, and museum education activities. **Word to the wise:** Traffic tends to get hectic and the Museum Campus congested on Chicago Bears game days (Soldier Field is just south of the Field Museum). Plan your visit accordingly. ⓘ *30 min., more if you visit some of the museums. 18th St. and Lake Shore Dr.* ☎ *312/742-PLAY (7529). www.chicagopark district.com. Bus: 12, 127, or 146.*

Park Planning

Chicago's lakefront is forever free and clear of development thanks in no small part to Daniel H. Burnham (1846–1912), a renowned architect and city planner. Burnham, architect of the Rookery, the Monadnock Building, the "White City" of the 1893 World's Columbian Exposition, New York's Flatiron Building, and Washington, D.C.'s Union Station, presented his most ambitious work, the *Plan of Chicago*, in 1909 with architect Edward H. Bennett. The plan set the standard for urban design in the United States and anticipated the city's need to control random urban growth and create a system of city parks and lakefront recreation areas.

Biking **Chicago**

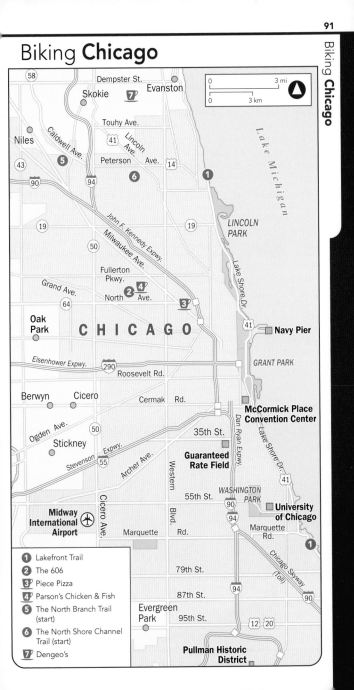

1 Lakefront Trail
2 The 606
3 Piece Pizza
4 Parson's Chicken & Fish
5 The North Branch Trail (start)
6 The North Shore Channel Trail (start)
7 Dengeo's

Aside from walking, biking around Chicago is the best way to to see the city, whether you're gearing up in spandex and hammering south on the 18-mile Lakefront Path or planning a progressive meal through Chicago's neighborhoods. The city is bike-friendly (although you'll need to follow the rules of traffic and be aware of drivers and pedestrians) and the terrain is flat, making for an easy and scenic ride. Don't feel limited by the trails below. Many Chicago residents rely on cycling as their primary form of transportation, so jump into the fray and hit the nearest bike lane. It's about as fast as taking the El—and a much better workout.

1 Lakefront Trail. The paved, 18-mile path that traces the shores of Lake Michigan is one of the things that active locals love most about Chicago—and it shows. If the weather is nice, the trail is packed with cyclists, walkers, strollers, in-line skaters, and more. The trail runs from Hollywood Beach in the north (the neighborhood of Edgewater) to the Museum of Science and Industry (Hyde Park) in the south, connecting the waterfront access points. It passes by Lincoln Park Zoo, Navy Pier, Grant Park, and the Museum Campus, along with plenty of beaches. Please note that regular users treat the path as

you would a street, keeping to the right side in either direction. Be aware of your surroundings at all times to avoid cyclist-on-cyclist and cyclist-on-pedestrian collisions. *From Ardmore Street (5800 N. Sheridan Rd.) to the north to 71st Street (7100 S. South Shore Dr.) to the south. www.chicagoparkdistrict.com*

2 The 606. It's frequently compared to New York's High Line. And while it is, indeed, a former railroad track (called the Bloomingdale Line) that's been converted to an elevated walking path, it's different in that it's not in an area that's highly trafficked by tourists. With that said, if you're looking for a

Cyclists along the 18-mile-long Lakefront Trail.

The 606 highline railway.

neighborhood adventure, consider the box checked. The landscaped, 3-mile trail runs through the west-side neighborhoods of Humboldt Park, Logan Square, Bucktown, and Wicker Park. You can access the easternmost part of the trail at Walsh Park, 1722 N. Ashland, and take it west to its terminus at Ridgeway and Lawndale. Then head back the way you came.

If you want to include some local eats in your cycling tour, hop off the trail at Damen Avenue (Churchill Park) and grab pizza at **3** ★ **Piece Pizza** (1927 W. North Ave.; ☎ 773/772-4422; www.piecechicago.com; $; p 105) or hop off at Humboldt Blvd. and bike over to **4** **Parson's Chicken & Fish** (2952 W. Armitage Ave.; ☎ 773/384-3333; www.parsonschickenandfish.com; $; p 115) for fried chicken on a bustling patio. *www.the606.org.*

5 The North Branch Trail. If you're feeling ambitious, this peaceful 20-mile path winds through Chicago parks and forest preserves, passing through McDonald Woods and Turnbull Woods before ending up at Chicago Botanical Garden, north of the city. That glorious garden is pay dirt for your efforts. It's 385 acres of sheer natural beauty, with islands, bridges and every kind of flower and plant you could possibly imagine. Parking here is usually $25–$30, so you're saving money by biking. *The trail starts at the Caldwell Forest Preserve (Devon and Caldwell avenues) and ends in Glencoe at Chicago Botanic Garden, 1000 Lake Cook Rd.* ☎ *847/835-6801. www.chicago botanic.org.*

6 The North Shore Channel Trail. This is one of my favorite bike paths in the city, in part because of the ever-changing views as you ride along the North Shore Channel, which is a drainage canal, but mostly because you won't encounter the traffic of the Lakefront Trail. The 7-mile paved trail starts at River Park, at Francisco and Lawrence avenues on the city's North Side. It winds through green parkland alongside the water and then past nearly 60 sculptures, which range from brightly colored horses to abstract works at the Skokie Northshore Sculpture Park. It ends at Green Bay Road in Skokie.

For fuel along the North Channel Trail, hit **7** **Dengeo's.** Known for its delicious gyros, it's located just across from the trail at McCormick Boulevard and Main Street, and you won't be judged if you show up in workout gear. Order at the counter and then take it back to the park for an impromptu picnic. *3301 Main St., Skokie.* ☎ *847/677-7911. www.dengeos.com. $.* ●

Finding Your Perfect Pedals

Divvy is the name of Chicago's bike-share program (www.divvy bikes.com) and, with nearly 600 stations and almost 6,000 bikes around town, it's an ideal way for visitors to grab two wheels and go. A single ride on a powder-blue cruiser, which includes 30 minutes on the bike, is $3, or you can get a 24-hour pass for $15. With the latter, you can spend 3 hours on the bike before you need to return it to a dock (you can then take it out again or exchange it for another bike after you check in). Download the Divvy app to purchase your pass and you'll get a code to unlock a bike. Just be sure to plan your route around Divvy stations, so you have one when you need it. Of the rides listed above, your best bet for Divvy station concentration is the Lakefront Path and the 606. *Note:* You'll need to bring your own helmet.

For a sportier bike (and a helmet), head over to **Bike and Roll Chicago** (☎ **312/729-1000;** www.bikechicago.com), which has staffed locations at Millennium Park and Navy Pier, and automated locations at the North Branch Trail and Dan Ryan Woods. Bike rentals start at $12.50 per hour and $35 for the day and feature shiny new Trek bicycles. The company also offers easy 2- to 3-hour bike tours of the lakefront and neighborhoods; tours start at around $45 for adults, $35 kids under 12. If you want to try something different, Bike and Roll also offers **Segway tours** of the lakefront and parks, at $75 for adults and $65 for people ages 12 to 20 for a 2-hour tour on the lakefront.

Dining Best Bets

Best **Diner**
★★★ Little Goat Diner $$
820 W. Randolph St. (p 103)

Best **Burger**
★★★ The Gage $$$
24 S. Michigan Ave. (p 102)

Best **Dim Sum**
★ Phoenix $$ *2131 S. Archer Ave.
(p 104)*

Best **Sushi**
★★★ Tanoshii $$$ *720 W.
Randolph St. (p 106)*

Best **Chicago-Style Pizza**
★★★ Lou Malnati's $ *439 N.
Wells St. (p 103)*

Best **Celebrity-Chef Meal**
★★★ Frontera Grill,
Topolobampo, and Xoco $$–$$$
445 N. Clark St. (p 102)

Best **Mind-Blowing
Presentation**
★★★ Alinea $$$$ *1723 N.
Halsted St. (p 100)*

Best **French Bistro**
★★★ Bistro Campagne $ *4518 N.
Lincoln Ave. (p 100)*

Best **Special Occasion Spot**
★★★ Somerset $$–$$$ *1112 N.
State St. (p 106)*

Best **Seafood**
★★ Shaw's Crab House $$$
21 E. Hubbard St. (p 106)

Best **Macanese Food**
★★★ Fat Rice $$ *2957 W.
Diversey. (p 101)*

Best **Old-School Italian**
★★ Topo Gigio $$ *1516 N.
Wells St. (p 106)*

Best **Steakhouse**
★★ Gibsons $$$ *1028 N. Rush St.
(p 102)*

Best **Hot Dog**
★ Portillo's $ *100 W. Ontario St.
(p 105)*

Best **Breakfast**
★ Orange $$$ *2413 N. Clark St.
(p 104)*

Best **Vegetarian**
★★ India House $ *59 W. Grand
Ave. (p 103)*

Best **Ice Cream**
★★★ Margie's Candies $ *1960 N.
Western Ave. (p 104)*

Best **View**
★★★ Everest $$$$ *440 S.
LaSalle St. (p 101)*

Best **Late-Night Dinner**
★★ Sushi-san $$ *63 W. Grand Ave.
(p 106)*

Previous page: Heaven on Seven. Above: Outdoor dining at Bistro Campagne.

Bucktown & Wicker Park Dining

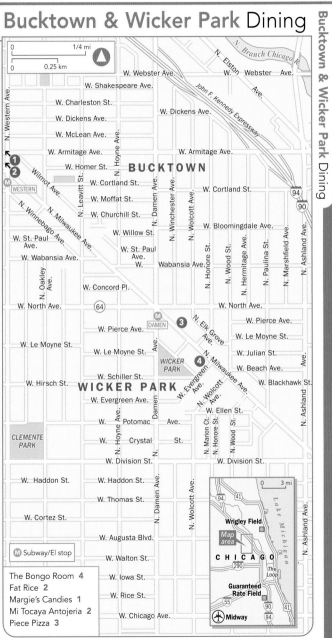

The Bongo Room **4**
Fat Rice **2**
Margie's Candies **1**
Mi Tocaya Antojeria **2**
Piece Pizza **3**

Ⓜ Subway/El stop

98

Chicago Dining

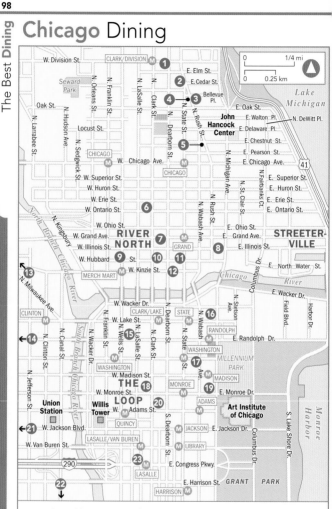

Lincoln Park Dining

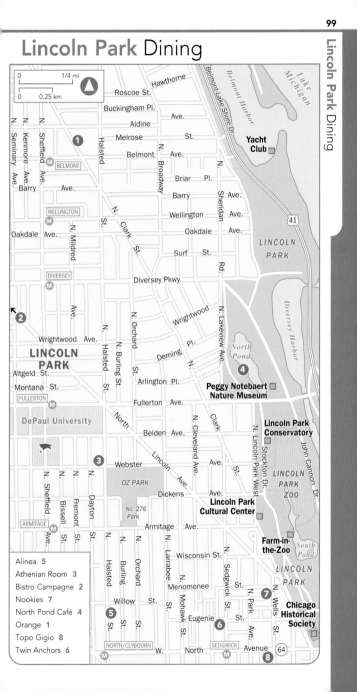

Alinea 5
Athenian Room 3
Bistro Campagne 2
Nookies 7
North Pond Café 4
Orange 1
Topo Gigio 8
Twin Anchors 6

Restaurants A to Z

★★★ Alinea LINCOLN PARK
MOLECULAR GASTRONOMY A 10-to-18-course tasting menu with wine pairings at Chef Grant Achatz's fine-dining Xanadu may cost as much as a mortgage payment, but think of it as dinner and a show. Serving vessels might be made of hand-carved ice; food could be smoking; dessert just may come in the form of an edible helium balloon. Three different options for dining are available: The poshest is the Kitchen Table, which overlooks the food preparation drama; next is The Gallery Menu, which is 16 to 18 courses; The Salon Menu is the most subdued (which isn't saying much!) at 10 to 12 courses. Make reservations online weeks if not months in advance. *1723 N. Halsted St.* ☎ *312/867-0110. www.alinearestaurant.com. Dinner: $185–$390. Wine pairings $135–$195. Dinner daily. El: Red Line to North/Clybourn. Map p 99.*

★ kids Athenian Room LINCOLN PARK *GREEK* Swing by this family-owned Greek taverna for chicken kalamata with a side of tasty fries smothered in olive oil, lemon, and red-wine vinegar, and topped with oregano, salt, and pepper. *807 W. Webster Ave. (at Halsted St.).* ☎ *773/348-5155. Entrees $8–$12. Lunch & dinner daily. El: Brown Line to Armitage. Map p 99.*

★★ Avec WEST LOOP *MEDITER-RANEAN* Dine at communal tables at this upscale classic, which features Mediterranean shared plates made with seasonal Midwestern ingredients. The wine list showcases unexpected European finds. *615 W. Randolph St. (at Jefferson St.).* ☎ *312/377-2002. www.avecrestaurant.com. $12–$27. Lunch Mon–Fri, brunch Sun, dinner daily. El: Green Line to Clinton. Map p 98.*

Communal tables at Avec.

★★★ Bistro Campagne
LINCOLN SQUARE *FRENCH* The coziest bistro in town sports a wood, Prairie-school interior with a lovely garden space for outdoor dining. Expect excellently prepared but simple fare in a charming neighborhood. *4518 N. Lincoln Ave.* ☎ *773/271-6100. www.bistrocampagne.com. Entrees $13–$38. Dinner daily; brunch Sun. El: Brown Line to Western. Map p 99.*

★ Bistronomic RIVER NORTH
FRENCH This bistro creates French dishes with ingredients from local(ish) farms, when possible, like

The bar at Bistronomic.

steak frites made with Midwestern beef. In true French fashion, there are also house-made pâté and cheese flights. *840 N. Wabash Ave. (at Pearson St.).* ☎ *312/944-8400. www.bistronomic.net. Entrees $18–$29. Lunch Wed–Fri, dinner nightly. El: Red Line to Chicago. Map p 98.*

★ kids The Bongo Room
WICKER PARK *BREAKFAST* The menu changes frequently at this brunch mecca, but recent scores include apple churros French toast and white chocolate and caramel pretzel pancakes. Two more locations are in Andersonville and the South Loop. *1470 N. Milwaukee Ave.* ☎ *773/489-0690. www.thebongo room.com. Entrees $7–$16. Breakfast/ lunch Mon–Fri until 2:30pm; brunch Sat–Sun until 2pm. El: Blue Line to Damen. Map p 97.*

★ Chicago q GOLD COAST
BARBECUE Chicago q is serious about barbecue. Portions of the baby back ribs, brisket, and smoked chicken are generous, as are the smoked sandwiches and creative salads. The potato chips and pickles that are served up while you wait are a bonus. Open 'til midnight Fridays and Saturdays for the post-bar crowd. *1160 N. Dearborn St. (at Division St.).* ☎ *312/642-1160. www.chicagoqrestaurant.com.*

Reservations recommended. Entrees $15–$35. Lunch Mon–Fri; brunch Sat–Sun; dinner daily. El: Red Line to Clark/Division. Map p 98.

★★ Cochon Volant Brasserie
LOOP *FRENCH* The top-notch French fare served here relies on fresh, seasonal ingredients, and servers are charming. Even better? The prices are shockingly reasonable—especially at lunch—for a downtown French restaurant. *100 W. Monroe St.* ☎ *312/754-6560. www. cochonvolantchicago.com. Entrees: $13–$57. Breakfast & lunch Mon–Fri; brunch Sat–Sun; dinner daily. El: Red or Blue Line to Monroe. Map p 98.*

★★★ Everest THE LOOP
FRENCH Forty stories above Chicago, Everest astounds with spectacular views and the multi-course Alsatian artistry of legendary Chef Jean Joho. *440 S. LaSalle St. (at Congress Pkwy.).* ☎ *312/663-8920. www. everestrestaurant.com. Reservations required. Prix fixe and tasting menu only: $59–$165. Dinner Tues–Sat. El: Brown Line to LaSalle/Van Buren or Red Line to Adams. Map p 98.*

★★★ Fat Rice LOGAN SQUARE
MACANESE If you've ever wondered what food from Macau tastes like, this beloved neighborhood spot, which blends influences from Africa, Brazil, China, India, and

The patio at Chicago q.

Portugal, has a compelling answer. Try the Arroz Gordo ("fat rice"), which is similar to paella. *2957 W. Diversey Ave.* ☎ *773/681-9170. www.eatfatrice.com. Shared plates $8–$48. Lunch Wed–Fri; brunch Sat–Sun; dinner Tues–Sat. El: Blue Line to Logan. Map p 97.*

★★ **Free Rein** LOOP *AMERICAN* The executive chef and pastry chef have both earned Michelin stars (at previous restaurants), so you're in skilled hands here. Seasonal dishes (seafood, steak, pasta) are artfully presented and flavors are complex at this Midwestern-influenced brasserie at the St. Jane Hotel. Cocktails beg for Instagram shares—mine had "Free Rein" scrolled across the top. *224 N. Michigan Ave. (in the St. Jane Hotel.).* ☎ *312/345-1000. www.stjanehotel.com. Entrees $25–$36. Breakfast, lunch & dinner daily. El: Red Line to Lake. Map p 98.*

★★★ **Frontera Grill, Topolobampo, and Xoco** RIVER NORTH *MEXICAN* At this trinity of Rick Bayless's eateries, Frontera Grill offers a casual atmosphere and well-prepared Mexican classics, while the dressier (and pricier) Topolobampo delivers more refined fare. Xoco's counter service is a must-do for lunch—or churros. *445 N. Clark St. (btw. Illinois and Hubbard sts.).* ☎ *312/661-1434. www.rickbayless. com. Reservations accepted at Topolobampo; Frontera takes a limited number of online reservations. Entrees: Frontera $15–$35; Topolobampo lunch $17–$30; dinner tasting menus $95–$140. Xoco breakfast, sandwiches, and soups $6–$14. Frontera Grill: Lunch Tues–Fri; brunch Sat; dinner Tues–Sat. Topolobampo: Lunch Tues–Fri; dinner Tues–Sat. Xoco: Tues–Thurs 8am–9pm; Fri–Sat 8am–10pm. El: Red Line to Grand/ State. Map p 98.*

★★★ **The Gage** LOOP *GASTRO-PUB* Go high-brow (rack of venison or lamb loin) or lower brow (the burger is amazing) at this always bustling gastropub across from Millennium Park. It's also a great late-night stop for a local beer or a hefty wine pour in a lovely, historic setting in an old millinery, with floor-to-ceiling windows and an ornate tin ceiling. *24 S. Michigan.* ☎ *312/372-4243. www.thegagechicago.com. Entrees $14–$65. Lunch Mon–Fri; brunch Sat–Sun; dinner daily. El: Red Line to Monroe. Map p 98.*

★★ **Gibsons Steakhouse** GOLD COAST *STEAKHOUSE* Chicagoans come to this steakhouse to see and be seen. Giant-size, well-aged steaks are the stars of the show. *1028 N. Rush St. (at Bellevue Place).* ☎ *312/266-8999. www.gibsons steakhouse.com. Entrees $24–$106. Lunch & dinner daily. El: Red Line to Clark/Division. Map p 98.*

★★★ **Girl & the Goat** WEST LOOP *AMERICAN* Wood-roasted pig face (it is exactly what it sounds like) is a popular order at this always-packed shared-plate restaurant, as is anything made of goat. Not to be overshadowed, the vegetable preparations of Chef Stephanie Izard, like the wood-grilled broccoli, are divine. *809 W. Randolph St.* ☎ *312/492-6262. www.girland thegoat.com. Shared plates: $7–$25. Dinner Sun–Thurs 4:30–11pm; 4:30pm–midnight Fri–Sat. El: Green or Pink Line to Morgan. Map p 98.*

★ kids **Harry Caray's** RIVER NORTH *ITALIAN/STEAKHOUSE* Named for the legendary Chicago Cubs announcer, this brick-lined restaurant showcases scores of baseball memorabilia. Wet- and dry-aged steaks, chops, and Italian dishes, including the Chicago-born chicken Vesuvio (baked with garlic, peas, white wine, and potatoes), are served in enormous portions, and bartenders spin a good yarn. *33 W. Kinzie St. (at Dearborn St.).* ☎ *312/828-0966. www.harrycarays.com. Entrees $15–$60. Lunch & dinner daily. El: Brown Line to Merchandise Mart or Red Line to Grand/State. Map p 98.*

★ kids **Heaven on Seven** THE LOOP *CAJUN* The best Cajun and Creole cooking north of New Orleans. Opt for the po' boy sandwiches (oyster and soft-shell crab). *111 N. Wabash Ave. (at Washington St.), 7th floor.* ☎ *312/263-6443. www.heavenonseven.com. Entrees $8–$15. No credit cards. Breakfast Mon–Fri; brunch Sat; dinner Thurs–Sat. El: Brown Line to Washington/Wabash; Red Line to Lake. Map p 98.*

★★ **India House** LOOP *INDIAN* Downtown workers love this refined Indian spot for its elaborate lunch buffet. Dinner, served a la carte, is also destination worthy. Be sure and order the Kashmiri naan, which is stuffed with cherries, cashews, and coconut and cooked in a tandoori oven. *59 W. Grand Ave.* ☎ *312/645-9500. www.indiahouse chicago.com. Lunch buffet: $15 Mon–Thurs, $18 Fri–Sun; dinner entrees $19–$40. Lunch & dinner daily. El: Red Line to Grand. Map p 98.*

★★★ kids **Little Goat Diner** WEST LOOP *DINER* The younger sister to Girl & the Goat, this diner by *Top Chef* winner Stephanie Izard serves one of the best and certainly the most inventive breakfasts in town, with options like bi bim bop made with cauliflower rice and a breakfast burrito rolled in paratha bread. Lunch and dinner put a chef-driven twist on casual comfort food, like the nachos, which consist of homemade masa chips piled with braised pork and pickled peppers. *820 W. Randolph (at Green St.).* ☎ *312/888-8455. www.littlegoat chicago.com. Breakfast/lunch $12–$16; dinner $18–$21. Breakfast, lunch & dinner daily. El: Green or Pink Line to Morgan. Map p 98.*

★★★ kids **Lou Malnati's** RIVER NORTH *PIZZA* Thin crust is as delish as the deep dish at this beloved local chain—but every visitor has to try the ungodly thick Chicago style at least once. *439 N. Wells St.* ☎ *312/828-9800. www.loumalnatis. com. Pizzas start at $9. Lunch & dinner daily. El: Brown Line to Merchandise Mart. Map p 98.*

★ kids **Lou Mitchell's** THE LOOP *AMERICAN/DINER* A Chicago tradition since 1923, this modest diner draws in local celebs and politicians for airy omelets served in sizzling skillets. *565 W. Jackson Blvd. (at Jefferson St.).* ☎ *312/939-3111. www. loumitchells.com. Entrees $8–$15. Breakfast & lunch daily. El: Blue Line to Clinton St. Map p 98.*

Lou Mitchell's diner.

★★★ kids **Margie's Candies**
BUCKTOWN *ICE CREAM* This
kitschy ice-cream parlor circa 1921
serves sundaes in giant conch shell
dishes and makes its own hot
fudge, butterscotch, and caramel.
Sandwiches and salads are available, too—but shouldn't you treat
yourself? *1960 N. Western Ave. (at
Armitage Ave.).* ☎ *773/384-1035.
www.margiesfinecandies.com.
Entrees $7–$9. Daily 9am–midnight.
El: Blue Line to Western. Map p 97.*

★ **Mi Tocaya Antojeria** LOGAN
SQUARE *MEXICAN Bon Appétit*
magazine gave props to this tiny
Mexican spot in Logan Square.
Shareable plates range from tacos
and artfully plated vegetables in
mole sauce to unexpected combi-
nations, like the peanut butter y
lengua (cow tongue drizzled with
peanut sauce). It all pairs well with a
mezcal margarita. *2800 W. Logan
Blvd.* ☎ *872/315-3947. www.mi
tocaya.com. Larger plates $10–$26.
Dinner Tues–Sun. El: Blue line to
California. Map p 97.*

★ kids **Naansense** LOOP *INDIAN
FAST FOOD* This popular, quick
lunch stop is like Chipotle, but with
Indian food. Choose naan tacos, a
salad, or a rice or quinoa bowl; pick
your protein or veggies and then
choose a sauce, like vindaloo,
korma, or tikka. If it's nice out, take
it a few blocks north and eat by the
river. *171 N. Wells St.* ☎ *312/578-
8825. www.eatatnaansense.com.
Entrees $7–$10. Lunch & dinner Mon–
Fri. El: Red Line to Lake. Map p 98.*

★★★ **Nico Osteria** GOLD
COAST *SEAFOOD* You can't
choose wrong here, from the elegant seafood to the inspired house-
made pasta. But it's bruschetta with
stracciatella and crispy Brussels
sprouts that has my heart. Everything is shareable, so plan on sampling. *1015 N. Rush St.* ☎ *312/994-
7100. www.nicoosteria.com. Entrees
$28–$50. Breakfast & lunch Mon–Fri,
brunch Sat–Sun, dinner daily. El: Red
Line to Chicago. Map p 98.*

★ kids **Nookies** OLD TOWN
BREAKFAST This small but per-
petually bustling cafe near Lincoln
Park Zoo is a neighborhood favorite. Three squares are available, but
breakfast is the biggest draw, with
homeruns like the croissant French
toast Napoleon (with vanilla mas-
carpone and strawberries) and the
artichoke frittata. *1746 N. Wells St.*
☎ *312/337-2454. www.nookies
chicago.com. $8–$13. Breakfast &
lunch daily. El: Brown Line to Sedge-
wick. Map p 99.*

★★ **North Pond Café** LINCOLN
PARK *AMERICAN* This secluded,
Arts and Crafts–style retreat offers
dramatic vistas from its location
inside Lincoln Park. Meals are
crafted from organic, locally grown
ingredients. *2610 N. Cannon Dr.
(south of Diversey Pkwy.).* ☎ *773/477-
5845. www.northpondrestaurant.com.
Entrees $37–$43. Dinner Tues–Sun;
brunch Sun. Bus: 151. Map p 99.*

★ kids **Orange** LAKEVIEW
AMERICAN A breakfast/lunch
appetizer is a must here in the form
of "frushi"—that's fresh fruit on sushi
rice—and it's Instagram-ably delicious. Also on the menu: pancake
flights, green eggs and ham (made
with pesto), and a variety of sandwiches and salads for lunch. *2413 N.
Clark (btw. Fullerton Ave. and Arlington Place).* ☎ *773/549-7833. www.
orangerestaurantchicago.com. Entrees
$8–$11. Breakfast & lunch daily. El:
Brown Line to Fullerton. Map p 99.*

★ kids **Phoenix** CHINATOWN
CHINESE/DIM SUM Expect
speedy, friendly service, immense
dining rooms, and tables of families
enjoying Cantonese cuisine, ranging
from shrimp dumplings to sizzling
beef tenderloin. Arrive early if you
want to sample the dim sum. *2131*

S. Archer Ave. ☎ 312/328-0848. www.chinatownphoenix.com. Entrees $9–$24. Breakfast, lunch & dinner daily. Dim sum service: Mon–Fri 9am–3pm, Sat–Sun 8am–3pm. El: Red Line to Cermak/Chinatown. Map p 98.

★★ **Piccolo Sogno** WEST TOWN *ITALIAN* The most beautiful alfresco dining spot in the city is a garden full of plants and trees at this Italian restaurant. Try the wood-fired white pizzas or wood-roasted pork. 464 N. Halsted St. (at Grand Ave.). ☎ 312/2421-0077. www. piccolosognorestaurant.com. Entrees $14–$36. Lunch Mon–Fri; dinner daily. El: Blue Line to Grand. Map p 98.

★ kids **Piece Pizza** WICKER PARK *PIZZA* Eat like a rock star, literally, at this pizza joint, which is owned by Cheap Trick guitarist Rick Nielsen. People go crazy for the New Haven–style pizza—thin crust, irregularly shaped, and served sans mozz (although you can order it with cheese). Try the white pizza with clam and bacon for real Connecticut immersion. 1927 W. North Ave. ☎ 773/772-4422. www. piecechicago.com. Pizza $8–$27. Lunch & dinner daily. El: Blue Line to Damen. Map p 97.

★ kids **Portillo's** RIVER NORTH *FAST FOOD* This beloved chain started in the 'burbs and has been encouraging Midwesterners' love of food on a bun since the 1960s. The Chicago-style dog is a must, and save room for a slice of the famous chocolate cake. Multiple locations, including 100 W. Ontario St. (at Clark St.). ☎ 312/587-8910. www. portillos.com. Hot dogs/sandwiches $3–$11. Lunch & dinner daily. El: Red Line to Grand/State. Map p 98.

★ kids **Potbelly Sandwich Works** MAGNIFICENT MILE *SANDWICHES* This popular local chain serves a mean grilled sub sandwich, prepared on a

Mixed shellfish dish at Piccolo Sogno.

homemade roll with turkey, Italian meats, veggies, and more. Patrons stop in specifically to buy their *giardiniera* (an Italian relish). 520 N. Michigan Ave. (in the shops at North Bridge). ☎ 312/6644-1008. www. potbelly.com. Sandwiches $4–$7. Lunch & dinner daily. El: Red Line to Grand/State. Map p 98.

★★★ **Purple Pig** MAGNIFICENT MILE *MEDITERRANEAN* The Purple Pig was serving small plates before they were trendy. Bring your sense of adventure and try the crispy pig's ears or opt for tamer, but still complex choices, like olive oil poached tuna, and grilled broccoli. 500 N. Michigan Ave. ☎ 312/ 464-1744. www.thepurplepigchicago. com. Shared plates $8–$35. Lunch & dinner daily. El: Red Line to Grand/ State. Map p 98.

★ kids **Revival Food Hall** THE LOOP *FOOD HALL* The food hall craze has hit Chicago, and Revival shows how it's done, bringing outposts of neighborhood favorites under one roof downtown. With ramen, tacos, fried chicken, poke bowls, craft cocktails, and more, it's a crowd pleaser for breakfast, lunch, or a quick dinner. *125 S. Clark St. (at Adams St.).* ☎ *773/999-9411. www.revivalfoodhall.com. Meals $6–$15. Breakfast, lunch & dinner Mon–Fri. El: Red Line to Monroe. Map p 98.*

★★ Shaw's Crab House RIVER NORTH SEAFOOD

A 1940s-style local institution, Shaw's has an extensive seafood menu featuring whatever is in season. Expect oysters, crab, lobster, fish, and even steaks. The raw bar at the more modern on-site Oyster Bar will please even the most sophisticated seafood lover, to a soundtrack of live jazz or blues. Brunch, with its glorious seafood stations, is a worthwhile splurge. *21 E. Hubbard St. (at State St.).* ☎ *312/527-2722. www.shawscrabhouse.com. Entrees $16–$78; brunch $65. Lunch Mon–Fri; brunch Sat–Sun; dinner daily. El: Red Line to Grand/State. Map p 98.*

★★★ Somerset GOLD COAST AMERICAN

Chef Lee Wolen can do no wrong. His roast chicken—which two can share here—is dream-worthy, and his smoked beet tartare, topped with cumin yogurt and goat Gouda, is a revelation, even for self-described beet haters. *1112 N. State St. (in Viceroy Hotel).* ☎ *312/586-2150. www. somersetchicago.com. Dinner entrees $16–$52. Breakfast & dinner daily; lunch Mon–Fri; brunch Sat–Sun. El: Red Line to Clark/Division. Map p 98.*

★★ Sushi-san GOLD COAST SUSHI

Turns out, loud hip hop and quality sushi go quite well together. Serving creative maki, nigiri, handrolls, and even a few grilled-meat options, this Japanese eatery caters to a later-night crowd (open 'til midnight Sun–Thurs and 1am Fri–Sat). *63 W. Grand Ave. (east of Clark St.).* ☎ *312/828-0575. www. sushisanrestaurant.com. Small plates $7–$30. Lunch Mon–Fri; dinner and late-night dining daily. El: Red Line to Grand/State. Map p 98.*

★★★ Tanoshii WEST LOOP SUSHI

This sushi restaurant serves a show-stopping *omakase* menu, which translates as dealer's choice for the chef. Blow torches, truffle oil, and fresh herbs make for a memorable sushi experience. *Be forewarned:* If you ask the chef what's in the roll you're eating, he's likely to respond with a cheeky answer: "Fish!" *720 W. Randolph.* ☎ *312/207-8894. www.tanoshii sushi.com. Omakase menu: $50–$70. Lunch Mon–Fri; dinner daily. El: Green or Pink Line to Morgan. Map p 98.*

★★ Topo Gigio OLD TOWN ITALIAN

If you're craving an old-school, red-sauce slinging kind of place, you won't do much better than Topo Gigio. The bread is heavenly, pastas are divine, and the fried calamari appetizer is the best I've had. Servings are enormous, so consider sharing. *1516 N. Wells St.* ☎ *312/266-9355. www.topogigio chicago.com. Entrees $14–$24. Lunch Mon–Sat; dinner daily. El: Brown Line to Sedgwick. Map p 99.*

★ kids Twin Anchors OLD TOWN BARBECUE

This unpretentious pub dates back to Prohibition and preserves old-school Chicago with its dark mahogany and serviceable Formica. The restaurant's slow-cooked baby back ribs (go for the zesty sauce) keep people coming back. *1655 N. Sedgwick St.* ☎ *312/266-1616. www.twinanchors ribs.com. Entrees $8–$32. Lunch Sat–Sun; dinner daily. El: Brown Line to Sedgwick. Map p 99.* ●

The Best Nightlife

Nightlife Best Bets

Best **Viennese Coffee**
★★ Julius Meinl Café,
3601 N. Southport Ave. (p 117)

Best **Tiki Bar**
★★★ Lost Lake, *3154 W. Diversey
Ave. (p 114)*

Best **Speakeasy**
★★★ Violet Hour, *1520 N. Damen
Ave. (p 116)*

Best **View**
★★ J Parker, *1816 N. Clark St. (p 114)*

Most **Dramatic Cocktails**
★★★ Aviary, *955 W. Fulton Market
(p 113)*

Best **Craft Brewery**
★★ Half Acre, *4257 N. Lincoln Ave.
(p 114)*

Best **Barcade**
★★ Headquarters Beercade,
312 W. Institute Place (p 114)

Best **Patio**
★ Parson's Chicken & Fish,
2952 W. Armitage Ave. (p 115)

Best **Blues Club**
★★★ Buddy Guy's Legends,
700 S. Wabash Ave. (p 116)

Best **Sports Bar**
★ Cubby Bear, *1059 W. Addison St.
(p 114)*

Best **Neighborhood Hangout**
★ Old Town Ale House,
219 W. North Ave. (p 115)

Best **Only-in-Chicago Bar**
★ Billy Goat, *430 N. Michigan Ave.
(p 114)*

Best **Champagne Bar**
★★ Pops for Champagne,
601 N. State St. (p 115)

Best **World Music Venue**
★★ Old Town School of Folk
Music, *4544 N. Lincoln Ave. (p 118)*

Best **Club**
★★★ Smart Bar, *3730 N. Clark St.
(p 118)*

Best **Mecca for Beer Lovers**
★ The Map Room, *1949 N.
Hoyne Ave. (p 115)*

Best **Local Music Hangout**
★★★ The Hideout, *1354 W.
Wabansia Ave. (p 118)*

Best **Hotel Bar**
★★★ Apogee, *in the Dana Hotel
and Spa, 2 W. Erie St. (p 113)*

Best **Jazz Club**
★★★ The Green Mill, *4802 N.
Broadway (p 118)*

*Previous page: A performance at the Old Town School of Folk Music. Above: Three
Dots and a Dash adds speakeasy style to its tiki bar setting.*

Bucktown Nightlife

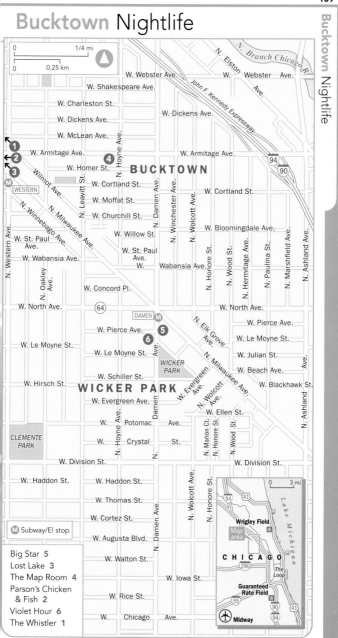

M Subway/El stop

Big Star **5**
Lost Lake **3**
The Map Room **4**
Parson's Chicken & Fish **2**
Violet Hour **6**
The Whistler **1**

Chicago Nightlife

Berlin 8
B.L.U.E.S. 11
Cubby Bear 5
Elbo Room 9
Goose Island Brewing
   Company 13
The Green Mill 1
Half Acre 7
The Hideout 12
J Parker 14
Julius Meinl Café 4
Kingston Mines 10
Old Town Ale House 15
Old Town School
   of Folk Music 6
Smart Bar 2
Uncommon Ground 3
Zebra Lounge 16

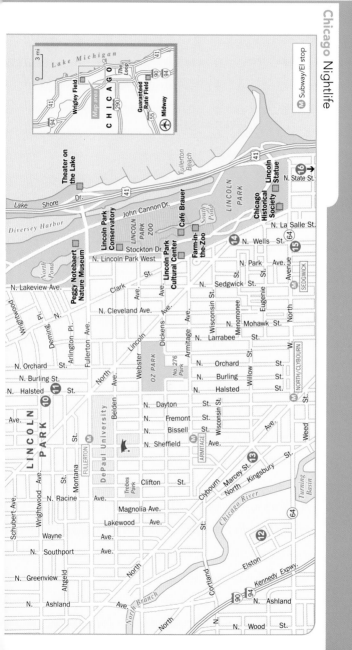

M Subway/El stop

River North Nightlife

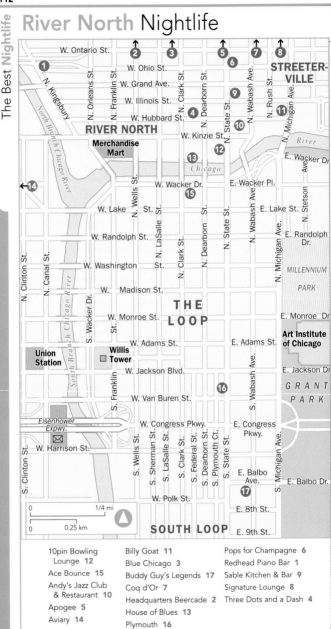

10pin Bowling Lounge **12**	Billy Goat **11**	Pops for Champagne **6**
Ace Bounce **15**	Blue Chicago **3**	Redhead Piano Bar **1**
Andy's Jazz Club & Restaurant **10**	Buddy Guy's Legends **17**	Sable Kitchen & Bar **9**
Apogee **5**	Coq d'Or **7**	Signature Lounge **8**
Aviary **14**	Headquarters Beercade **2**	Three Dots and a Dash **4**
	House of Blues **13**	
	Plymouth **16**	

Nightlife A to Z

Bars

★ **10pin Bowling Lounge** RIVER NORTH   A modern interpretation of the classic bowling alley, this lounge is tucked away behind the Marina Towers complex. There's a full menu of cocktails, craft beer, and gastropub snacks, served lane-side or in two lounges. Low lighting and giant video screens overlooking the 24 bowling lanes give the place a nightclub vibe. *330 N. State St. (btw. Kinzie St. and the Chicago River).* ☎ *312/644-0300. www.10pinchicago. com. El: Red Line to Grand or Brown Line to Merchandise Mart. Map facing page.*

★ **Ace Bounce** THE LOOP   Imagine loud music, a trendy craft cocktail bar in an industrial-ish setting, and, well, balls flying everywhere (expect to get pelted!) and you've got Ace Bounce, a quirky ping-pong bar relatively new to the Chicago nightlife scene. Staff are on standby to walk you through the basics. If you get hungry, the food, which is several notches above bar fare, is excellent. *230 N. Clark St. (at Wacker Dr.).* ☎ *773/219-0900. www.acebounce. com. $15–$22 per table/half-hour. El: Brown or Red Line to Lake. Map facing page.*

★★★ **Apogee** RIVER NORTH   It's quite the scene on the rooftop of

the Dana Hotel, with indoor/outdoor access, twinkling city views, and an alluring firepit. But it's not just about the eye candy here. The drinks are on point. Each beverage is served in dreamy drinkware (it may resemble a mushroom or coconut) with huge hunks of ice. A popular standby is the Weston, which is a bourbon drink with coffee essence and pipe tobacco. The Dana's lobby bar, called Leviathan, also serves remarkable cocktails with a maritime theme. *In the Dana Hotel and Spa, 2 W. Erie St. (at State St.), 26th floor.* ☎ *312/202-6060. www.apogeechicago.com. El: Red Line to Chicago. Map facing page.*

★★★ **Aviary** WEST LOOP   Dramatic is the best word to describe the drinks here. One might be smoking. Another may be encapsulated within ice and released with a mini sling shot. Take a group; the surprise presentation is the best part. *955 W. Fulton Market (at Morgan St.).* ☎ *312/226-0868. www.theaviary.com. El: Green Line to Morgan. Map facing page.*

★★ **Big Star** WICKER PARK   This hipster honky tonk is known for whiskey, beer, tequila, and tacos. Lest you think that the booze begets the food ordering, the reverse is more often true. The

Ace Bounce features 16 ping-pong tables.

Big Star.

chef-driven tacos, like the Taco de Panza with crispy pork belly, are the real siren's song. While I prefer this original location, a second location opened across from Wrigley Field, and it's packed before and after games. *1531 N Damen Ave.* ☎ *773/235-4039. www.bigstarchicago.com. El: Blue Line to Damen. Map p 109.*

★ **Billy Goat** LOOP You may know if from the "cheezborger" *Saturday Night Live* skit, but regulars at the original subterranean location are more likely to stop in for a beer and camaraderie first, and then opt for the mediocre cheezborger ("no fries—cheeps!") to soak up the suds. *430 N Michigan Ave. (at Hubbard St.), lower level.* ☎ *312/222-1525. www.billygoattavern.com. El: Red Line to Grand/State. Map p 112.*

★ **Cubby Bear** WRIGLEYVILLE Drinking at this rollicking Cubs bar is practically a rite of passage for visitors. The tri-level landmark is packed before and after games, as beer guzzlers play pool and darts, watch sports on TV and, at night, rock out to live music. *1059 W. Addison St. (across from Wrigley Field).* ☎ *773/327-1662. www.cubbybear. com. Concert tickets under $10. El: Red Line to Addison. Map p 110.*

Goose Island Brewing Company LINCOLN PARK This brewpub was making craft beer well before the recent renaissance. Relax in the taproom, where there's a full

food menu with suggested beer pairings, or take the informative, hour-long tour ($12; yes, there's beer along the way). The brewery was acquired by Anheuser-Busch a few years ago, but it still packs them in. It doesn't hurt that it's surrounded by a busy shopping area in Lincoln Park, making it an ideal place to put your feet up, mid-spree. *1800 N. Clybourn (at Willow St.).* ☎ *312/915-0071. www.gooseisland.com. El: Red Line to North/Clybourn. Map p 110.*

★★ **Half Acre** NORTH CENTER Daisy Cutter has long been Chicago-speak for "craft beer." Drink the piney pale ale and other inspired brews right where they were created, at this small but mighty North Side brewery and taproom. There's a second location a couple of miles north. *4257 N. Lincoln Ave.* ☎ *773/754-8488. www.halfacrebeer.com. El: Brown Line to Montrose. Map p 110.*

★★ **Headquarters Beercade** RIVER NORTH The beercade/barcade scene—think arcade with adult beverages—is booming in Chicago, and this location is the most convenient for visitors. Suck on a boozy "freezer pop" while playing Centipede or 60-plus other vintage games. If you work up an appetite, there's also a full food menu. *213 West Institute Place.* ☎ *312/291-8735. www.hqrivernorth.com. El: Brown Line to Chicago. Map p 112.*

★★ **J Parker** LINCOLN PARK The views at this rooftop lounge at Hotel Lincoln are among the best in town, and it gets packed in gorgeous weather. Take in Lake Michigan, Lincoln Park Zoo, and downtown while sipping rosé. *1816 N Clark St., 13th floor.* ☎ *312/254-4747. www.jparkerchicago.com. Bus: 22 or 36. Map p 110.*

★★★ **Lost Lake** LOGAN SQUARE If you assume tiki drinks are overly sweet, think again. Lost Lake serves

Parson's Chicken & Fish.

fruit-forward, strong, balanced cocktails in a bar filled with bamboo and palm fronds. The banana daiquiri is even topped with a banana cut to look like a dolphin. *3154 W Diversey Ave.* ☎ *773/293-6048. www.lostlaketiki.com. El: Blue Line to Logan Square. Map p 109.*

★ **The Map Room** BUCKTOWN/WICKER PARK Nearly 200 beers from around the world are available at this travel-themed tavern, where maps double as art along the walls. Beer education is part of the experience, so don't be shy about asking the nerdy beer staff about your suds. In the morning, this is a coffee bar with excellent espresso and pastries; the taps start flowing at 11am. *1949 N. Hoyne Ave. (at Armitage Ave.).* ☎ *773/252-7636. www.maproom.com. El: Blue Line to Western. Map p 109.*

★ **Old Town Ale House** OLD TOWN This legendary saloon has played host to many a Second City comedian, including John Belushi, who commanded the pinball machines here during his Second City (p 126) days. It's a bit dingy, but full of local flavor—especially the weird wall paintings, which you just need to see for yourself. *219 W. North Ave. (at Wells St.).* ☎ *312/944-7020. www.theoldtownalehouse.com. Cash only. El: Brown Line to Sedgwick. Map p 110.*

★ **Parson's Chicken & Fish** LOGAN SQUARE This gas station-turned-bar-and-fried-chicken-shack brought to Chicago the Negroni slushy, and for that, the town is grateful. Weather-permitting, the boozy slushies, beer cocktails, and even Parson's own eponymous beer are best sipped on the enormous patio, which is loaded with picnic tables, bleachers, ping-pong, and Negroni-happy guests. *2952 W Armitage Ave.* ☎ *773/384-3333. www.parsonschickenandfish.com. El: Blue Line to California. Map p 109.*

Plymouth THE LOOP There's no theme, no dress code, no fancy cocktail menu. Plymouth is just a good, friendly, no-frills bar with solid drink specials and friendly servers. Thanks to its central Loop location, it's popular with the after-work crowd—especially in the summertime, when it's nice enough to have drinks on the rooftop. *327 S. Plymouth Ct. (at Van Buren St.).* ☎ *312/362-1212. www.plymouthgrill.com. El: Brown Line to Harold Washington Library. Map p 112.*

★★ **Pops for Champagne** RIVER NORTH A hot date spot for all ages, this romantic lounge offers more than 250 labels of bubbly, plus free, live jazz at 9pm (Sun–Tues) in the downstairs jazz lounge. Bottles of sparkling start at $45. With a courtyard and sidewalk cafe, raw bar, jazz lounge—Pops has it all. *601 N. State St. (at Ontario St.).* ☎ *312/266-7677. www.popsforchampagne.com. El: Red Line to Grand/State. Map p 112.*

★★ **Sable Kitchen & Bar** RIVER NORTH The outstanding happy hour might lure people in ($6 cocktails from 4–6pm during the week), but it's the book-length booze list and chatty bartenders that keep them at this bar at the Hotel

Palomar. Judging by the ratio of locals to visitors, you'd never guess it's a hotel bar. *505 N State St. (at Illinois St.).* ☎ *315/755-9704. www.sablechicago.com. El: Red Line to Grand/State. Map p 112.*

★★★ Signature Lounge MAG-NIFICENT MILE

Skip the ticket and line for 360 CHICAGO, which is the observation deck on the 94th floor of the John Hancock Building, and just head to this 96th floor lounge. Order a martini and soak in the views. *875 N. Michigan Ave.* ☎ *312/787-9596. www.signatureroom.com/lounge. El: Red Line to Chicago. Map p 112.*

★ Three Dots and a Dash RIVER NORTH

Take the alley. Follow the blue light. Down the stairs. Past the skulls. Into the basement. It's not as scary as it sounds. The speakeasy style adds to the allure of this "secret" tiki bar, where the fruit-filled drinks come by the themed glass or the bowl. *435 N Clark St. (at Hubbard St.).* ☎ *312/610-4220. www.threedotschicago.com. El: Red Line to Grand/State. Map p 112.*

★★★ Violet Hour WICKER PARK

Treat this speakeasy-style bar as you would a nice restaurant. Study the menu. Don't rush. Appreciate all of the flavors. Cocktails here take time to make, but that's okay. Patrons are allowed to enter through a semi-camouflaged door (you'll know it by

the perpetual line out front) only when a table is available, in order to quaff without feeling rushed. *1520 N. Damen Ave.* ☎ *773/252-1500. www.theviolethour.com. El: Blue Line to Damen. Map p 109.*

Jazz & Blues Clubs

★★ Andy's Jazz Club & Restaurant RIVER NORTH

Just a couple of blocks off of frenzied Michigan Avenue, Andy's has a kind of mellow, real-life feel behind the brick storefront. Make a dinner reservation for a guaranteed seat at the nightly shows. *11 E. Hubbard St. (at State St.).* ☎ *312/642-6805. www.andysjazzclub.com. Admission $10–$15. El: Red Line to Grand/State. Map p 112.*

★ Blue Chicago RIVER NORTH

This intimate club, with exposed brick walls and a stellar sound system, showcases top blues talent—often female—singing their hearts out. *536 N. Clark St.* ☎ *312/661-0100. www.bluechicago.com. Cover $10–$12. El: Red Line to Grand/State. Map p 112.*

B.L.U.E.S. LINCOLN PARK

Live music plays 365 days a year in this tiny, laid-back club that seats patrons super close to the performers. *2519 N. Halsted St. (at Wrightwood Ave.).* ☎ *773/528-1012. Cover $5–$10. El: Brown Line to Diversey. Map p 110.*

★★★ Buddy Guy's Legends THE LOOP

If Chicago is the body and soul of blues music, then this

Enjoy dinner and a show at Andy's Jazz Club.

House of Blues.

club—owned and operated by rock-'n'-roll Hall of Famer Buddy Guy—is its heart. The club's renowned guitar collection features instruments played by the likes of Eric Clapton and John Lee Hooker. Menu includes southern favorites such as étouffée and Cajun meatloaf. *700 S. Wabash Ave. (at Balbo).* ☎ *312/427-1190. www.buddyguy.com. Cover $10–$20. El: Red Line to Harrison. Map p 112.*

★★★ **House of Blues** RIVER NORTH   Listen to A-list acts and local faves blast some of the city's best sound systems. Walls are adorned with Southern-style art, and guests sway every Sunday during the ever-popular gospel brunch, with chicken, waffles, and worship ($43; seatings at 10am and 12:30pm; reservations highly recommended). *329 N. Dearborn St. (at Kinzie St.).* ☎ *312/923-2000. www.houseof blues.com. Tickets $10–$35. El: Red Line to Grand/State. Map p 112.*

★ **Kingston Mines** LINCOLN PARK   This veteran roadhouse attracts hardcore fans and celebs with two stages' worth of down-home blues. Performances last past 4am on Saturdays. *2548 N. Halsted St. (at Wrightwood Ave.).* ☎ *773/477-4646. www.kingstonmines.com. Cover $12–$15. El: Brown Line to Diversey. Map p 110.*

Cabaret & Piano Bars
Coq d'Or MAGNIFICENT MILE   This piano bar and lounge

showcases pianists and vocalists on weekends, from 9pm to 1am Friday and Saturday. It's a classy place, where you can sip a martini with the older crowd and ruminate on the bar's history, dating back to 1933. *In The Drake Hotel, 140 E. Walton St.* ☎ *312/787-2200. www.thedrakehotel.com. No cover. El: Red Line to Chicago/State. Map p 112.*

Redhead Piano Bar RIVER NORTH   A favorite with locals, this upscale lounge features top-notch pianists and makes a great spot for after-dinner cocktails. Dress well. *16 W. Ontario.* ☎ *312/640-1000. www.redheadpianobar.com. El: Red Line to Grand/State. Map p 112.*

★ **Zebra Lounge** GOLD COAST Black-and-white striped walls are the key to the decor at this shoe-box-size piano bar. The multigenerational, loyal crowd gets raucous late in the evening; arrive by 9:30pm if you want to get a seat. *1220 N. State Pkwy. (btw. Division and Goethe sts.).* ☎ *312/642-5140. www.thezebralounge.net. Subway/El: Red Line to Clark/Division. Map p 110.*

Cafes
★★ **Julius Meinl Café** LAKEVIEW   The venerable Austrian coffee empire chose Chicago for its first attempt at re-creating a Viennese coffeehouse in the U.S. and has since expanded. The rich coffee is served with class, on a silver tray with a glass of water and a cookie.

But don't let that stop you from ordering dessert. *3601 N. Southport Ave. (at Addison St.) and 4115 N. Ravenswood Ave.* ☎ *773/868-1857. www.meinl.com. El: Brown Line to Southport. Map p 110.*

★★★ Uncommon Ground

WRIGLEYVILLE This bohemian cafe's soul-warming bowls of coffee are accompanied by California-influenced cuisine that's heavy on vegetarian, vegan, and gluten-free dishes, accompanied by live music nightly. A second location is an option in Edgewater. *3800 N. Clark St. (at Grace St. (☎ 773/929-3680), and 1401 W. Devon Ave. (☎ 773/465-9801). www.uncommonground. com. El: Red Line to Addison. Map p 110.*

Live Music

Elbo Room LINCOLN PARK The eclectic acts at this small live music venue range from hip-hop to Goth to rockabilly. The crowds are equally diverse. *2871 N. Lincoln Ave. (at George St.).* ☎ *773/549-5549. www. elboroomlive.com. Cover $9–$10; no cover for upstairs lounge. El: Brown Line to Diversey. Map p 110.*

★★★ The Green Mill UPTOWN

Famous for offering eclectic live jazz in a historical setting, this former speakeasy was established in 1907 and frequented by infamous mobster Al Capone. Today you can hear Latin jazz, big-band jazz, jazz piano, and more. On Sunday nights it hosts the famous Uptown Poetry Slam with Marc Kelly Smith. *4802 N. Broadway (at Lawrence Ave.).* ☎ *773/878-5552. www.greenmill jazz.com. Free to $15 cover. El: Red Line to Lawrence. Map p 110.*

★★★ The Hideout WEST TOWN

Head to this friendly, downhome tavern for the best lineup of folk and alt country bands in the city. Many bartenders here have gone on to become famous. Heard of Neko Case? *1354 W. Wabansia Ave. (btw. Elston Ave. and Throop St.).* ☎ *773/227-4433. www.hideoutchi cago.com. Cover usually $8–$10. El: Blue Line to Damen. Map p 110.*

★★ Old Town School of Folk Music LINCOLN SQUARE Known

around the world, this venerable school and concert venue brings in all types of folk talent, from Joan Baez to Afro beat ensembles. Discover new music at the free weekly concert, World Music Wednesdays. *4544 N Lincoln Ave.* ☎ *773/728-6000. www.oldtownschool.org. Tickets $15–$48. El: Brown Line to Western. Map p 110.*

Nightclubs

★ Berlin BOYSTOWN This Boys-

town dance club is a retro favorite for anyone—gay, trans, straight, etc.—looking to get their freak on. Music spans the eras, with '80s, house, disco, and more. *954 W. Belmont Ave.* ☎ *773/348-4975. www. berlinchicago.com. Fri-Sat cover $7–$10. El: Red Line to Belmont. Map p 110.*

★★★ Smart Bar WRIGLEYVILLE

One of the coolest clubs in Chicago is tucked away in the dimly lit basement of Metro, one of Chicago's popular live rock venues. DJs here do some serious spinning. *3730 N. Clark St.* ☎ *773/549-4140. www.smartbarchicago.com. Usually free to $17 cover. El: Red Line to Addison. Map p 110.*

★★ The Whistler LOGAN

SQUARE Part music venue, part record label, all cocktail destination, this lounge is as surprising as they come, with DJs and live entertainment nightly. *2421 N. Milwaukee Ave.* ☎ *773/227-3530. www.whistler chicago.com. No cover. El: Blue Line to California. Map p 109.* ●

Arts & Entertainment Best Bets

Best **Theater Company**
★★★ Steppenwolf Theatre Company, *1650 N. Halsted St. (p 129)*

Best **Cutting-Edge Productions**
★★★ Lookingglass Theatre Company, *821 N. Michigan Ave. (p 129)*

Best **Fancy Theater Experience**
★★★ Goodman Theatre, *170 N. Dearborn Ave. (p 128)*

Best **Opera Company**
★★★ Lyric Opera of Chicago, *20 N. Wacker Dr. (p 127)*

Best **Ballet**
★★ Joffrey Ballet of Chicago, *10 E. Randolph St. (p 126)*

Best **Modern Dance**
★★ Hubbard Street Dance Chicago, *1147 W. Jackson Blvd. (p 126)*

Best **Symphony**
★★ Chicago Symphony Orchestra, *220 S. Michigan Ave. (p 125)*

Best **Late-Night Comedy**
★ The Infinite Wrench, *5153 N. Ashland Ave. (p 128)*

Best **Guaranteed Laugh**
★★★ Blue Man Group, *3133 N. Halsted St. (p 128)*

Best **Up-and-Coming Comedians**
★★ iO Theater, *1501 N. Kingsbury St. (p 126)*

Best **Free Live Music Performances**
★★★ Jay Pritzker Pavilion, *201 E. Randolph St. (p 125)*

Wackiest **Place to Watch a Film**
★★★ Music Box Theatre, *3733 W. Southport Ave. (p 127)*

Best **Movie Theater for Cinema Buffs**
★ Gene Siskel Film Center, *164 N. State St. (p 127)*

Best **Venue for World-Premiere Theater**
★★★ Victory Gardens Theater, *2433 N. Lincoln Ave. (p 130)*

Best **Children's Film Festival**
Facets Multi-Media, *1517 W. Fullerton Ave. (p 126)*

Best **Dinner Theater Show**
Tommy Gun's Garage, *2114 S. Wabash Ave. (p 129)*

Best **Sports Experience**
★★★ Wrigley Field, *1060 W. Addison St. (p 128)*

Best **Summer Music Destination**
★★★ Ravinia Festival, *418 Sheridan Rd. (p 125)*

Best **Improv**
★★★ The Second City, *1616 N. Wells St. (p 126)*

Best **Children's Theater**
★★ Emerald City Theatre Company, *2540 N. Lincoln Ave. (p 128)*

Previous page: Wrigley Field.

The Loop Entertainment

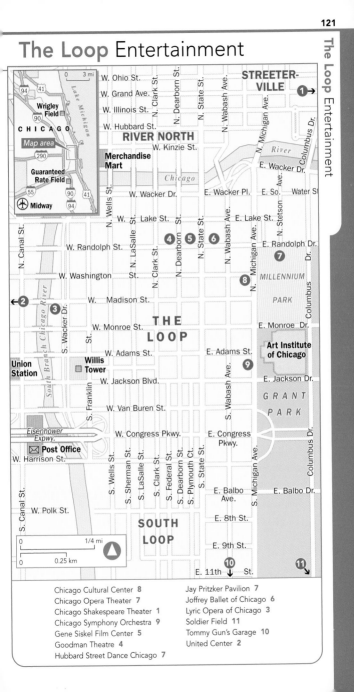

Chicago Cultural Center **8**
Chicago Opera Theater **7**
Chicago Shakespeare Theater **1**
Chicago Symphony Orchestra **9**
Gene Siskel Film Center **5**
Goodman Theatre **4**
Hubbard Street Dance Chicago **7**

Jay Pritzker Pavilion **7**
Joffrey Ballet of Chicago **6**
Lyric Opera of Chicago **3**
Soldier Field **11**
Tommy Gun's Garage **10**
United Center **2**

Lincoln Park Entertainment

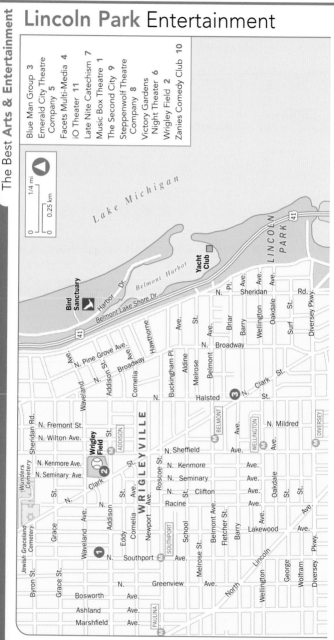

Blue Man Group 3
Emerald City Theatre Company 5
Facets Multi-Media 4
iO Theater 11
Late Nite Catechism 7
Music Box Theatre 1
The Second City 9
Steppenwolf Theatre Company 8
Victory Gardens Night Theater 6
Wrigley Field 2
Zanies Comedy Club 10

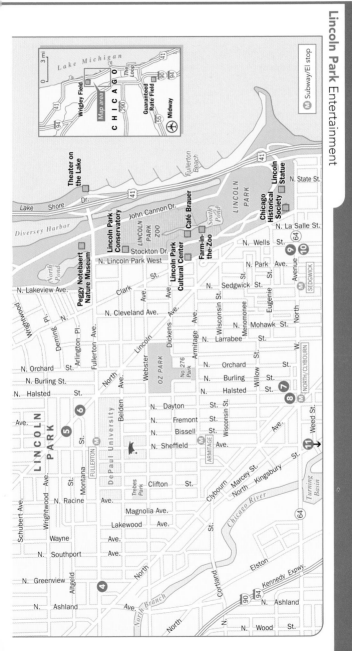

Chicago Arts & Entertainment

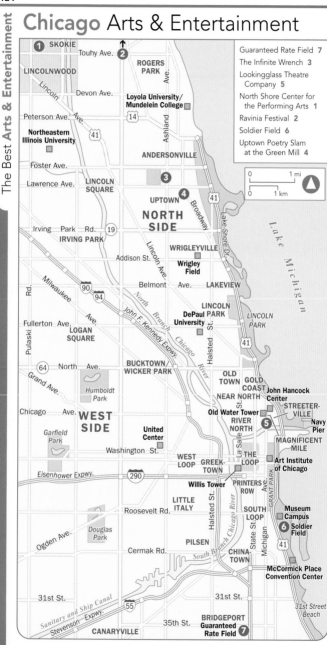

Guaranteed Rate Field **7**
The Infinite Wrench **3**
Lookingglass Theatre Company **5**
North Shore Center for the Performing Arts **1**
Ravinia Festival **2**
Soldier Field **6**
Uptown Poetry Slam at the Green Mill **4**

1 SKOKIE
LINCOLNWOOD
Touhy Ave. 2
ROGERS PARK
Devon Ave.
Loyola University/ Mundelein College
Peterson Ave.
Northeastern Illinois University
14
Foster Ave.
ANDERSONVILLE
Lawrence Ave.
LINCOLN SQUARE
3
UPTOWN
4
NORTH SIDE
Irving Park Rd.
IRVING PARK
19
Addison St.
WRIGLEYVILLE
Wrigley Field
Belmont Ave.
LAKEVIEW
Lincoln Ave.
LINCOLN PARK
DePaul University
LINCOLN PARK
Milwaukee
Fullerton Ave.
LOGAN SQUARE
Halsted St.
North Branch Chicago River
90 94
John F. Kennedy Expwy.
Pulaski
64
North Ave.
BUCKTOWN/ WICKER PARK
Grand Ave.
Humboldt Park
OLD TOWN
GOLD COAST
John Hancock Center
NEAR NORTH
STREETER-VILLE
Chicago Ave.
WEST SIDE
Old Water Tower
RIVER NORTH
5
Navy Pier
Garfield Park
United Center
MAGNIFICENT MILE
Washington St.
WEST LOOP
GREEK-TOWN
THE LOOP
La Salle St.
Art Institute of Chicago
Eisenhower Expwy.
290
Willis Tower
PRINTERS ROW
GRANT PARK
LITTLE ITALY
Roosevelt Rd.
Halsted St.
South Branch Chicago River
SOUTH LOOP
Museum Campus
6 Soldier Field
Douglas Park
Ogden Ave.
PILSEN
Cermak Rd.
CHINA-TOWN
State St.
Michigan
41
McCormick Place Convention Center
31st St.
Sanitary and Ship Canal
55
31st St.
31st Street Beach
Stevenson Expwy.
CANARYVILLE
35th St.
BRIDGEPORT
Guaranteed Rate Field
7

Lake Michigan
Lake Shore Dr.
Broadway
Ashland Ave.
Lincoln Ave.
41

0   1 mi
0   1 km

Arts & Entertainment A to Z

Chicago Cultural Center.

Classical Music & Concerts

Chicago Cultural Center THE LOOP This former public library is now a cultural institution, with free concerts, art exhibits, lectures, films, and the world's largest Tiffany glass dome. Free tours are available and Dame Myra Hess Memorial classical concerts are every Wednesday at noon. *78 E. Washington St. ☎ 312/744-6630, www.choosechicago.com for weekly events. El: Brown Line to Washington/Wabash or Red Line to Lake. Map p 121.*

★★ Chicago Symphony Orchestra THE LOOP One of the best and oldest symphony orchestras in the world performs a varied repertoire of classical works at Orchestra Hall from September to June. The "Symphony Center Presents" series features top jazz, world

beat, Latin, and cabaret artists. *Symphony Center, 220 S. Michigan Ave. (at Jackson St.). ☎ 312/294-3000. www.cso.org. Tickets $35–$200. El: Brown Line to Adams or Red Line to Monroe. Map p 121.*

★★★ Jay Pritzker Pavilion LOOP Gospel, jazz, salsa, world music, rock—you name it and you're likely to find it at this beloved outdoor venue at Millennium Park during the summer. See website for concert dates. *201 E. Randolph St. ☎ 312/742-1168. www.cityofchicago. org. Free. El: Red Line to Lake, or Brown Line to Randolph. Map p 121.*

★ North Shore Center for the Performing Arts SUBURBAN SKOKIE Opened in 1996, this state-of-the-art complex has earned comparisons to Washington, D.C.'s Kennedy Center. It's home of the respected Northlight Theater, the Skokie Valley Symphony Orchestra, an educational arts series touring acts, including comics, dance troupes, and children's programs. *9501 Skokie Blvd. (at Golf Rd.). ☎ 847/673-6300. www.northshorecenter.org. Tickets $10–$60. Take I-90 to Old Orchard Rd. exit; turn right on Old Orchard Rd., and drive past Old Orchard Mall. Turn right on Skokie Blvd. Map p 124.*

★★★ Ravinia Festival SUBURBAN HIGHLAND PARK Locals pack in elaborate picnics, complete with candelabras, at this outdoor pavilion

The Jay Pritzker Pavilion.

North Shore Center for the Performing Arts.

all summer long. Concerts range from Joshua Bell to 50 Cent, and it's the summer home of the Chicago Symphony Orchestra. *418 Sheridan Rd., Highland Park.* ☎ *847/266-5100. www.ravinia.org. Tickets $10 for lawn seating, $25–$135 for the pavilion. Metra: UP North line to Ravinia. Map p 124.*

Comedy Clubs

★★ **iO Theater** LINCOLN PARK Tina Fey and Amy Poehler got their start here, and the remarkable improv talent streak continues today across four stages. Get ready for laughter exhaustion. *1501 N. Kingsbury St.* ☎ *773/929-2401. www.ioimprov.com. Cover $5–$16. El: Red Line to North. Map p 122.*

★★★ **The Second City** OLD TOWN The star-studded history includes Bill Murray, Chris Farley, Dan Aykroyd, and too many to list at this Chicago institution. Two sketch-comedy productions run on the main stage and at ETC (et cetera), a smaller venue. If you just want a quick sampling, free improv sessions take place every night except Friday, after the late show, around 10:15pm (no ticket necessary). *1616 N. Wells St. (at North Ave.).* ☎ *877/778-4707 or 312/337-3992. www.secondcity. com. Cover $26–$48. El: Brown Line to Sedgwick. Map p 122.*

Zanies Comedy Night Club OLD TOWN High-caliber comedians treat sold-out houses to the best in traditional stand-up. *1548 N. Wells St. (at North Ave.).* ☎ *312/337-4027. www.chicago.zanies.com. Cover $25–$30, with a 2-item food/drink minimum. 21 or older to enter. El: Brown Line to Sedgwick. Map p 122.*

Dance

★★ **Hubbard Street Dance Chicago** THE LOOP This 17-member troupe, Chicago's best-known contemporary dance company, is known for exhilarating performances that reference an array of genres. You can catch three to four performances each season at different theatres around town. *Office: 1147 W. Jackson Blvd.* ☎ *312/635-3799. www.hubbardstreetdance. com. Tickets $25–$110. Map p 121.*

★★ **Joffrey Ballet of Chicago** SOUTH LOOP Founded in 1956 in New York, the Joffrey moved into the Joffrey Tower in 2008, and does about 6 weeks of performances in its hometown, including the ever popular *Nutcracker* in December. Known for boundary-pushing works and diverse dancers, performances take place in the stunning Auditorium Theater, which was designed by Dankmar Adler and Louis Sullivan with the help of a young Frank Lloyd Wright. If you've always dreamed of dancing like the pros, you can drop in on an adult dance class at Joffrey Academy of Dance for $15. *10 E. Randolph St.* ☎ *312/386-8905. www.joffrey.org. Tickets about $35–$204. Map p 121.*

Film

kids Facets Multi-Media LAKEVIEW This nonprofit group screens independent and experimental films from around the world at its modest Cinematheque Theatre. Its collection of children's films is the most extensive in the U.S., and it also hosts the Chicago International Children's Film Festival (Oct/Nov), the oldest and largest such festival in the country. In old-school fashion, you can even rent artsy DVDs here. *1517 W. Fullerton Ave.* ☎ *773/281-9075; 773/281-4114 for program information and show times. www.facets.org. Tickets around $10. El: Red or Brown line to Fullerton. Map p 122.*

★ Gene Siskel Film Center THE
LOOP Named after the late *Chicago Tribune* film critic, this theater for serious film buffs is part of the School of the Art Institute of Chicago. It offers an array of foreign, art, and experimental films, as well as lectures and discussions with filmmakers. *164 N. State St.* ☎ *312/846-2800. www.siskelfilmcenter.org. Tickets $8–$11. El: Red Line to Washington or Brown Line to Randolph. Map p 121.*

★★★ Music Box Theatre
LAKEVIEW This atmospheric movie house, designed to re-create the open-air feeling of an Italian courtyard, opened in 1929. Its funky, shabby feel is part of its charm. The now-restored theater screens cult, independent, classic, and foreign films. *3733 W. Southport Ave.* ☎ *773/871-6604. www.musicbox theatre.com. Tickets $9–$11. El: Brown Line to Southport. Map p 122.*

Opera

Chicago Opera Theater THE LOOP A focus on often-neglected and new works, plus relatively low ticket prices, makes this not-for-profit opera company appealing to a broad audience. The November to April season includes three operas. *At the Studebaker Theater, 410 S. Michigan Ave., and Harris Theatre, 205 E. Randolph.* ☎ *312/704-8414. www.chicagooperatheater.org. Tickets $45–$145. El: Red Line to Harrison (Studebaker); Red Line to Randolph (Harris). Map p 121.*

★★★ Lyric Opera of Chicago
THE LOOP One of the country's premier opera companies stages lavish productions headlined by the world's top talent in a stunning, 3,500-seat theater. *Tip:* Discounted children's tickets ($20–$50) are available by phone when purchasing an adult ticket. *Civic Opera House, 20 N. Wacker Dr.* ☎ *312/827-5600. www.lyricopera.org. Tickets $37–$258. El: Brown Line to Washington. Map p 121.*

Spectator Sports

Guaranteed Rate Field BRIDGEPORT Home of the Chicago White Sox and their blue-collar, Cubs-loathing South Side fans. The ballpark features excellent sightlines, and tickets are easier to come by here than at Wrigley (diehards still call it Comiskey Park). *333 W. 35th St.* ☎ *312/674-1000. www.whitesox.mlb.com. Tickets $7 and up. El: Red Line to Sox/35th St. Map p 124.*

Soldier Field SOUTH LOOP Renovations have vastly improved the amenities at the home of the NFL's oldest team, the venerable Chicago Bears (and occasional soccer and rugby games). Ticket prices are demand-based and can be very expensive. *1410 S. Museum Campus Dr.* ☎ *312/235-7000. www.soldier field.net. Tickets $40–$700 and up. Bus: 130 or 146. Map p 121.*

Lyric Opera of Chicago.

United Center NEAR WEST Yes, the Chicago Bulls glory days of Michael Jordan are gone, but the team is still full of talent and games at this massive stadium are a blast. During hockey season, games here can get downright rowdy watching the NHL's Chicago Blackhawks, who won the Stanley Cup in 2015. *1901 W. Madison St.* ☎ *312/455-4500. www.unitedcenter.com. Tickets start at $12 and climb, depending on the event. El: Blue Line to Illinois Medical District. Map p 121.*

★★★ **Wrigley Field** WRIGLEY-VILLE Whether the Cubs win or lose, a visit to their home field is a don't-miss Chicago experience. This baseball mecca is pure magic, from its ivy-covered walls to the hand-operated scoreboard and views of shimmering Lake Michigan from the upper deck. Fans are more dedicated than ever since the Cubs won the 2016 World Series. *1060 W. Addison St.* ☎ *800/THE-CUBS (843-2827). www.cubs.mlb. com. Tickets $37 and up. El: Red Line to Addison. Map p 122.*

Theater

★★★ **Blue Man Group** LINCOLN PARK Originally an off-Broadway show that ripped early 1990s performance art (all in good fun), the Blue Man Group's mix of percussion, mime, and music has taken on a life of its own. The troupe has been so successful that they bought their own theater—so expect them to be in Chicago a good long while. *At Briar Street Theatre, 3133 N. Halsted St. (at Briar St.).* ☎ *773/348-4000. www. blueman.com. Tickets $49–$89. El: Brown Line to Wellington. Map p 122.*

★★★ **Chicago Shakespeare Theater** NAVY PIER Patterned loosely after the Swan Theatre in Stratford-upon-Avon, this stunning theater is the backdrop for top-notch performances of Shakespeare's works. Avoid the upper balcony seats if you're not fond of heights. *800 E. Grand Ave. (at the tip of Navy Pier).* ☎ *312/595-5600. www.chicago shakes.com. Tickets $50–$90. El: Red Line to State/Grand, then free trolley to Navy Pier. Map p 121.*

★★ **kids Emerald City Theatre Company** LAKEVIEW It's all about kids at this neighborhood, nonprofit theater company, which seeks to show babies to teens just how exciting theater can be. Recent shows, which play at different theaters, include Mother Goose and Knuffle Bunny. *Frequently at the Apollo Theater, 2540 N. Lincoln Ave.* ☎ *773/529-2690. www.emeraldcity theatre.com. Tickets $15 for adults, $12 for kids. El: Red or Brown Line to Fullerton. Map p 122.*

★★★ **Goodman Theatre** THE LOOP The internationally recognized Goodman is queen of the Chicago theater scene, producing both original works and familiar standards in a custom-designed home (p 33, ⓓ). The Albert is the main stage, and you'll see locals don their finest furs here; the Owen is the smaller, less formal hall. *170 N. Dearborn St. (at Randolph St.).* ☎ *312/443-3800. www.goodmantheatre.org. Tickets $35–$90. El: Red Line to Washington/ State, or Brown or Orange line to Clark/Lake. Map p 121.*

★ **The Infinite Wrench** NORTH SIDE If you don't like the performance, wait a minute—actually, 2 minutes—and it'll change. So it goes with this spirited production, which consists of a series of 2-minute plays, one after another, all written by ensemble members. Drama, comedy, surrealism—it's all here. *At the Neo-Futurarium, 5153 N. Ashland Ave.* ☎ *773/878-4557. www.neofuturists.org. Shows run Fri– Sat 11:30pm, Sun 7pm. Tickets $10– $20. El: Red Line to Berwyn. Map p 124.*

Scoring Discounted Tickets

Bargain hunters rejoice: The League of Chicago Theatres operates **Hot Tix** (☎ 312/554-9800; www.hottix.org), which sells half-price tickets for the current week and for future performances. Get tickets online or at two Loop locations: inside the Block 37 Shops at 108 N. State St. and at 72 E. Randolph St. The site **Broadway in Chicago** (☎ 312/977-1700; www.broadwayinchicago.com) operates a deeply discounted lottery for popular shows and sells a limited number of discount tickets. The site **Goldstar** (www.goldstar.com) is another go-to for discounts, although you're unlikely to find the hottest tickets in town there. Also, the **Today Tix** app (www.todaytix.com) showcases last-minute savings on shows.

Steppenwolf Theatre Company sells 20 same-day seats for $20 at 11am the day of the show by phone (☎ 312/335-1650); if a show doesn't sell out, half-price tickets are available for purchase in-person an hour before the performance at the box office. At the Goodman Theatre, if a show doesn't sell out, half-price tickets for that day's performance are available at noon at the box office or at www.goodmantheatre.org with the promo code MEZZTIX.

Late Nite Catechism LINCOLN PARK Catechism class is in session every weekend (though not late-night) at this long-running show where you can laugh your sins off. Audience participation is part of the experience, so be prepared to make your own true confessions to the nuns. *At the Royal George Theatre Center, 1641 N. Halsted St. ☎ 312/988-9000. 5pm Sat, 2pm Sun. www.theroyalgeorgetheatre. com. Tickets $22–$30. El: Red Line to North/Clybourn. Map p 122.*

★★★ Lookingglass Theatre Company MAGNIFICENT MILE Original shows and unusual literary adaptations in a highly physical, imaginative style are the forte of this Tony Award–winning company. Lookingglass stages several productions each year, many of which are world premieres. The intimate theater seats a max of 240, and there's not a bad seat in the house (the balcony seats are especially good). It's located within an architectural landmark, the Water Tower Pumping Station, which withstood the Great Chicago Fire of 1871. *821 N. Michigan Ave. ☎ 312/337-0665. www.lookingglasstheatre.org. Tickets $30–$60. El: Red Line to Chicago/State. Map p 124.*

★★★ Steppenwolf Theatre Company LINCOLN PARK Known for its original, edgy drama, this veteran company has launched the careers of many well-respected actors, including Joan Allen, John Malkovich, and Gary Sinise—and nabbed 12 Tony Awards along the way. *1650 N. Halsted St. (at North Ave.). ☎ 312/335-1650. www.steppenwolf.org. Tickets $20–$99. El: Red Line to North/Clybourn. Map p 122.*

Tommy Gun's Garage SOUTH LOOP A cut above the usual tourist fare, this dinner theater puts on a vaudeville show filled with 1920s-era gangsters, flappers, and gigolos.

The Victory Gardens Theater.

The food's not bad, either, but hooch (alcohol, silly) will cost you extra. *2114 S. Wabash Ave. (at E. 21st St.).* ☎ *312/225-0273. Shows run Thurs–Sun nights. 3-course dinner and show $67–$77. Subway/El: Red Line to Cermak/Chinatown. Map p 121.*

★★ Uptown Poetry Slam at The Green Mill UPTOWN
Poets vie for an open mic to roast and ridicule each other's work every Sunday night at a former speakeasy that's a real Chicago treasure. *At The Green Mill. 4802 N. Broadway (at Lawrence Ave.).* ☎ *773/878-5552. Cover $7. Subway/ El: Red Line to Lawrence. Map p 124.*

★★★ Victory Gardens Theater
LINCOLN PARK   This is the third Chicago theater of five (after the Steppenwolf and the Goodman) to win a Tony Award for sustained excellence by a regional theater. All the shows staged here, on the main stage in the historic Biograph Theater, are world premieres (usually by developing playwrights), and they're always provocative and well acted. *2433 N. Lincoln Ave. (at Belden Ave.).* ☎ *773/871-3000. www.victorygardens. org. Tickets $30–$60. El: Red or Brown line to Fullerton. Map p 122.* ●

Finding Out What's Playing

Connect to the Chicago fine-arts scene by perusing the *Chicago Tribune* (www.chicagotribune.com) and its dining/entertainment/ nightlife website, www.metromix.com; the *Chicago Sun-Times* (www.suntimes.com); and the *Daily Herald* (www.dailyherald.com) newspapers, which offer comprehensive weekly listings in their Friday entertainment sections and online.

Other reliable sources of reviews and commentary are *Chicago* (www.chicagomag.com) and *Make It Better* (www.makeitbetter.net) magazines. For out-of-the-mainstream performances, pick up the *Chicago Reader* (www.chicagoreader.com) and *New City* (www.new citychicago.com), the leading free alternative newspapers, and check out the local online guide, *Time Out* (www.timeout.com/chicago). The site Theatre in Chicago (www.theatreinchicago.com) rounds up what's playing where, and even offers discounted tickets.

Hotel Best Bets

Chicago. Most **Luxurious**
★★★ The Langham $$$–$$$$$
330 N. Wabash Ave. (p 140)

Best **Business Hotel**
★★ Loews Chicago Hotel
$$–$$$$ *455 North Park Dr. (p 140)*

Best **Views**
★★ Chicago Athletic Association
$$–$$$$$ *12 S. Michigan Ave. (p 137)*

Best **Historic Hotel**
★★ The Blackstone $$–$$$$$
636 S. Michigan Ave. (p 136)

Best **Hotel for Millennials**
★ Moxy $$ *530 N. LaSalle Dr. (p 141)*

Best **Hostel**
★ Freehand Chicago $
19 E. Ohio St. (p 144)

Best **Hotel Away from the Magnificent Mile**
★★★ Viceroy $$–$$$
1118 N. State St. (p 143)

Best **Moderately Priced Hotel**
★ Best Western Plus Hawthorne Terrace $–$$$ *3434 N. Broadway (p 136)*

Best **Family Hotel**
Homewood Suites $–$$$$
40 E. Grand Ave. (p 138)

Best **Local Secret**
★★ Talbott Hotel $–$$
20 E. Delaware Pl. (p 142)

Best **Cheap Bed**
★ Hotel Felix $$–$$$$$
111 W. Huron St. (p 138)

Best **Swimming Pool**
★ InterContinental Chicago
$$–$$$$$ *505 N. Michigan Ave. (p 139)*

Most **Quirky and Fun**
★★★ ACME Hotel $$–$$$
15 E. Ohio St. (p 136)

Most **Instagrammable**
★★ Hotel EMC2 $$–$$$
228 E. Ontario St. (p 138)

Best **Lobby**
Palmer House Hilton $$–$$$
17 E. Monroe St. (p 141)

Best **Boutique Hotel**
★★★ Kimpton Gray $$–$$$$
122 W. Monroe St. (p 140)

Best **Hotel Bar(s)**
★★ Dana Hotel and Spa
$$–$$$$$ *660 N. State St. (p 137)*

Best **Hotel for Cubs Fans**
★ Hotel Zachary $$–$$$
3630 N. Clark St. (p 139)

Best **Spa**
★★★ JW Marriott $$$–$$$$
151 W. Adams St. (p 140)

Best **Neighborhood Hotel**
★★ Hotel Lincoln $$–$$$
1816 N. Clark St. (p 139)

Best **Rooftop**
★ LondonHouse Chicago $$–$$$$
85 E. Upper Wacker Dr. (p 141)

Previous page: Lobby of the Ritz-Carlton Chicago.

River North & Magnificent Mile Hotels

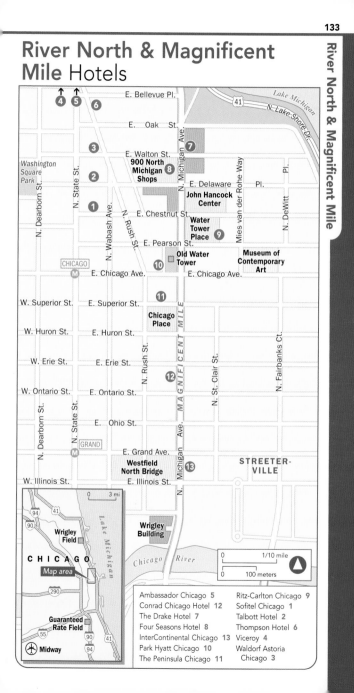

Ambassador Chicago **5**
Conrad Chicago Hotel **12**
The Drake Hotel **7**
Four Seasons Hotel **8**
InterContinental Chicago **13**
Park Hyatt Chicago **10**
The Peninsula Chicago **11**

Ritz-Carlton Chicago **9**
Sofitel Chicago **1**
Talbott Hotel **2**
Thompson Hotel **6**
Viceroy **4**
Waldorf Astoria
  Chicago **3**

The Loop Hotels

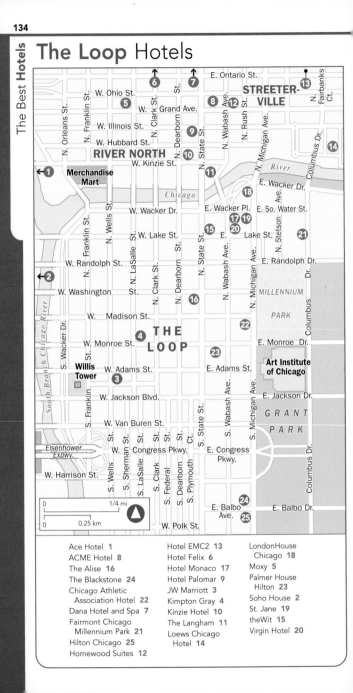

Ace Hotel **1**
ACME Hotel **8**
The Alise **16**
The Blackstone **24**
Chicago Athletic
  Association Hotel **22**
Dana Hotel and Spa **7**
Fairmont Chicago
  Millennium Park **21**
Hilton Chicago **25**
Homewood Suites **12**

Hotel EMC2 **13**
Hotel Felix **6**
Hotel Monaco **17**
Hotel Palomar **9**
JW Marriott **3**
Kimpton Gray **4**
Kinzie Hotel **10**
The Langham **11**
Loews Chicago
  Hotel **14**

LondonHouse
  Chicago **18**
Moxy **5**
Palmer House
  Hilton **23**
Soho House **2**
St. Jane **19**
theWit **15**
Virgin Hotel **20**

Hotels **Beyond Downtown**

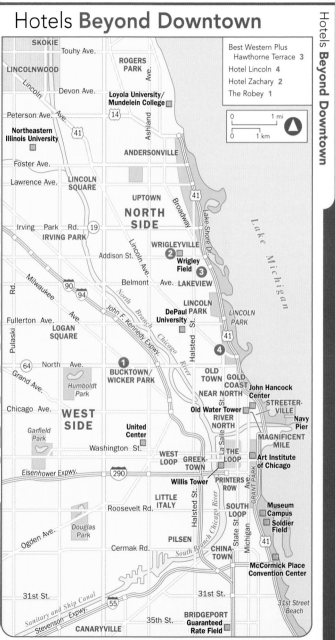

Best Western Plus
Hawthorne Terrace **3**
Hotel Lincoln **4**
Hotel Zachary **2**
The Robey **1**

Hotels A to Z

Ace Hotel WEST LOOP This youthful brand, located across the street from Google, appeals to trendsters looking for a minimalist aesthetic in rooms (think: dorm room chic) coupled with excellent food and coffee and rooftop cocktail options on-site. *311 N. Morgan St. (just north of W. Fulton Market).* ☎ *312/548-1177. www.acehotel.com/chicago. 159 units. Doubles $199–$409. El: Green or Pink Line to Morgan. Map p 134*

★★★ ACME Hotel RIVER NORTH If a property were to have a sense of humor, it would be ACME, a quirky boutique hotel where night lights appear as lips on bathroom mirrors and the basement hot tub room—called Bunny Slope—is straight out of a ski lodge. Bonus: rates are reasonable and staff couldn't be nicer. *15 East Ohio St. (at State St.).* ☎ *312/894-0800. www.acmehotelcompany.com. 130 units. Doubles $179–$372. El: Red Line to Grand/State. Map p 134.*

★★ The Alise THE LOOP One of the world's first skyscrapers, D. H. Burnham's Reliance Building

The ACME Hotel.

(p 11, ③) is now home to this historic boutique hotel, Chicago's most distinctive for architecture buffs. Ask for a high room facing east for lake views. *1 W. Washington St. (at State St.).* ☎ *312/940-7997. www.staypineapple.com/chicago. 122 units. Doubles $199–$450. El: Red Line to Lake. Map p 134.*

Ambassador Chicago GOLD COAST The former Ambassador East Hotel, a historic hotel to the stars, places guests in a posh neighborhood near the lake amid gorgeous brownstone mansions. The renovated property offers guest rooms that are bright, artsy, and welcoming, though hallways are oddly dim and a little creepy. The restaurant, Booth One, is a perpetual scene. *1301 N. State Pkwy.* ☎ *312/787-3700. www.ambassadorchicago.com. 285 units. Doubles $179–$309. El: Red Line to Clark/Division. Map p 133.*

★ kids Best Western Plus Hawthorne Terrace LAKEVIEW A fantastic bargain for travelers who don't mind staying a bit north of the beaten track, this hotel offers plenty of space in a walkable neighborhood about a mile from Wrigley Field. If you're driving to Chicago, overnight parking is a (relative) bargain at $45. *3434 N. Broadway Ave.* ☎ *888/860-3400. www.hawthorneterrace.com. 83 units. Doubles and suites $96–$400. Rates include breakfast. El: Red Line to Belmont. Map p 135.*

★★ The Blackstone SOUTH LOOP This Beaux Arts–style hotel dates back to 1910 and roosts on Michigan Ave. overlooking Grant Park and Lake Michigan. Marble and crystal chandeliers bedazzle the lobby, while the sizeable rooms are modern, with decor and art that

Chicago Athletic Association Hotel.

nod to the property's storied past. Let's just say that if the walls could talk, you'd get an earful here about gangsters, politicians, and movie stars who've been guests. *636 S. Michigan Ave. (at Balbo Dr.).* ☎ *312/447-0955. www.theblackstonehotel. com. 335 units. Doubles $179–$629. El: Red Line to Harrison. Map p 134.*

★★ Chicago Athletic Association Hotel LOOP This Venetian

Gothic beauty was once a chic men's club. Today, the athletic theme seeps into the rooms (like that pommel horse at the foot of the bed), and ornate touches are around every corner. Locals wait in line to get into Cindy's, a scene-y rooftop lounge peeping out at Lake Michigan. *12 S. Michigan Ave. (at Madison St., across from Millennium Park).* ☎ *312/940-3552. www.chicagoathletichotel.com. 241 units. Doubles $269–$1,200. El: Red Line to Monroe. Map p 134.*

★★ Conrad Chicago Hotel

MAGNIFICENT MILE Peering down on Michigan Avenue, rooms are large at this luxury Hilton brand, and the restaurant, Baptiste & Bottle, serves flaming cocktails and inventive American fare. *101 E. Erie St. (at Michigan Ave.).* ☎ *312/667-6700. www.conradchicagohotel.com. 289 units. Doubles $199–$409. El: Red Line to Grand/State. Map p 133.*

★★ Dana Hotel and Spa RIVER

NORTH Reasonable rates, tranquil rooms, an inviting spa, a creative seafood restaurant, and two bars serving dramatic cocktails (with tinctures and multicolored ice) make this boutique hotel a score that many locals don't even know about. *660 N. State St. (at Erie St.).* ☎ *312/202-6000. www.danahotel andspa.com. 216 units. Doubles $189–$689. El: Red Line to Chicago/ State. Map p 134.*

The Conrad rooftop.

★ kids **The Drake Hotel** MAG-NIFICENT MILE This quietly elegant grande dame (the landmark opened in 1920) still features gracious style and boundless charm. Rooms have high ceilings, polished woodwork, and marble bathrooms. Don't miss out on afternoon tea in the Palm Court during your stay; it's pricey at $50 per person, but worth it—and a treat for kids. *140 E. Walton Place (at Michigan Ave.).* ☎ *800/55-DRAKE (553-7253) or 312/787-2200. www.thedrakehotel.com. 535 units. Doubles $129–$339. El: Red Line to Chicago/State. Map p 133.*

★ **Fairmont Chicago Millennium Park** LOOP Overlooking Millennium Park, this opulent hotel is popular with politicos and the business set. The exceptionally large guest rooms feature dressing rooms; walk-in closets; and marble bathrooms with huge tubs, separate showers, and TVs. *200 N. Columbus Dr. (at Lake St.).* ☎ *800/257-7544 or 312/565-8000. www.fairmont.com. 687 units. Doubles $149–$449. El: Brown or Red line to Lake. Map p 134.*

★★★ **Four Seasons Hotel** MAGNIFICENT MILE Consistently ranked among the best hotels in the world, the Four Seasons offers lavish decor and stellar service. Discreetly located between the 30th and the 46th floors of the 900 North Michigan Shops (translation:

The Four Seasons' luxe spa.

amazing views!), the hotel has spacious rooms packed with extras (L'Occitane toiletries, for one). *120 E. Delaware Place (at Michigan Ave.).* ☎ *800/332-3442 or 312/280-8800. www.fourseasons.com. 345 units. Doubles $395–$895. El: Red Line to Chicago/State. Map p 133.*

kids **Hilton Chicago** SOUTH LOOP A great choice for families thanks to its indoor pool and nearby Grant Park, this hotel sprawls over an entire block. Many of the rooms feature two bathrooms, and spacious public areas abound with shops, bars, restaurants, and artwork. *720 S. Michigan Ave. (at Balbo Dr.).* ☎ *800/HILTONS (445-8667) or 312/922-4400. www.hilton.com. 1,544 units. Doubles $108–$407. El: Red Line to Harrison/State. Map p 134.*

kids **Homewood Suites** RIVER NORTH An excellent choice for families, this simple-yet-comfy hotel offers two-room suites, each with a full kitchen and affordable rates. Bonus points for the free breakfast, evening receptions, and top-floor pool. *40 E. Grand Ave. (at Wabash St.).* ☎ *800/CALL-HOME (225-5466) or 312/644-2222. www.homewood suites3.hilton.com. 233 units. Doubles $87–$503. Rates include breakfast. El: Red Line to State/Grand. Map p 134.*

★★ **Hotel EMC2** STREETERVILLE Art and science is the theme at this delightfully unconventional boutique hotel, part of Marriott's Autograph Collection. In-room showers look like 1920s wet labs, Alexa doubles as concierge, and robots deliver bottled water or a toothbrush on request. *228 E. Ontario St. (at N. St. Clair St.).* ☎ *844/205-3939 or 312/915-0000. www.hotelemc2.com. 195 units. Doubles $249–$349. El: Red Line to State/Grand. Map p 134.*

★ **Hotel Felix** RIVER NORTH Rooms are tiny, but rates can be, too. The hotel was the first in the city to claim Silver LEED status, and that eco-appeal is noticeable in decor made from recycled items. While energy saving is a focus, it's never carried out at the expense of comfort. *111 W. Huron (at N. Clark St.).* ☎ *877/848-4040 or 312/447-3440. www.hotelfelixchicago.com. 228 units. Doubles $129–$799. El: Red or Brown Line to Chicago/State. Map p 134.*

★★ **Hotel Lincoln** LINCOLN PARK The neighborhood-y location is fantastic at this youthful boutique hotel with a slightly quirky style. You won't want to leave the amazing rooftop lounge, with its views of Lake Michigan and downtown. *1816 N. Clark St.* ☎ *855/514-8112 or 312/254-4700. www.jdvhotels.com. 184 units. Doubles $129–$329. Bus: 22 or 36. Map p 135.*

★ **Hotel Monaco** THE LOOP A playful vibe sashays through the rooms at this hat-factory-turned-hotel, from the cushy window seats to the swirly pink and brown color scheme. It's a Kimpton, which means a free nightly wine reception, bikes to borrow, and a welcoming pet policy. *225 N. Wabash Ave. (at Wacker Pl.).* ☎ *866/610-0081 or 312/960-8500. www.monaco-chicago.com. 191 units. Doubles $179–$479. El: Brown or Red Line to Lake. Map p 134.*

★★★ **Hotel Palomar** RIVER NORTH This boutique Kimpton hotel stands apart from the competition thanks to its large rooms, 17th-floor indoor pool, and free nightly

wine hour. Request a corner room for maximum light coming through the floor-to-ceiling windows. Sable, the restaurant, is a locals' after-work favorite for its impressive cocktail list. *505 N. State St. (at Illinois St.).* ☎ *877/731-0505 or 312/755-9703. www.hotelpalomar-chicago.com. 261 units. Doubles $209–$489. El: Red Line to Grand/State. Map p 134.*

★ **Hotel Zachary** LAKEVIEW It's so close to Wrigley Field, some rooms give a glimpse of the baseball action. Cubs fans are rejoicing at the tasteful boutique hotel, new in 2018, and named for the architect of the famous stadium. The multiple bars and restaurants here are mobbed before and after games. *3630 N. Clark St.* ☎ *773/302-2300. www.hotelzachary.com. 173 units. Doubles $209–$409. El: Red Line to Addison. Map p 135.*

★ **InterContinental Chicago** MAGNIFICENT MILE Formerly the luxurious Medinah Athletic Club, this enormous hotel, built in 1929, is a touch eccentric. While rooms are modern, the decor throughout ranges from medieval English to Mesopotamian (ask the concierge for an iPod tour). The Roman-style pool—the best in the city—and multilevel gym further set it apart. *505 N. Michigan Ave. (at Illinois St.).* ☎ *800/628-2112 or 312/944-4100. www.icchicagohotel.com. 792 units. Doubles $140–$730. El: Red Line to Grand/State. Map p 133.*

A suite at the InterContinental Chicago.

JW Marriott's king suite.

★★★ JW Marriott THE LOOP
Twentieth-century opulence lives on in this hotel, formerly a bank designed by architect Daniel Burnham. With Corinthian columns and endless marble in the lobby, and a spa with a hammam, it's forgivable that rooms feel a touch corporate. *151 W. Adams St. (at Wells St.).* ☎ *312/660-8200. www.marriott.com. 610 units. Doubles $329–$509. El: Red or Blue Line to Monroe. Map p 134.*

★★★ Kimpton Gray THE LOOP
Tucked into the historic New York Life Insurance Building, the entryway is swimming in the Georgia gray marble that inspired the hotel's name. Rooms are quite smart, with a rich blue and gray palette; king "spa" rooms have dramatic freestanding soaking tubs. *122 W. Monroe St. (at LaSalle St.).* ☎ *877/771-7031 or 312/750-9012. www.grayhotelchicago.com. 293 units. Doubles $219–$519. El: Blue or Red Line to Monroe. Map p 134.*

Kinzie Hotel RIVER NORTH
Another lesser-known score, this boutique hotel gets high marks for its proximity to the Loop; colorful, natural-light filled rooms; modest rates; and plentiful perks, including a free cocktail reception with an impressive spread of food and free breakfast. *20 W. Kinzie St. (at Dearborn St.).* ☎ *877/569-3742 or 312/315-9000. www.kinziehotel.com. 215 units. Doubles $94–$379. El: Red Line to Grand/State. Map p 134.*

★★★ The Langham RIVER NORTH
With a team of butlers on staff and an museum-worthy art collection, The Langham, housed in a boxy skyscraper designed by Ludwig Mies van der Rohe, takes luxury to a new stratosphere. If you have money to burn, this is a great place to set it alight. *330 N. Wabash Ave. (at the Chicago River).* ☎ *312/923-9988. www.langhamhotels.com. 316 units. Doubles $395–$1,200. El: Red Line to Grand/State. Map p 134.*

★★ Loews Chicago Hotel STREETERVILLE
"Corporate luxury" is a good descriptor for this towering glass building near the lake and river. The Craftsman-inspired lobby is especially inviting, and with a rooftop restaurant, indoor lap pool, fitness center, and spa, it covers all the five-star bases. *455 North Park Dr.* ☎ *877/648-1305 or 312/840-6600.*

Loews Chicago's seasonal rooftop restaurant, Streeterville Social.

www.loewshotels.com/chicago-downtown. 400 units. Doubles $129–$499. El: Red Line to Grand/State. Map p 134.

★ **LondonHouse Chicago** THE LOOP   Rooms are a touch small but views are phenomenal if you're facing the river. Head up to the 22nd floor for a rooftop cocktail while gazing at 180 degrees of Chicago in all her glory. 85 E. Wacker Dr. (at Michigan Ave.). ☎ 312/357-1200. www.londonhousechicago.com. 452 units. Doubles $159–$499. El: Brown or Red Line to Lake. Map p 134.

★ **Moxy** RIVER NORTH   Quarters are unabashedly tight, er, "European-style" at this trendy, millennial-minded Marriott brand, with the assumption that you'll just be sleeping there. The lobby doubles as a co-working/hangout space, and a taco counter serves grub 24/7. Tip: Request a corner room and your bed will be surrounded by windows. 530 N. LaSalle Dr. (at Grand Ave.). ☎ 312/605-8708. www.moxy-hotels.marriott.com. 156 units. Doubles $170–$200. El: Red Line to State/Grand. Map p 134.

Palmer House Hilton THE LOOP   You could get lost in the never-ending hallways, and rooms can be small and service can be harried, but for history buffs (and, often, bargain hunters), this hotel has an intriguing tale to tell as the country's oldest continuously operating hotel. At minimum, drop by the grand lobby to see the ceiling frescoes and order a brownie—it was invented here. 17 E. Monroe St. (at State St.). ☎ 800/HILTONS (445-8667) or 312/726-7500. www.palmerhousehiltonhotel.com. 1,641 units. Doubles $129–$339. El: Red Line to Monroe. Map p 134.

★★★ **Park Hyatt Chicago** MAGNIFICENT MILE   The building is part hotel, part condo, all luxury (which you'll pay for). Spacious

The Robey's rooftop pool.

rooms have window seats and lovely views, which you can also gaze upon from the deep soaking tub in the bathroom. 800 N. Michigan Ave. (at Chicago Ave.). ☎ 800/233-1234 or 312/335-1234. www.hyatt.com. 198 units. Doubles $350–$695. El: Red Line to Chicago/State. Map p 133.

★★★ **The Peninsula Chicago** MAGNIFICENT MILE   Service is practically a religion at this Art Deco bastion of luxury. Rooms are enormous, and in-room tech, which allows guests to control the lights, TV, curtains, and room temperature via a tablet, is also worthy of worship. 108 E. Superior St. (at Michigan Ave.). ☎ 866/288-8889 or 312/337-2888. www.peninsula.com. 339 units. Doubles $399–$850. El: Red Line to Chicago/State. Map p 133.

★ **Ritz-Carlton Chicago** MAGNIFICENT MILE   Set above the shops at Water Tower Place (p 83), this celebrity magnet is known for its tip-top service—and families love it for the pool. The atrium is the perfect spot for afternoon tea or an evening aperitif. 160 E. Pearson St. (just east of N. Michigan Ave.). ☎ 800/542-8680 or 312/266-1000. www.ritzcarlton.com. 434 units. Doubles $259–$699. El: Red Line to Chicago/State. Map p 133.

The Robey WICKER PARK   This boutique hotel exudes coolness, with its triangular shape, rooftop pool, location in hipster Wicker Park, and this: rooms with bunks that can sleep up to four. 2018 W.

North Ave. (at Milwaukee Ave.).
☎ 872/315-3050. www.therobey.
com. 89 units. Doubles $135–$495.
Blue line to Damen. Map p 135.

Sofitel Chicago RIVER NORTH
Sofitel, drawing on the city's tradition
of great architecture, built this soar-
ing, triangular tower with a glass-and-
aluminum facade that sparkles in the
sun. The interior has a European
vibe—you'll be greeted in French—
and with 32 floors, odds are the view
from your mid-size room will be
decent. Wake up early to take advantage of the top-notch free breakfast
pastries. *20 E. Chestnut St. (at Wabash
St.).* ☎ *800/SOFITEL (763-4835) or
312/324-4000. www.sofitel.com. 415
units. Doubles $136–$348. El: Red
Line to Chicago/State. Map p 133.*

★ Soho House WEST LOOP
Prepare to feel like you're staying
at your cool friend's apartment—
which happens to have a rooftop
pool that's quite a scene, and an
enormous gym complete with a
boxing ring. *113 N. Green St. (at
Randolph St.).* ☎ *312/521-8000.
www.sohohousechicago.com. 40
units. Doubles $300–$400. El: Green
or Pink Line to Morgan. Map p 134.*

*The Carbide and Carbon building is an
excellent example of Art Deco architecture at the St. Jane.*

The Talbott's 20 East restaurant.

★ St. Jane LOOP   Another score
for architecture buffs. The green
and gold-leaf Carbide and Carbon
building resembles a giant champagne bottle, and the decor within
carries out the Art Deco theme.
The hotel has 38 floors, and views
up Michigan Avenue are ever so
Instagrammable. Just be sure to
draw the curtains in the shower, or
neighboring office dwellers can
peer right in. *230 N. Michigan Ave.
(at E. Wacker Place).* ☎ *312/345-
1000. www.stjanehotel.com. 365
units. Doubles $249–$599. El: Red or
Brown Line to Lake. Map p 134.*

★★ Talbott Hotel GOLD COAST
Built as an apartment building in
the 1920s, the recently renovated
hotel itself has a residential vibe—no
cookie-cutter decor here. Vintage
fixtures and velvety textiles in the
generous-size rooms are a nod to its
Roaring '20s past. It's just west of the
Magnificent Mile, but far enough
from the heavy tourist action that it
feels like a local secret, often at bargain rates. *20 E. Delaware Pl. (at State
St.).* ☎ *800-TALBOTT (825-2688) or
312/944-4970. www.talbotthotel.com.
178 units. Double $119–$209. El: Red
Line to Chicago/State. Map p 133.*

★★ theWit LOOP   This slightly
quirky hotel loves its urban setting
and makes the most of it: Two-
story-high lobby windows look
directly onto a bustling El station.
Part of the Doubletree family (free

Mixologist at work at theWit.

cookies!), theWit is popping with personality (bird songs are piped into the hallway and the voice of Al Capone can deliver a wake-up call) and its popular top-floor bar, Roof, brings a little taste of Miami Beach to the Loop. *201 N. State St. (at Lake St.).* ☎ *866/318-1514 or 312/467-0200. www.thewithotel.com. 310 units. Doubles $109–$499. El: Red or Brown Line to Lake. Map p 134.*

★★ **Thompson Hotel** GOLD COAST This slender, 22-floor building in the Gold Coast offers an excellent excuse to leave downtown for leafy green streets amid old-money mansions. The hotel, itself, has an air of fun sophistication. Its lobby is filled with bookshelves, its bar has a living plant wall, higher-up rooms offer gorgeous views, and some suites even have balconies.

The seafood-centric restaurant, Nico Osteria, is a must. *21 E. Bellevue Place (at Rush St.).* ☎ *800/606-8188 or 312/266-2100. www.thompsonhotels. com. 247 units. Doubles $149–$649. El: Red Line to Chicago. Map p 133.*

★★★ **Viceroy** GOLD COAST Visual surprises abound: the tree-lined neighborhood location, the poetry wall in the lobby, and the gilded wallpaper art in the mid-century-esque rooms. The hotel opened in 2017 and it's just stunning. *1118 N. State St. (at Elm St.)* ☎ *888/712-2712 or 312/586-2000. www.viceroyhotelsandresorts.com. 180 units. Doubles $209–$399. El: Red Line to Clark/Division. Map p 133.*

★ **Virgin Hotel** LOOP It's what you'd expect from a Richard Branson project: tech-driven (control the

A spacious bathroom in a Viceroy suite.

The Waldorf Astoria's Gold Coast Suite.

room temp with an app) and a little bit whimsical. Rooms can be divided by a sliding door that separates the bathroom/vanity and sleeping area for maximal privacy. The clubby rooftop bar is quite popular with locals after work. *203 N. Wabash Ave. (at Lake St)* ☎ *855/946-6600 or 312/940-4400. www.virginhotels.com. 250 units. Doubles $179–$379. El: Brown or Red Line to Lake. Map p 134.*

★★★ Waldorf Astoria Chicago

GOLD COAST   Plan on being spoiled with enormous rooms—many with fireplaces and deep soaking tubs—at an überposh address just west of Michigan Avenue. Chef Michael Mina's Margeaux Brasserie serves stellar French fare, which you can burn off in the pool and generous health club. *11 E. Walton St. (at State St.).* ☎ *312/646-1300. www.waldorfastoriachicago hotel.com. 215 units. Doubles $268–$545. El: Red Line to Chicago. Map p 133.* ●

Beyond Hotels

While hotels are the most obvious—and plentiful—option, cost-saving alternatives abound. As in any major city, vacation rentals have been a game changer. The city regulates these (or tries to) so look for homeowners that mention a license on Airbnb, etc.

For a traditional B&B, the site **Chicago Bed and Breakfasts** (www.bedandbreakfast.com) lists the availability and rates for bed and breakfasts. Prices range from about $99 to $200 a night.

And a handful of hostels are centrally located bargains. The **Freehand Chicago**, 19 E. Ohio St. (☎ **312/940-3699;** www.freehandhotels.com), is a trendy River North hotel that also has quad hostel rooms, with bed rates as low as $30 a night. At **HI Chicago,** The J. Ira and Nicki Harris Family Hostel, just off Michigan Avenue (24 E. Congress Pkwy.; ☎ **312/360-0300;** www.hiusa.org), beds in minimalist shared rooms start at $28 and private suites start at $85 per night.

Oak Park

1. Oak Park Visitor Center
2. Frank Lloyd Wright Home & Studio
3. Wright Around Oak Park
4. Historic Neighborhood Walking Tour
5. Unity Temple
6. Petersen's Ice Cream
7. Historic Pleasant Home
8. Hemingway Birthplace Museum
9. Johnny's Beef

Previous page: Entrance to Northwestern University.

This historic and scenic suburb on the western fringe of Chicago was Ernest Hemingway's birthplace and boyhood home, as well as the location of Frank Lloyd Wright's first home and studio. It's home to the country's largest concentration of houses and buildings designed and built by Wright. START: **Take the El (Green Line) to Harlem Ave., about a 25-min. ride from downtown. Get off the train at Harlem and walk 2 blocks north to the Oak Park Visitor Center at Lake St.**

❶ Oak Park Visitor Center.

Pick up useful maps of the area before tackling the historic district, located just a few blocks away. You can also purchase special event tickets, souvenirs, and themed tours. *1010 Lake St.* ☎ *888/OAK-PARK (625-7275). www.visitoakpark.com. Mon–Sat 10am–5pm; Sun 10am–4pm.*

❷ ★★★ Frank Lloyd Wright Home & Studio.

For the first 20 years of Wright's career, this remarkable complex served first and foremost as the sanctuary from which the famous architect designed and executed more than 130 of his 430 completed buildings. The home began life as a simple shingled cottage that Wright (1867–1959) built for his bride in 1889 at the age of 22, but it became a work in progress, as Wright remodeled it constantly until 1911 (though he left the house in 1909 after separating from his wife). The home was Wright's

showcase and laboratory for his famous Prairie style, but it also embraces many idiosyncratic features, including a barrel-vaulted children's playroom and a studio with an octagonal balcony suspended by chains. It has been restored to its 1909 appearance. ⏱ *1 hr. 951 Chicago Ave.* ☎ *312/994-4000. www.flwright.org. Admission $18 adults, $15 seniors, students, and military; free for kids 3 and under. Admission to Home & Studio is by guided tour only; tours depart from the Ginkgo Tree Bookshop daily 10am–4pm (every 20 min.); Closed Thanksgiving, Dec 24–25, and Jan 1. Facilities for people with disabilities are limited; call in advance. Not recommended for kids younger than 8.*

❸ ★★ Wright Around Oak Park.

For superfans, this tour is as in-depth as they come. Limited to small groups of 10 or fewer, the tour starts in Frank Lloyd Wright's

The Frank Lloyd Wright Home & Studio.

House and peeks into exclusive areas, like the octagonal studio balcony. Then, you'll walk around Oak Park, passing nearly a dozen FLW homes, before visiting Unity Temple. Over the course of 3 hours, docents have the time to delve deeply into the architect's life and work, and to answer questions. ⏱ *3 hrs. 951 Chicago Ave.* ☎ *312/994-4000. www.flwright.org. Admission $60. Noon daily Apr–Oct; 9:30am Tues June–Sept. Closed Thanksgiving, Dec 24–25, and Jan 1. Facilities for people with disabilities are limited; call in advance. Not recommended for kids younger than 8*

④ ★ Historic Neighborhood Walking Tour. On this detailed but self-guided audio tour, you can go at your own pace and check out the exteriors of the houses designed by Wright, as well as the charming Victorian homes that he hated so intensely. ⏱ *40–50 min. Tours depart from the Ginkgo Tree Bookshop in the Frank Lloyd Wright Home & Studio, 951 Chicago Ave.* ☎ *312/994-4000. www.flwright.org. Audio tours $15 adults, $12 seniors, students, and*

military. Daily 9am–4:15pm. Closed Thanksgiving, Dec 24–25, and Jan 1.

⑤ ★★ Unity Temple. This National Historic Landmark's reinforced concrete exterior is as forbidding as a mausoleum. Built between 1905 and 1908 for the Unitarian Universalist Congregation, the Cubist-style church is one of Wright's greatest masterpieces and the only public building from his "Golden" period that still stands. The considerably cheerier interior contains the entire architectural alphabet of the Prairie School of architectural design, from the skylight to the prominent use of wood trim. ⏱ *30 min. 875 Lake St.* ☎ *312/994-4000. www.flwright.org. Self-guided tours $10 adults; $8 seniors, students, and military. Mon–Thurs 9am–4:15pm; Fri 9am–3:15pm; Sat 9am–11:15am; 30–40 minutes. Guided tours $18 adults; $15 seniors, seniors, and military. Mon–Thurs 10am–4pm; Fri 10am–3pm; Sat 10am–11am; 1 hr. Closed Thanksgiving, Dec 24–25, and Jan 1. Church events can alter schedule; call in advance.*

Unity Temple interior.

where repeated decorative motifs are incorporated into every facet of the home. ⏱ *1 hr. for a guided tour. 217 Home Ave.* ☎ *708/383-2654. www.pleasanthome.org. Guided tour is $10 adults; $8 seniors and students; $5 kids 5–18; Thurs, Fri, Sun at noon and 1pm; Sat at 11am, noon, and 1pm. Self-guided tours is $5 per person; Fri–Sun 2–4pm; on Thurs self-guided tour is free.*

8 Ernest Hemingway Birthplace Museum. This lovely Queen Anne home, with a wraparound porch and turrets, has been restored to replicate its appearance at the end of the 19th century. The home was built in 1890 for Hemingway's grandfather, Ernest Hall. Hemingway was born here on July 21, 1899, though the author actually spent most of his youth at 600 N. Kenilworth Ave., a few blocks away (that house is privately owned). This is an appealing stop for fans of historic houses, whether you're a Hemingway fan or not. The docents are wonderful Hemingway buffs, and can fill you in on the author's life, from his first job out of high school as a young reporter with the *Kansas City Star* to his work as a war correspondent in Europe during World War II. *339 N. Oak Park Ave.* ☎ *708/848-2222. www.hemingwaybirthplace.com. Admission $15 adults, $13 seniors, students, and those under 18. Sun–Fri 1–5pm; Sat 10am–5pm.*

Hemingway was born here in 1899.

☕ **★★★ Petersen's Ice Cream Parlour & Sweet Shoppe** has been serving up classic American favorites since 1919. There's wonderfully rich ice cream (I recommend the Mackinac Island Fudge in a fresh waffle cone), as well as espresso and other hot and iced coffee drinks. *1100 W. Chicago Ave.* ☎ *708/386-6131. $.*

7 ★ Historic Pleasant Home. Named for its location at Pleasant and Home streets, this opulent, 30-room mansion is a must-see for fans of architecture and historic homes. It was built in 1897 by prominent Prairie School architect George W. Maher (1864–1926) for investment banker and philanthropist John W. Farson. Of some 300 structures that Maher designed, it's the only one open to the public and was designated a National Historic Landmark in 1996. You'll see colorful art glass, custom furniture and light fixtures, and Maher's unique use of his "motif-rhythm" theory,

You hear a lot about Chicago-style pizza and hot dogs, but don't forget to try the Italian beef! 🥪 **Johnny's Beef** ranks as one of the best, serving up tender, juicy meat on a crusty Italian roll, dipped in au jus (upon request) and topped with sweet or hot peppers. The barebones grill is a trek from Chicago, but, if you're driving, it's just a quick 3-mile jaunt from Oak Park. *7500 W. North Ave.* ☎ *708/452-6000. $.*

Evanston

1 Grosse Pointe Lighthouse and Maritime Museum

2 Northwestern University

3 Shakespeare Garden

4 The Mary and Leigh Block Museum of Art

5 Charles Gates Dawes Mansion

6 Willard House

7 Edzo's Burger Shop

The oldest suburb of Chicago, Evanston is home to a Mayberry of a downtown, grand old homes, and the Northwestern University campus. It combines the peaceful feeling and green space of suburban life with the culture and lively atmosphere that you'd expect of a college town. START: **Catch the Metra North train line from Northwestern Station in the Loop for the 20-min. ride to the Davis St. station. Walk east on Davis St. into the heart of downtown Evanston.**

The Grosse Point Lighthouse.

❶ Grosse Point Lighthouse and Maritime Museum. This

lighthouse served as a beacon when Lake Michigan still teemed with cargo-laden ships. Be sure to stroll the scenic grounds. If you're here during the summer, it's worth taking a tour of the lighthouse's interior—you get to climb the 141 steps to the top of the tower and are rewarded with a wonderful view. If you're here between Memorial Day and Labor Day, you'll have to pay to frolic on the beach ($8 adults, $6 children 1–11), but it's a great place for a (free) stroll on a

sunny spring or fall day. ① *45 min. 2601 Sheridan Rd.* ☎ *847-328-6961. www.grossepointlighthouse.net. Lighthouse admission $6 adults, $3 children 8–12; children 7 and under not admitted for safety reasons. Tours of the interior conducted June–Sept weekends only at 2, 3, and 4pm; grounds year-round daily. Closed July 4 and Labor Day.*

❷ Northwestern University.

This world-class university makes its home on a beautiful lakefront campus, and its architecturally significant buildings make it worthy of several hours of exploration. Don't miss the sublime stained-glass facade of the **Alice Millar Chapel.** Other standouts include the Norman Gothic **Deering Library** and the Romanesque **Revival Fisk Hall.** ① *1–2 hr. Sheridan Rd. (at Chicago Ave.) and continuing north and east along Sheridan Rd.* ☎ *847-491-3741. www.northwestern.edu. Free admission.*

❸ Shakespeare Garden. In

1915, the Drama League of America asked its members to come up with ways to commemorate the 300th anniversary of Shakespeare's death. Noted Chicago landscape architect Jens J. Jensen responded with this gem: a National Historic Landmark that features several memorials to the Bard and more than 50 plants that were either mentioned in Shakespeare's plays or common in Tudor England. ① *10 min. At*

Charles Gates Dawes Mansion.

Northwestern University, east of Sheridan Rd., entrance off Garrett Place. ☎ *847/491-3741. www.north western.edu. Free admission.*

④ The Mary and Leigh Block Museum of Art. This fine-arts haven offers a top-notch collection of prints, photographs, and drawings, as well as always intriguing temporary exhibitions. Don't miss the outdoor sculpture garden. ⏱ *30 min. At Northwestern University, 40 Arts Circle Dr.* ☎ *847/491-4000. www.blockmuseum.north western.edu. Free admission with a suggested $5 donation. Tues, Sat, Sun 10am–5pm; Wed–Fri 10am–8pm.*

⑤ Charles Gates Dawes Mansion. Dawes was a wealthy financier who served as vice president under Calvin Coolidge and won the 1925 Nobel Peace Prize for his smooth handling of German reparations after World War I on behalf of the League of Nations. Dawes's former home—completed in 1896—now houses the Evanston History Center, which offers tours of this restored landmark. The 25-room home was designed in the manner of a French château and features a collection of historic costumes, decorative arts, and antiques. ⏱ *1 hr. 225 Greenwood St.* ☎ *847/475-3410. www.evanston historycenter.org. Admission $10, kids under 10 are free. Tours Thurs–Sun 1–4pm, starting at 1, 2, and 3pm.*

⑥ Willard House. Frances Willard (1839–98), social reformer and founder of the Women's Christian Temperance Union (WCTU), spent most of her adult life in Evanston. Nine of the 17 rooms have been converted into a museum of period furnishings and temperance memorabilia. Among the personal effects on display is the bicycle Willard affectionately called "Gladys" and learned to ride late in life—spurring women across the country to do the same. The headquarters of the WCTU is still located on-site. ⏱ *1 hr. 1730 Chicago Ave.* ☎ *847/328-7500. www.franceswillardhouse. org. Admission $10 adults, $5 students, children 6 and under are free. Open Sun Mar–Dec 1–4pm with tours at 1, 2, and 3pm; in July tours are also available Thurs 1–4pm.*

Every college town deserves a burger joint as great as **⑦ Edzo's Burger Shop.** The menu seems basic, with burgers, fries, hot dogs, and shakes. But here's the Portlandia-style Evanston twist: you can "upgrade" your burger by choosing the farm the meat comes from. *1571 Sherman Ave.* ☎ *847/864-3396. www.edzos.com. $.* ●

The Savvy Traveler

Before You Go

Government Tourist Offices

The city's tourism bureau, called **Choose Chicago**, has a **Visitor Information Center** in Macy's, 111 N. State Street (☎ **312/567-8500**; www.choosechicago.com), and dispenses information to both domestic and international visitors.

You can also contact the **Illinois Office of Tourism** (☎ **TTY 800/406-6418**; www.enjoyillinois.com) for city and state info.

The Best Times to Go

The ideal time to visit Chicago is in summer or fall. Summer offers a nonstop selection of special events and outdoor activities, though you will face crowds and the occasional period of hot, muggy weather. In autumn, days are generally sunny and crowds at major tourist attractions grow thinner. Snow generally doesn't start falling until November.

Spring is extremely unpredictable, with dramatic fluctuations between cold and warm weather, and usually lots of rain. Winter, though not any worse than in many other northern cities, is generally cold—sometimes frigid—and snowy. That said, museum lovers and those on a tight budget might find winter a good time to visit: You'll find no lines at museums, lots of sales in the stores, and the cheapest rates at hotels.

Festivals & Special Events

Choose Chicago (☎ **877/CHI-CAGO** [244-2246]; www.choosechicago.com) produces a *Chicago Visitors Guide*, available online and at Visitor Information Centers. The City's **Department of Cultural Affairs and Special Events** is also a good resource to learn about cultural events and festivals (☎ **312/744-3316**; www.cityofchicago.org/specialevents).

JAN. The latest boats and recreational vehicles are put on display at the **Chicago Boat, RV & Sail Show** (☎ **312/946-6200**; www.chicagoboatshow.com), which also features trout fishing, a sailing simulator, boating safety seminars, and big-time entertainment. The action takes place in early-January.

Grab a prix-fixe meal for a steal during **Chicago Restaurant Week,** sponsored by **Choose Chicago** (☎ **312/567-8500**; www.choosechicago.com). Lunch and dinner is priced at $22, $33, or $44 at participating restaurants around town. Make a reservation—the most popular spots fill quickly during the 2-week event.

FEB. True, many attendees will get to the **Chicago Auto Show** (☎ **630/495-2282**; www.chicagoautoshow.com) via public transportation. Irony aside, it's the largest auto show in North America and winter is a great time to peruse 1,000 shiny new vehicles on display at McCormick Place. You can get inside them for a closer look, and some you can even drive around an obstacle course.

MAR. The Chicago River is dyed green for the **St. Patrick's Day Parade** (www.choosechicago.com), a Chicago tradition since the 1840s that's held on the Saturday before March 17. The parade route is Columbus Drive from Balbo Drive to Monroe Street. The **South Side Irish Parade** (www.southsideirishparade.org), which is more community oriented, happens the day after

---

Previous page: Biking around Chicago.

the downtown parade, on Western Avenue from 103rd to 115th streets.

APR. Join the enthusiastic fans of the **Cubs** (☎ 773/404-CUBS [2827]; www.cubs.mlb.com) or the **White Sox** (☎ 312/674-1000; www.whitesox.mlb.com) on **Opening Day.** Be sure to get your tickets early for this eagerly awaited day, and go prepared with warm gear, because it's usually freezing cold in early April.

The **Chicago Improv Festival** features big names and lesser-known comedians converging for a celebration of spontaneous hilariousness, with both large main-stage shows and smaller, more experimental performances at different venues (☎ 773/472-3492; www.chicagoimprovfestival.org). The biennial festival is in early April on odd years.

MAY. On the third Saturday in May, you can take the annual **Wright Plus Housewalk** (☎ 312/994-4000; www.flwright.org/wrightplus), a rare look at the interiors of notable buildings in Oak Park. Tickets go on sale January 1 and can sell out within a few weeks.

Lakeshore Drive (aka LSD) shuts down to cars and opens to bikes one morning a year for the annual **Bike the Drive** (☎ 312/427-3325; www.bikethedrive.org). Cyclists can ride for a few miles or opt for a 30-mile loop with unbeatable views of Lake Michigan and the downtown skyline. Sunday morning, Memorial Day weekend.

Highland Park's **Ravinia Festival** (☎ 847/266-5100; www.ravinia. org) is the open-air summer home of the Chicago Symphony Orchestra and many first-rate visiting orchestras, chamber ensembles, pop artists, dance companies and so forth. It runs from late May to September.

JUNE. The largest free literary fest in the midwest, **Printers Row Lit Fest** (http://printersrowlitfest.org)

features more than 200 booksellers displaying new, used, and antiquarian books for sale. Add in readings and signings by big-name authors and panel discussions on how to pen your first novel, and you've got a full day of entertainment. It takes place the second weekend in June.

Dozens of acts perform over 3 days at **Chicago Blues Festival** (☎ 312/744-3370; www.chicago bluesfestival.us) in Millennium Park. Many of Chicago's legendary musicians show off their stuff at Chicago's largest music festival. All shows are free, so get there early to nab a good spot on the lawn, along with hundreds of thousands of other fans. Second weekend in June.

The **Grant Park Music Festival** (☎ 312/742-7638; www.grant parkmusicfestival.com) at Pritzker Pavilion in Millennium Park offers free outdoor musical concerts from June to August. One of the city's best bargains, the concerts feature musicians from the Grant Park Orchestra and Chorus. Bring a picnic and enjoy dinner beforehand with a view of the Chicago skyline.

The floats and marching units at the **LGBTQ Pride Parade** (☎ 773/348-8243; www.chicagopride calendar.org) are the definition of over-the-top. Halsted Street is always mobbed; Grab a spot on Broadway to be on the outskirts. The parade runs between Addison and Diversey, mostly along Halsted, the last Sunday in June. A 2-day Pride Fest takes place the weekend prior in the Boystown neighborhood.

The annual **Old St. Patrick's World's Largest Block Party** (☎ 312/648-1021; www.worlds largestblockparty.com) is a beloved blowout at the city's oldest church, an Irish Catholic landmark in the West Loop area, in late June. Beer flows and rock bands perform over 2 nights. Bonus: Proceeds benefit social justice causes.

Late June through late August, the city's Department of Cultural Affairs hosts **Chicago Summerdance** (☎ 312/742-4007; www.chicago summerdance.org). A 4,900-square-foot outdoor dance floor is the venue for 1-hour lessons followed by open dancing, from ballroom to samba. Thursday, Friday, and Saturday from 6 to 9:30pm and Sunday 4 to 7pm. Free admission.

JULY. Enticing smells waft through downtown during **Taste of Chicago** (☎ 312/744-3316; www.tasteof chicago.us), the gigantic outdoor festival that draws more than 1 million to nosh on top city offerings—well beyond pizza and ribs—served al fresco and priced ala carte (admission is free). An A-list of headliners makes for a rollicking nightly soundtrack (admission required) throughout the 5-day event.

More than 80 homeowners open their backyards to visitors at the annual **Sheffield Garden Walk** (www.sheffieldgardenwalk.com) in the Lincoln Park neighborhood near DePaul University. Intersplice your self-guided garden tour with guided architectural tours and breaks for food, drinks, kid's activities, and live music at the street festival held in tandem with the walk. Third weekend in July.

AUG. Grab your fedora and festival gear for **Lollapalooza** (☎ 888/512-SHOW [7469]; www.lollapalooza.com), which brings 3 days of big-name bands to Grant Park. Beyond the music (more than 150 bands on 8 stages), there are after-shows, artisans, and incredible food offerings from local chefs. Early August.

The U.S. Air Force Thunderbirds and U.S. Navy Leap Frogs usually put in an appearance at the **Chicago Air & Water Show** (☎ 312/744-3316; www.chicago airandwatershow.us), which is held the third weekend in August. Admission is free to this hugely popular aquatic and aerial spectacular at North Avenue Beach.

Northalsted Market Days (☎ 773/883-0500; www. northalsted.com) is the city's largest street festival, drawing nearly 200,000 to the heart of this gay neighborhood. Centered on Halsted Street between Belmont Avenue and Addison Street, the 2-day extravaganza includes food, crafts, DJs, dancing, and plenty of pride.

SEPT. National headliners are always on hand at the **Chicago Jazz Festival** (☎ 312/744-3316; www. chicagojazzfestival.us). The free event, which includes an art fair, takes place in Millennium Park Labor Day weekend.

One of my favorite festivals of the year is the **Fulton Market Harvest Festival** (☎ 888/512-SHOW [7469]; fultonmarketharvestfest.org) Organized by the talented Chef Stephanie Izard (of Girl & the Goat and Little Goat Diner), the fest has booths from top restaurants, author readings, and live music. There's even a Champagne booth. Admission is free; food costs $4 to $12. Mid-September.

OCT. The oldest U.S. festival of its kind, the **Chicago International Film Festival** (☎ 312/683-0121; www. chicagofilmfestival.org) screens films from around the world—including shorts, documentaries, indies, noir, local films, and more—at various theaters over 2 weeks in October.

The **Chicago Marathon** (☎ 312/904-9800; www.chicago marathon.com) has become a major event on the international long-distance running circuit. Held Columbus Day weekend, the marathon begins and ends in Grant Park, but can be viewed along any of the many vantage points along the route (Lincoln Park provides some of the best).

NOV. Magnificent Mile Lights Festival (☎ 312/409-5560; www. magnificentmile.com) kicks off the

CHICAGO'S AVERAGE TEMPERATURES & PRECIPITATION						
	JAN	FEB	MAR	APR	MAY	JUNE
High °F	20	34	44	59	70	79
Low °F	14	18	28	39	48	58
High °C	–7	1	7	15	21	26
Low °C	–10	–8	–2	4	9	14
Rainfall (in.)	1.60	1.31	2.59	3.66	3.15	4.08
Rainfall (cm)	4.06	3.33	6.58	9.30	8	10.36
	JULY	AUG	SEPT	OCT	NOV	DEC
High °F	85	82	76	64	48	35
Low °F	63	62	54	42	31	20
High °C	29	28	24	18	9	2
Low °C	17	17	12	6	–1	–7
Rainfall (in.)	3.63	3.53	3.35	2.28	2.06	2.10
Rainfall (cm)	9.22	8.94	8.51	5.79	5.23	5.33

holiday season by lighting up Michigan Avenue at dusk the Saturday before Thanksgiving. But it's more than just lights. There's also a parade of Disney characters, carolers, elves, minstrels, Santa, and family-friendly activities Friday evening and all day Saturday.

DEC. The esteemed Joffrey Ballet of Chicago performs **The Nutcracker** (☎ 312/386-8905; www.joffrey. com) with a twist: the plot revolves around Chicago's 1893 World's Fair. A family holiday tradition, performances begin after Thanksgiving and continue through the end of December.

Christkindlmarket, Daley Plaza, in the Loop (☎ 312/494-2175; www.christkindlmarket.com), is an annual holiday event inspired by traditional German Christmas festivals, with vendors flying in from Germany to sell handcrafted ornaments and decorations. Don't miss the hot spiced wine, beer, and sausages. Open Thanksgiving Day through Christmas Eve. For a smaller, less crowded version—complete with ice skating—head to Gallagher Way at Wrigley Field.

Goodman Theatre's *A Christmas Carol* (☎ 312/443-3800; www.goodmantheater.org) is a seasonal favorite, performed from Thanksgiving through December.

The Weather

Withstanding extreme weather—particularly those blustery, cold winters—is a point of pride with Chicagoans. They're rewarded for their hardiness every summer—at least, on those few picture perfect days locals lives for. When visiting, bring layers and hope for the best.

While the city has a reputation for extremely cold winters, in reality it doesn't get much colder than any comparable northern city. (Though blustery winds do blow in from Lake Michigan, Chicago's nickname, the Windy City, is due to the hot air generated by its politicos, not its weather.) Still, days of subzero temperatures, snowstorms, and freezing wind chills are not unheard of. If you arrive in winter, a hat, down coat, and a good pair of boots are musts.

Summer in Chicago can be tough to take as well: Temperatures can soar past 90°F (32°C) for several days at a stretch, and the humidity can rise to stifling proportions. That said, thanks to Lake Michigan breezes, it's always cooler near the lake.

As close to your departure as possible, check the local weather forecast at the websites of the *Chicago Tribune* newspaper (www.chicagotribune.com); WGN-TV, whose Tom Skilling is a very well-known meteorologist (www.wgntv.com); or The Weather Channel (www.weather.com).

Useful Websites

- **www.chicago.metromix.com**: Comprehensive entertainment and nightlife listings from the *Chicago Tribune*. A good place to check reviews and get an early look at new bars and nightclubs.

- **www.do312.com**: Another reliable events website that clues you in to concerts, festivals, comedy, and events; its sister site, **www.rainbow.do312.com**, shares LGBTQ listings.

- **www.choosechicago.com**: Run by Choose Chicago, which is the city's tourism arm, this site gives a good overview of festivals, parades, and other events.

- **www.blockclubchicago.org**: Want to see what issues have Chicagoans all riled up? Check out this sounding board for local news, which covers everything from government corruption scandals to neighborhood news.

- **www.chicagoplays.org**: The League of Chicago Theatres runs a comprehensive site where you can search specific dates to see what's playing.

Mobile Phones

If you're from another country, it's a good bet that your cellphone will work in Chicago if you have an international plan, although we do have a fragmented cellular system so it's helpful to check with your carrier. If your phone is unlocked, you can purchase a SIM card from Best Buy or one of the mobile carriers (T-Mobile, AT&T, and Best Buy have stores downtown and throughout the city); alternatively, you can simply purchase an inexpensive, pay-as-you-go or pre-paid phone service from a company such as **TracFone** (☎ 800/867-7183; www.tracfone.com).

You can also forgo the cell phone hassle—if it is a hassle—and rely on Wi-Fi and Skype or other VOIP services to stay connected. Most hotel lobbies offer free Wi-Fi, as does Harold Washington Library, which also has computers available to the public for free.

Car Rentals

Unless you plan on taking a day trip from Chicago, I recommend that you don't rent a car. And even if you do plan on leaving the city limits during your stay, rent a car only for the day you'll need one. You're far better off sticking to public transportation, taxis, and your own two feet. Parking in Chicago is scarce and expensive, and gasoline (petrol) isn't cheap.

If you still want to rent a car, the best deals are usually found at rental-car company websites, although all the major online travel agencies also offer rental-car reservations services.

Getting There

By Plane

Chicago is served by two major airports. **O'Hare International Airport** (☎ 800/832-6352; www.flychicago.com; online airport code ORD) has long battled with Atlanta's Hartsfield-Jackson Airport for the title of the world's busiest airport. It's located about 15 miles northwest of the Loop. Though taxis are plentiful (a cab ride into town averages about $50) and ride shares, such as Uber and Lyft, are readily available, traffic can be horrendous (the ride can last an hour or more, and the longer you sit in traffic in a taxi, the higher the fare will be). If you arrive around rush hour and aren't carting around lots of luggage, I recommend taking the El (see "Getting Around," below) as it's both cheaper and faster. The 45-minute trip on the El's Blue Line from O'Hare to downtown costs $5. If you are staying around Michigan Avenue, you'll want to switch to the Red Line, which will add another 10 to 15 minutes to your trip.

Midway International Airport (☎ 773/838-0600; www.flychicago. com; online airport code MDW) is located 10 miles southwest of downtown Chicago. Although fewer airlines operate routes here, Midway is closer to the Loop and attracts more discount airlines, so you may be able to get a cheaper fare if you fly here. Taxis are available, as are Uber and Lyft, and a cab ride (about $30) from Midway to the Loop usually takes about 20 minutes (though in bad traffic, the journey can take considerably longer). Again, I recommend taking public transportation. The 20- to 30-minute trip on the El's Orange Line from Midway to the downtown area costs $2.50. *Note:* The train station at Midway is a significant walk from the terminal—without the benefit of O'Hare's moving sidewalks—so be prepared if you've got heavy bags.

Another transportation option at both airports is **GO Airport Express** (☎ 888/2-THEVAN [284-3826]; www.airportexpress.com). This shuttle's green-and-white vans service most first-class hotels in Chicago; ticket counters are located at both airports near the baggage claim (outside Customs at the international terminal at O'Hare). For transportation to the airport, reserve a spot at

your hotel (check with the bell captain). The cost is $35 one-way ($50 round-trip) to or from O'Hare and around $24 one-way (around $40 round-trip) to or from Midway. Group rates for two or more people traveling together are less expensive than sharing a cab, and children under 6 are free and ages 6 to 12 ride for $15 each. The shuttles operate from 4am to 11:30pm.

By Car
Interstate highways from all major points in the U.S. either run through or terminate in Chicago. **I-80** and **I-90** approach from the west, crossing the northern sector of Illinois, with I-90 splitting off and emptying into Chicago via the **Skyway** and the **Dan Ryan Expressway.** From Chicago, I-90 runs through Wisconsin, following a northern route to Seattle.

I-55 snakes up the Mississippi Valley from the vicinity of New Orleans and enters Chicago from the west along **the Stevenson Expressway.** In the opposite direction it provides an outlet to the southwest. **I-57** originates in southern Illinois and forms part of the interstate linkage to Florida and the South, connecting within Chicago on the west leg of the Dan Ryan. **I-94** links Detroit with Chicago, arriving in Chicago as the **Calumet Expressway** and leaving the city as the **Kennedy Expressway** en route to the Northwest.

By Train
A national rail hub, Chicago is served by a plethora of Amtrak trains. Contact **Amtrak** (☎ 800/USA-RAIL [872-7245]; www.amtrak.com) for tickets or to get the company's useful travel planner, which includes information on train accommodations and package tours.

Trains pull into **Union Station,** 210 S. Canal St. (between Adams and Jackson sts.; ☎ 312/655-2385).

Bus nos. 1, 60, 125, 151, and 156 all stop at the station, which is just west across the river from the Loop. The nearest El stop is at Clinton Street and Congress Parkway (on the Blue Line), which is 3 blocks away. **Ogilvie Transportation Center**, 500 W. Madison St., where you can catch the often-overlooked **Metra** commuter rail line (☎ **312/322-6777;** www. metrarail.com), is a 5-minute walk.

By Bus

Greyhound (☎ **800/231-2222;** www.greyhound.com), the sole nationwide bus line, has a downtown Chicago terminal at 630 W. Harrison St. (☎ **312/408-5821**). The location is not within walking distance of the major hotel zones, so you'll need to book a ride or public transportation to get to your accommodations.

Getting **Around**

By Public Transportation

The **Chicago Transit Authority** (CTA; ☎ **312/836-7000;** www. transitchicago.com) operates an extensive system of trains and buses throughout the city. Aside from walking, using public transportation is the quickest and most economical way to move about Chicago. Fares are $2.50 for the train and $2.25 for the bus ($2.50 if you pay cash), regardless of how far you go. For an additional 25¢, you can transfer to the bus or take a different 'L' ride within 2 hours. Children 6 and under ride free, and those between the ages of 7 and 11 pay $1.25 for the El and $1.10 for the bus. Seniors can also receive the reduced fare if they have the appropriate reduced-fare permit (call ☎ **312/913-3110** for details on how to obtain one, although this is probably not a realistic option for the short-term visitor).

You can get a transit card, called a Ventra card, from a vending machine at any of the train stations and choose either a single-ride ticket ($3), a 1-day ticket ($10), or a refillable, pay-as-you-go card ($5, which you can use as transit fare but only if you register the card within 90 days). You can also purchase a 3-day card ($20) at an airport vending machine. If you're going to be riding the bus and train quite a bit, I recommend

getting the 1- or 3-day card. They will quickly pay for themselves, and you don't have to worry about returning to the machine to reload when you're trying to catch a train.

Subways and elevated trains (known as the El) are generally safe and reliable, although it's advisable to avoid long rides through unfamiliar neighborhoods late at night. Most lines run 24 hours a day, though some do have limited hours, and some stations close down during the evening. The rush-hour crush occurs roughly 6 to 9:30am and 3 to 7pm.

Other than on foot or bicycle, the best way to get around Chicago's warren of neighborhoods is by riding the El. To get a gander, find a Brown line station and take it north from downtown, towards Kimball. This train line is elevated (they aren't all raised, despite the name) and, between admiring the beautiful brownstone homes and tree-lined streets, you can peer into office and residential windows and feel like bit like a voyeur.

The bus is also a convenient sightseeing tool, especially if you're staying near the lakefront, where the trains don't run. A few buses that are particularly handy for many visitors are the **no. 146 Inner Drive/ Michigan,** an express bus from Belmont Avenue on the North Side that cruises down North Lake Shore Drive (and through Lincoln Park during nonpeak times) to North Michigan Avenue, State Street, and the Grant Park museum campus; the **no. 151 Sheridan,** which passes through Lincoln Park en route to inner Lake Shore Drive and then travels along Michigan Avenue as far south as Adams Street, where it turns west into the Loop (and stops at Union Station); and the **no. 156 LaSalle,** which goes through Lincoln Park and then into the Loop's financial district on LaSalle Street. Note that many bus routes shut down late at night (when you're probably better off taking a cab anyway).

To plan your route, the CTA's website offers a trip planner that allows you to type in point A and B (or more) and it'll show you the routes you can take and the time it will take to get there. You can also download the Ventra app to your phone for planning purposes (www.ventrachicago.com). The CTA operates a useful information line that will help you find the bus or El train that will get you to your destination: ☎ **312/836-7000** or TTY 888/282-8891. The line is staffed from 7am to 7pm. Excellent CTA comprehensive maps, which include both El and bus routes, are usually available at subway or El stations, or by calling the CTA.

If you plan to head to Evanston (p 150), you'll need to take the Union Pacific line of the **Metra** commuter railroad (☎ **312/322-6777** or TTY 312/322-6774; Mon–Fri 8am–5pm; at other times, call the Transit Information Center at ☎ **312/836-7000** or TTY 312/836-4949; www.metrarail.com), out of **Ogilvie Transportation Center** at Madison and Canal streets (☎ **312/496-4777).**

By Taxi or Rideshare

Taxis and rideshares, such as Uber and Lyft, are a convenient way to get around the Loop and to get to the dining, shopping, and entertainment options found beyond downtown. With Uber and Lyft, simply download the app (find them at www.uber.com and www.lyft.com) and you can schedule a car to meet you where you are. Rates with Uber and Lyft vary. There are different options for each company that range from sharing a car with strangers to riding in a luxury car. For a standard ride that's comparable to a taxi, the fare is usually lower for a ride-share. If you're in a traffic-filled area downtown, I find it's easier to just hail a cab. That way, there's no confusion in finding which car is for you. Cabs are easy to hail in the Loop, on the Magnificent Mile and the Gold Coast, in River North, and in Lincoln Park, but if you go much beyond these key areas, you might need to call. Cab companies include **Flash Cab** (☎ **773/561-4444), Yellow Cab** (☎ **312/TAXI-CAB** [829-4222]), and **Checker Cab** (☎ **312/ CHECKER** [243-2537]).

The meter in Chicago cabs currently starts at $3.25 for the first mile and costs $2.25 for each additional mile, with a $1 surcharge for the first additional rider and 50¢ for each person after that. When leaving the airport, there's an additional fee of $4 tacked on. And should you vomit in the cab, you'll pay $50 for the cleaning fee.

By Car

Try to avoid driving in Chicago if possible; it's easier and cheaper to get around by hopping public transportation or a taxi. If you must drive, you'll find that Chicago is laid out in a grid pattern so logical that it's relatively easy to get around by car.

For information on parking in the city, see "Parking," below.

Fast **Facts**

AREA CODES The 312 area code applies to the Loop and the neighborhoods closest to it, including River North, North Michigan Avenue, and the Gold Coast. The codes for the rest of the city are 773 and 872. Suburban area codes are 847 (north), 708 (west and southwest), and 630 (far west).

B&BS **At Home Inn Chicago** (☎ 800/375-7084 or 312/640-1050; www.athomeinnchicago.com), offers a centralized reservations service for corporate housing and vacation rentals, from high-rise and loft apartments to guest rooms in private homes. Alternatively, the **Chicago Bed and Breakfast Association** (www.chicago-bed-breakfast. com) runs a website that links to various properties around the city.

BABYSITTING Check first with the concierge or desk staff at your hotel; many hotels maintain lists of reliable sitters and babysitting services. Many top hotels work with **American Child-Care Service** (☎ 312/644-7300; www.americanchildcare.com), a state-licensed and insured babysitting service that can match you with a sitter. All of its sitters are required to pass background checks, must provide multiple child-care references, and are trained in infant and child CPR. It's best to make a reservation 24 hours in advance; the office is open from 9am to 5pm. Rates are $35 per hour, with a 4-hour minimum.

BANKING HOURS Banking hours in Chicago normally run from 9am (8am in some cases) to 5pm Monday through Friday, with select banks remaining open later on specified afternoons and evenings.

CONSULATES & EMBASSIES All embassies are located in the nation's capital, Washington, D.C. Some consulates are located in major U.S. cities, and most nations have a mission to the United Nations in New York City. If your country isn't listed below, call for directory information in Washington, D.C. (☎ **202/555-1212**), or do a search on the State Department's site, www.state.gov.

The embassy of **Australia** is at 1601 Massachusetts Ave. NW, Washington, DC 20036 (☎ **202/797-3000;** http:// usa.embassy.gov. au/). There are consulates in Chicago, Honolulu, Houston, Los Angeles, New York, and San Francisco.

The embassy of **Canada** is at 501 Pennsylvania Ave. NW, Washington, DC 20001 (☎ **202/682-1740;** http:// travel.gc.ca/assistance/embassies-consulates/united-states). Canadian consulates are in a number of cities, including Chicago, Detroit, Los Angeles, New York, and Seattle.

The embassy of **Ireland** is at 2234 Massachusetts Ave. NW, Washington, DC 20008 (☎ **202/462-3939;** www.embassyofireland.org). Consulates are in Boston, Chicago, New York, San Francisco, and other cities.

The embassy of **New Zealand** is at 37 Observatory Circle NW, Washington, DC 20008 (☎ **202/328-4800;** www.nzembassy.com). Consulates are in Los Angeles and Honolulu.

The embassy of the **United Kingdom** is at 3100 Massachusetts Ave. NW, Washington, DC 20008 (☎ **202/588-6500;** http://ukinusa. fco.gov.uk). Consulates are in Atlanta, Boston, Chicago, Cleveland, Houston, Los Angeles, Miami, New York, and San Francisco.

DENTISTS The referral service of the **Chicago Dental Society** (☎ **312/836-7300;** www.cds.org) can refer you to an area dentist. Your hotel concierge may also keep a list of dentists.

DINING You'll save money on often expensive room service by going out for breakfast. Most restaurants begin serving lunch by 11:30am, some as early as 11am. Dinner service usually starts at 5pm, with the last seating at 9:30pm, as many kitchens close around 10pm.

The dress code in most Chicago restaurants is usually quite relaxed. For men, an open-collared shirt and khakis should be just fine, even in the nicer restaurants. A few places still maintain a coat-and-tie dress code.

If you're planning on doing some fine dining at an in-demand restaurant, you may need to book up to 3 months in advance. Otherwise, most restaurant reservations can be made by calling the restaurant directly during the week that you're visiting; you can always walk in, but waits may be long. Another option is to make a reservation through **www.opentable.com**, a free online reservations service.

DOCTORS In the event of a medical emergency, your best bet—unless you have friends who can recommend a doctor—is to rely on your hotel physician or go to the nearest hospital emergency room or an urgent care facility. If you prefer to stay at your hotel, the service **Chicago Express Doctors** (☎ 312/929-4492; www.chicagoexpress doctors.com) makes house calls (expect to pay a premium for the convenience). Also see "Emergencies," below.

DRINKING LAWS The legal age for the purchase and consumption of alcoholic beverages is 21; proof of age is required and often requested at bars, nightclubs, and restaurants, so it's always a good idea to bring ID when you go out. In Chicago, beer, wine, and other alcoholic beverages are sold at liquor stores and supermarkets. Bars may sell alcohol until 2am, although some nightclubs have special licenses

that allow alcohol sales until 5am. Do not carry open containers of alcohol in your car or any public area that isn't zoned for alcohol consumption. The police can fine you on the spot. And nothing will ruin your trip faster than getting a citation for DUI (driving under the influence), so don't even think about driving while intoxicated.

ELECTRICITY Like Canada, the United States uses 110–120 volts AC (60 cycles), compared to 220–240 volts AC (50 cycles) in most of Europe, Australia, and New Zealand. Downward converters that change 220–240 volts to 110–120 volts are difficult to find in the United States, so bring one with you. Some hotels may have converters available for guests to borrow.

EMERGENCIES For fire and police emergencies, call ☎ **911.** This is a free call. If it is a medical emergency, a city ambulance will take the patient to the nearest hospital emergency room. The nonemergency phone number for the Chicago Police Department is ☎ **311.** If you desire a specific, nonpublic ambulance, call **Vandenberg Ambulance** (☎ 773/521-7777). A centrally located emergency room in Chicago is **Northwestern Memorial Hospital,** 251 E. Huron St. (☎ **312/926-2000;** www.nmh. org), a state-of-the-art medical center right off North Michigan Avenue. The emergency department (☎ **312/926-5188,** or 312/926-6363 for TTY access) is located at 250 E. Erie St. near Fairbanks Court.

EVENT LISTINGS Every Thursday, the *Chicago Reader* (☎ **312/222-6920;** www.chicagoreader.com), a free weekly, publishes current entertainment and cultural listings. The Friday edition of the *Chicago Tribune* (☎ **312/222-3232;** www. chicagotribune.com) and the *Chicago Sun-Times* (☎ **312/321-3000;**

www.suntimes.com) also feature extensive event listings.

Also, see "Useful Websites," earlier in this chapter.

FAMILY TRAVEL Look for items tagged with a "kids" icon in this book. You can pick up a free copy of *Chicago Parent* magazine (www.chicagoparent.com) at any local bookstore, public library, or park district building. The magazine includes a calendar of events geared to families with kids.

GAY & LESBIAN TRAVELERS Chicago is a very gay-friendly city. The neighborhood commonly referred to as "Boystown" (roughly from Belmont Ave. north to Irving Park Ave., and from Halsted St. east to the lakefront) is the center of gay nightlife (and plenty of daytime action, too). **Gay and Lesbian Pride Week** (☎ 773/348-8243; www.chicago pridecalendar.org), highlighted by a lively parade on the North Side, is a major event on the Chicago calendar each June. You also might want to stop by **Unabridged Books,** 3251 N. Broadway (☎ 773/883-9119; www.unabridgedbookstore.com), an excellent independent bookseller with a large lesbian and gay selection. Here and elsewhere in the Lakeview neighborhood, you can pick up *Windy City Times*, a weekly print publication that's free and available in news boxes and has an extensive website as well (www.windycitytimes.com). The **Center on Halsted,** 3656 N. Halsted St. (☎ 773/472-6469; www.centeronhalsted.org), is a gay social service agency and community center that's become an informal gathering place for Boys Town residents. Inside, you'll find an organic grocery store, a rooftop terrace, and plenty of couches for hanging out and taking advantage of the free Wi-Fi.

HOLIDAYS Banks, government offices, and post offices are closed on the following legal national holidays: January 1 (New Year's Day), the third Monday in January (Martin Luther King Day), the third Monday in February (Presidents' Day), the last Monday in May (Memorial Day), July 4 (Independence Day), the first Monday in September (Labor Day), the second Monday in October (Columbus Day), November 11 (Veterans Day), the fourth Thursday in November (Thanksgiving Day), and December 25 (Christmas). Also, the Tuesday following the first Monday in November is Election Day and is a federal government holiday in presidential-election years (held every 4 years, and next in 2020). Stores, museums, and restaurants are open most holidays, except for Thanksgiving, Christmas, and New Year's Day.

HOSPITALS See "Emergencies" and "Doctors," above.

INSURANCE Although it's not required of travelers, health insurance is highly recommended. International visitors should note that, unlike many European countries, the United States does not usually offer free or low-cost medical care to its citizens or visitors. Doctors and hospitals are expensive, and in most cases will require advance payment or proof of coverage before they render their services. Good policies will cover the costs of an accident, repatriation, or death. **Europ Assistance** offers global coverage and **Generali Global Assistance (GGA)** (☎ 800/777-8710; http://us.generaliglobalassistance.com) is the agent for Europ Assistance in the United States. Some credit card policies also include travel insurance, so check your policy before booking.

Canadians should check with their provincial health-plan offices, or call Health Canada (☎ 866/225-0709; www.hc-sc.gc.ca) to find out the extent of your coverage and what documentation and receipts you must take home in case you are treated in the United States.

Travelers from the U.K. should carry their European Health Insurance Card (EHIC) as proof of entitlement to free/reduced-cost medical treatment abroad (☎ **0844/567-8196;** www.ehic.org.uk). Note, however, that the EHIC covers only "necessary medical treatment," and for repatriation costs, lost money, baggage, or cancellation, travel insurance from a reputable company should always be sought.

The cost of **travel insurance** varies widely, depending on the destination, the cost and length of your trip, your age and health, and the type of trip you're taking, but expect to pay between 5% and 8% of the vacation itself. You can get estimates from various providers through **InsureMyTrip.com.** Enter your travel cost and dates, your age, and other information for prices from more than a dozen companies.

For information on traveler's insurance, trip cancellation insurance, and medical insurance while travelling, visit www.frommers.com/planning.

INTERNET ACCESS Hotels, resorts, airports, cafes, and retailers throughout the Chicago area have gone Wi-Fi, becoming "hotspots" that offer free high-speed access or charge a small fee for usage.

In the Loop, **Millennium Park; Daley Plaza** (along Washington St. between Dearborn and Clark sts.); the **Chicago Cultural Center,** 78 E. Washington St.; and the **Harold Washington Library Center,** 400 S. State St., all have wireless access (the library also has computers that the public can use). Elsewhere in downtown Chicago, Starbucks, the sandwich chain Cosi, and McDonald's have numerous locations with Wi-Fi access, as do many locally owned bars and cafes. You can also rely on most hotel lobbies to have free Wi-Fi—and you don't have to purchase anything to take advantage.

Many Chicago hotels also have business centers equipped with computers available for guests' use.

To find more hotspots in Chicago, download an app, such as **OpenSignal** (https://opensignal.com), and you'll be online in a jiffy.

LIMOS For limo service from either O'Hare or Midway, call **Carey Limousine of Chicago** (☎ 800/336-4646; www.carey.com) or **Chicago Limousine Services** (☎ 847/962-3308; www.chicagolimo.com).

MAIL At press time, domestic postage rates were 35¢ for a postcard and 50¢ for a letter. For international mail, a first-class letter of up to 1 ounce costs $1.15; a first-class postcard costs the same as a letter. For more information, go to www.usps.com.

PARKING Parking can be a nightmare, and regulations are vigorously enforced throughout the city. The streets around Michigan Avenue have no-parking restrictions during rush hour—believe me, your car will be towed immediately. Many neighborhoods have adopted resident-only parking that prohibits others from parking on their streets, usually after 6pm each day (even all day in a few areas, such as Old Town). The neighborhood around Wrigley Field is off-limits during Cubs night games, so look for yellow sidewalk signs alerting drivers about the dozen-and-a-half times the Cubs play under lights. Downtown, there are plenty of parking garages to choose from, such as **Millennium Park Garage** (enter on Columbus Dr., 1 block east of Michigan Ave., between Monroe and Randolph sts.) and **Grant Park North and South Garages,** with one entrance at Michigan Avenue and Van Buren Street and the other at Michigan Avenue and Madison Street (☎ **312/616-0600** for all three garages). But expect to pay $23 and up for the first hour or $30 to \$40 for the full day. Your best hope to snag a deal is to download a parking app. **ParkWhiz** (www.parkwhiz.com) and **SpotHero** (www.spothero.com) allow you to put in an address, search for nearby parking, and reserve a spot. The parking spaces are in garages, hotels, condo buildings, and other lots, and sometimes even have a valet option. These services can run at less than half of the price you'll pay pulling into a garage, and since it's reserved, you don't have to worry about finding a space.

PASSES The Chicago **CityPass** gets you into the city's biggest attractions (The Art Institute, Field Museum of Natural History, Shedd Aquarium, Adler Planetarium, Museum of Science and Industry, Skydeck Chicago, and 360 Chicago Observation Deck). The cost at press time was \$106 for adults and \$89 for kids, which is about 50% cheaper than paying all the museums' individual fees. You can buy a CityPass at any of the museums listed above, or purchase one online before you get to town (www.citypass.com).

PASSPORTS For Residents of Australia: Contact the **Australian Passport Information Service** at ☎ **131-232,** or visit www.passports.gov.au.

For Residents of Canada: Contact the central **Passport Office,** Department of Foreign Affairs and International Trade, Ottawa, ON K1A 0G2 (☎ **800/567-6868;** www.cic.gc.ca/english/passport).

For Residents of Ireland: Contact the **Passport Office,** Knockmaun House, 42-47 Lower Mount St., Dublin 2 (☎ **01/671-1633;** www.foreignaffairs.gov.ie).

For Residents of New Zealand: Contact the **Passports Office,** Department of Internal Affairs, 70 Molesworth St., Wellington 6011 (☎ **0800/225-050** in New Zealand

or 04/474-8100; www.passports.govt.nz).

For Residents of the United Kingdom: Visit your nearest passport office, major post office, or travel agency, or contact the **Identity and Passport Service,** 89 Eccleston Square, London SW1V 1PN (☎ **0300/222-0000;** www.gov.uk/browse/abroad/passports).

PHARMACIES Located on the Magnificent Mile just south of the Water Tower, **Walgreens,** 757 N. Michigan Ave., at Chicago Avenue (☎ **312/664-8686;** www.walgreens.com), is open 24 hours.

SAFETY Chicago has all the crime problems of any urban center, so use your common sense and stay cautious and alert. After dark, try to stick to well-lighted streets along the Magnificent Mile, River North, Gold Coast, and Lincoln Park, which are all high-traffic areas, even late into the night. You can feel safe walking around many of Chicago's neighborhoods, too, but keep that common sense in check: stick to lighted areas, be alert, don't wear headphones, stow your phone away while walking. If you find yourself in an area that does feel unsafe, you can always call an Uber or Lyft to come and pick you up. Muggings can—and do—happen anywhere. When in doubt, ask your hotel's concierge.

The El is generally quite safe, even at night, although some of the downtown stations can feel eerily deserted late in the evening. Buses are a safe option, too, especially nos. 146 and 151, which pick up along North Michigan Avenue and State Street and connect to the North Side via Lincoln Park.

SHOPPING Shops generally keep normal business hours, 10am to 6pm Monday through Saturday. Most stores stay open late at least 1 evening a week, usually on Thursday. Certain shops, such as bookstores, stay open during the evening hours all week. Most shops and malls (other than those in the Loop) open on Sunday, usually from noon to 5pm. Malls generally stay open to 7pm the rest of the week. Note that the local sales tax, a steep 10.25%, is the highest of all major cities in the United States.

SMOKING Smoking is banned in all public buildings in Chicago, including offices, restaurants, and bars. Hotels are still allowed to have smoking rooms available.

SPECTATOR SPORTS Chicago fans are nothing if not loyal, and, for that reason, attending a home game in any sport is an uplifting experience. The **Chicago Bears** (☎ 847/615-2327; www.chicagobears.com) are not the celebrated NFL team of the past, but that doesn't stop locals from partying out at Soldier Field in freezing "Bear Weather."

The **Chicago Bulls** (☎ 312/455-4000; www.nba.com/bulls) aren't the NBA team of Michael Jordan's heyday, but on the plus side, it's a lot easier to get tickets. The NHL's **Chicago Blackhawks** (☎ 312/455-7000; www.chicagoblackhawks.com) have a devoted, impassioned following that continues to grow after multiple recent Stanley Cup wins (2010, 2013, 2015). Expect them to work themselves into a frenzy, whether there are on-ice heroics or not.

It took 108 years for the perennially losing **Chicago Cubs** (☎ 773/404-CUBS [2827]; www.cubs.mlb.com) to win a World Series, and now Chicago can't get enough of their hometown champs (for the record, they were loved even when losing). A trip out to Wrigley Field is a special Chicago experience and tickets go fast; most weekend and night games are sold out by Memorial Day. The **Chicago White Sox** (☎ 312/674-1000; www.whitesox.mlb.com) don't command the kind of loyalty the Cubs do, but do offer a newer stadium and obtainable tickets.

TAXES The United States has no value-added tax or other indirect tax at the national level. Every state, county, and city may levy its own local tax on all purchases, including hotel and restaurant checks and airline tickets. These taxes will not appear on price tags.

The local sales tax is 10.25%, the highest in the country, and the hotel room tax is 17.4%.

TAXIS See "By Taxi" in "Getting Around," earlier in this chapter.

TICKETS Theater tickets should always be obtained as far in advance as possible; if you're set on seeing the latest touring Broadway production, you might need to book up to 3 months in advance. Tickets for most major Chicago events are sold through **Ticketmaster** (☎ 800/745-3000; www.ticketmaster.com). **Hot Tix** (☎ 312/977-9483; www.hottix.org), operated by the League of Chicago Theatres, sells half-price tickets. For more information on buying discount tickets in advance, see p 129.

TIPPING Tips are a very important part of certain workers' income, and gratuities are the standard way of showing appreciation for the services provided. (Tipping is certainly not compulsory if the service is poor!)

In hotels, tip bellhops at least $1 per bag ($2–$3 if you have a lot of bags) and tip the chamber staff $1 to $2 per day (more if you've left a disaster area). Tip the doorman or concierge only if he or she has provided you with some specific service (for example, calling a cab for you or obtaining difficult-to-get theater tickets). Tip the valet-parking attendant $2 to $5 every time you get your car.

In restaurants, bars, and nightclubs, tip service staff and bartenders 15% to 20% of the check, tip checkroom attendants $1 per garment, and tip valet-parking attendants $2 to $5 per vehicle.

As for other service personnel, tip cab drivers 15% of the fare; tip skycaps at airports at least $1 per bag; and tip hairdressers and barbers 15% to 20%.

TOILETS You won't find public toilets or restrooms on the streets. Your best bet for good, clean facilities are hotel lobbies, bars, fast-food restaurants, museums, malls, libraries, and department stores. Restaurants and bars in heavily visited areas may reserve their restrooms for patrons.

TOURIST OFFICES **Choose Chicago** is the name of the official tourism arm of Chicago, and the **Visitor Information Center** is in Macy's, 111 N. State St. (☎ 312/567-8500; www.choosechicago.com).

TOURIST TRAPS & SCAMS If you're planning on attending sporting or concert events, beware of ticket scalpers. Buy your tickets in advance from a legitimate source, as many of the tickets sold by scalpers are counterfeit.

TOURS **Chicago Architecture Center,** 111 E. Wacker Dr. (☎ 312/922-3432; www.architecture.org), leads insightful tours by foot, bus, boat, and train, peeking in and around the design and history of Chicago's marvelous buildings. Tours run $15 to $55.

The **Chicago Greeter** (☎ 312/744-8000; www.chicagogreeter.com) is a free program matching tourists with local Chicagoans who serve as volunteer guides. Visitors may request a specific neighborhood or theme (everything from Polish heritage sites to Chicago movie locations), and a greeter gives them a 2- to 4-hour tour. (Greeters won't escort groups of more than six people.) Specific requests should be made at 10 days in advance, but "InstaGreeters" are also available on for regular downtown and

neighborhood tours (Millennium Park, the Loop, Uptown and the Riverwalk) Fridays, Saturdays and Sundays. See chicagogreeter.com for starting points and times.

Chicago Trolley Company (☎ 773/648-5000; www.chicagotrolley.com) offers guided tours on a fleet of rubber-wheeled "San Francisco–style" trolleys that stop at 14 spots around the city. You can stay on for the full ride or get on and off at each stop. An all-day hop-on, hop-off pass costs $39 adults, $19 kids 3 to 11.

Started in 1935, **Wendella Sightseeing Boats** (☎ 312/337-1446; www.wendellaboats.com) operates a 75-minute tour along the Chicago River and a 1½-hour tour along the river and out onto Lake Michigan, pointing out architectural highlights along the way. Tours run April to October. Tickets $39 adults, $35 seniors, $18 kids 3 to 11.

TRAVELERS WITH DISABILITIES Thanks to provisions in the Americans with Disabilities Act, most public places in Chicago comply with disability-friendly regulations. Almost all public establishments, including restaurants, hotels, and museums, provide accessible entrances and other facilities for those with disabilities.

Pace (☎ 312/836-7000; www.pacebus.com), the company that runs bus routes between Chicago and its suburbs, offers paratransit services throughout the area for travelers with disabilities. Visitors must be registered with a similar program in their home city.

Several of the Chicago Transit Authority's (CTA's) El stations on each line are fitted with elevators. Call the CTA at ☎ 312/836-7000 for a list of those that are accessible. All city buses are equipped to accommodate wheelchairs. For specific information on facilities for people with disabilities, call or write the **Mayor's Office for People with Disabilities,** 121 N. LaSalle St., Room 1104, Chicago, IL 60602 (☎ **312/744-7050** for voice; 312/744-4964 for TTY; www.cityof chicago.org/disabilities).

Horizons for the Blind, 125 Erick St., Crystal Lake, IL 60014 (☎ **815/444-8800;** www.horizons-blind.org), is a social-service agency that can provide information about local hotels equipped with Braille signage and cultural attractions that offer Braille signage and special

tours. **Illinois Relay** (www.itactty.org/illinois-relay) enables hearing- and speech-impaired TTY callers to call individuals or businesses without TTYs 24 hours a day. Calls are confidential and billed at regular phone rates. Call TTY at ☎ **800/526-0844** or voice 800/526-0857.

WEATHER For current weather conditions, check the weather online at www.wgntv.com (television's Channel 9), www.chicago tribune.com, or www.weather.com.

Chicago: **A Brief History**

1673 French explorers Marquette and Joliet discover portage at Chicago linking the Great Lakes region with the Mississippi River valley.

1779 Afro-French-Canadian trapper Jean Baptiste Point du Sable establishes a trading post on the north bank of the Chicago River. A settlement follows 2 years later.

1818 Illinois is admitted to the Union as the 21st state.

1833 Town of Chicago is officially incorporated, with little more than 300 residents.

1837 Chicago is incorporated as a city, with about 4,000 residents.

1847 *Chicago Tribune* begins publishing.

1848 The 96-mile Illinois and Michigan Canal is opened, linking the Great Lakes with the Mississippi River.

1865 Chicago stockyards are founded.

1871 Great Chicago Fire burns large sections of the city; rebuilding begins while the ashes are still warm.

1882 The 10-story Montauk Building, the world's first skyscraper, is erected.

1885 William Le Baron Jenney's nine-story Home Insurance Building, the world's first steel-frame skyscraper, is built.

1886 Dynamite bomb explodes during a political rally near Haymarket Square, causing a riot in which eight policemen and four civilians are killed, and almost 100 are wounded.

1892 The city's first elevated train goes into operation.

1893 Chicago hosts its first World's Fair, the World's Columbian Exposition.

1900 The flow of the Chicago River is reversed to end the dumping of sewage into Lake Michigan.

1919 "Black Sox" bribery scandal perpetrated by eight Chicago White Sox players stuns baseball.

1920–33 During Prohibition, Chicago becomes a "wide-open town"; rival mobs battle violently throughout the city for control of distribution and sale of illegal alcohol.

1924 University of Chicago students Nathan Leopold and Richard Loeb murder 14-year-old Bobby Franks. They are defended by famed attorney Clarence Darrow in the "Trial of the Century."

1929 On St. Valentine's Day, Al Capone's gang murders seven members of rival George "Bugs" Moran's crew in a Clark Street garage.

1931 Al Capone finally goes to jail for tax evasion.

1933 Chicago Mayor Anton Cermak, on a political trip to Miami, is shot and killed during an attempt on president-elect FDR's life.

1933–34 Chicago hosts its second World's Fair, "A Century of Progress."

1934 Bank robber and "Public Enemy Number One" John Dillinger is gunned down by police outside the Biograph Theater.

1942 Scientists, led by Enrico Fermi, create the world's first nuclear chain reaction under Stagg Field at the University of Chicago.

1953 Chicago native Hugh Hefner starts publishing *Playboy* (the original Playboy Mansion was located in Chicago's Gold Coast neighborhood).

1955 Richard J. Daley begins term as mayor; he is widely regarded as the "last of the big-city bosses."

1966 Civil rights leader Martin Luther King, Jr., moves to Chicago to lead a fair housing campaign.

1968 Anti–Vietnam War protests in conjunction with the Democratic National Convention end in police riot and a "shoot to kill" order by Mayor Richard J. Daley.

1974 The 1,454-foot Sears Tower is completed, becoming the tallest building in the world.

1979 Jane Byrne becomes the first woman elected mayor of Chicago.

1983 Harold Washington becomes the first African-American mayor of Chicago.

1986 The Chicago Bears win their only Super Bowl.

1989 Richard M. Daley, the son of the long-serving mayor, is elected mayor.

1996 The city patches up its turbulent political history by hosting the Democratic National Convention, its first national political gathering in 3 decades. That same year, a young community organizer named Barack Obama is elected to the Illinois State Senate.

2001 Chicago's second airport, Midway, opens a new $800-million terminal.

2004 Barack Obama is elected to the U.S. Senate. That same year, Millennium Park, Chicago's largest public works project in decades, opens at the north end of Grant Park.

2007 Spertus Institute, 610 S. Michigan Ave. (☎ **312/322-1747;** www.spertus.edu), added another example of eye-catching architecture to Michigan Avenue with the opening of its new building dedicated to Jewish history, art, and culture in fall 2007.

2008 Barack Obama is the first African American elected to the United States presidency.

2011 Richard M. Daley's last day in office is May 16, making him the longest-serving mayor in Chicago history (he was first elected in 1989). Mayor Rahm Emanuel takes office.

Chicago's **Architecture**

Although the Great Chicago Fire leveled almost 3 square miles of the downtown area in 1871, it did clear the stage for Chicago's emergence as the country's preeminent city for architecture.

To learn more about Chicago's architecture, take a tour by foot, boat, or bus with the Chicago Architecture Center (see p 18, ②.)

Richardsonian Romanesque (1870–1900)

Boston-based architect Henry Hobson Richardson (1838–86) explored designs and forms based on the Romanesque (a style distinguished by rounded arches, thick walls, and small windows). His structures, ranging from university and civic buildings to railroad stations and homes, were marked by a simplification of form and the elimination of extraneous ornament and historical detail—features that set his buildings apart from others of the period. The overall effect depended on mass, volume, and scale.

Richardsonian Romanesque buildings share the following characteristics:

- A massive quality
- Arched entrances
- Squat towers
- Deeply recessed porches and doorways
- Heavy masonry exteriors
- Use of rough-hewn stone

Richardson's **John J. Glessner House,** 1800 S. Prairie Ave. (1885–87), an elegant urban residence, still stands on Chicago's Near South Side. It had a strong influence on Chicago architects, notably Louis Sullivan. The most celebrated example of Richardson's influence is the **Auditorium Building,** 430 S. Michigan Ave. (1887–89), an important early example of the emerging Chicago skyscraper.

Early Skyscrapers (1880–1920)

Experimentation with cast and wrought iron in the construction of

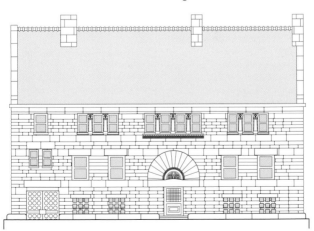

John J. Glessner House.

interior skeletons in the 1840s eventually allowed buildings to rise to previously unattainable heights. Following the Great Chicago Fire of 1871, important technical innovations—involving safety elevators, electricity, fireproofing, foundations, plumbing, and telecommunications—combined with advances in skeletal construction to create a new building type, the skyscraper. These buildings were spacious, cost-effective, efficient, and quickly erected—in short, the perfect architectural solution for Chicago's growing downtown.

Solving the technical problems of the skyscraper did not resolve how the building should look. Most solutions relied on historical precedents, including decoration reminiscent of the Romanesque, with its rounded arches; Gothic, with its spires, pointy arches, and even buttresses; or Beaux Arts, with its exuberant classical details. Louis Sullivan (1865–1924) was the first to formalize a vision of a tall building based on the parts of a classical column. His theories inspired the **Chicago school of architecture,** examples of which still fill the city's downtown.

Features of the Chicago school include:

- A rectangular shape with a flat roof
- Tripartite divisions of the facade similar to that of a classical column with a base (usually of two stories), shaft (midsection with a repetitive window pattern), and capital (typically an elaborate terra-cotta cornice)
- Exterior expression of the building's interior skeleton through an emphasis on horizontal and vertical elements
- Large windows made possible by the development of load-bearing interior skeletons; particularly popular are Chicago windows (large windows flanked by two narrow ones with double-hung sashes)
- Use of terra-cotta, a light and fireproof material that could be cast in any shape and attached to the exterior, often for decoration

A good example of the development of the skyscraper is the **Monadnock Building,** 53 W. Jackson Blvd. (1889–93). Built in two parts, the northern section has masonry load-bearing walls, while the southern half has a steel frame clad in terra-cotta. To support its 17 stories, the northern section has 6-foot-thick walls at its base. The entire building is notable for its clean, contemporary lines.

An excellent example of the Chicago school is the restored **Reliance Building** (p 11, ❸), now The Alise (p 32), 1 W. Washington St. (1891–95), outstanding for its use of glass and decorative spandrels (the horizontal panel below a window).

A good later example (taller and more technically sophisticated than its earlier incarnations) that most visitors will pass at some point during their visit is the Tribune Tower 435 N. Michigan Ave. (1923–25). As I type its being transformed from a hallowed newspaper hall into, you guessed it, condos.

Second Renaissance Revival (1890–1920)

Buildings in this style show a definite studied formalism. A relative faithfulness to Renaissance precedents of window and doorway treatments distinguish it from the much looser adaptations of the Italianate, a mid-19th-century style that took its inspiration from Italian architecture. Scale and size, in turn, set the Second Renaissance Revival apart from the first, which occurred from about 1840 to 1890. The grand buildings of the Second Renaissance Revival, with their textural richness, well suited the tastes of the wealthy Gilded Age.

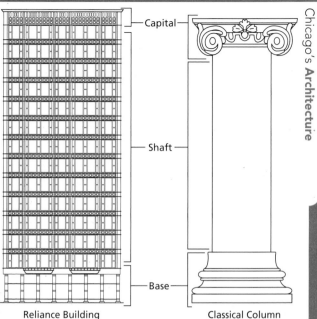

Reliance Building

Classical Column

Reliance Building and Classical Column.

The style was used primarily on the East Coast but also in Chicago for swank town houses, government buildings, and private clubs.

Typical features include:

- A cubelike structure with a massive, imposing quality

- Symmetrical arrangement of the facade, including distinct horizontal divisions

- A different stylistic treatment for each floor, with different column capitals, finishes, and window treatments on each level

- Use of rustification (masonry cut in massive blocks and separated from each other by deep joints) on the lowest floor

- The mixing of Greek and Roman styles on the same facade (Roman arches and arcades may appear with Greek-style windows with

straight-heads or pediments, a low-pitched triangular feature above a window, door, or pavilion)

- A cornice (a projecting feature along the roofline) supported by large brackets

- A balustrade (a railing supported by a series of short posts) above the cornice

A fine example of this style is the **Chicago Cultural Center** (p 21, ⑪), 78 E. Washington St. (1897), originally built as a public library. This tasteful edifice, with its sumptuous decor, was constructed in part to help secure Chicago's reputation as a culture-conscious city.

Beaux Arts (1890–1920)

This style takes its name from the Ecole des Beaux-Arts in Paris, where a number of prominent American architects (including H. H. Richardson

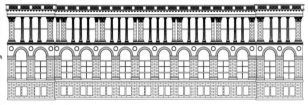

Chicago Cultural Center.

and Louis Sullivan) received their training, beginning around the mid–19th century. These architects adopted the academic principles of the Ecole, which emphasized the study of Greek and Roman structures, composition, and symmetry, and the creation of elaborate presentation drawings. Because of the idealized origins and grandiose use of classical forms, the Beaux Arts in America was seen as the ideal style for expressing civic pride.

Grandiose compositions, an exuberance of detail, and a variety of stone finishes typify most Beaux Arts structures. Particular features include:

- A pronounced cornice topped by a parapet (a low wall), balustrade, or attic story

- Projecting pavilions, often with colossal columns grouped in pairs

- Windows framed by free-standing columns, a sill with a balustrade, and pediments or decorative keystones (the central stone of an arch)

- Grand staircases

- Grand arched openings

- Classical decoration: freestanding statuary, ornamental panels, swags, and medallions

Chicago has several Beaux Arts buildings, exhibiting the style's main features. Examples include the oldest part of the **Art Institute of Chicago,** Michigan Avenue at Adams Street, which was built for the World's Columbian Exposition in 1893; and the gleaming white **Wrigley Building,** 400–410 N. Michigan Ave. (1919–24), which serves as a gateway to North Michigan Avenue.

Art Deco (1925–33)

Art Deco is a decorative style that took its name from the Exposition Internationale des Arts Décoratif, held in Paris in 1925. One of the first widely accepted styles not based on historic precedents (the jazzy style embodied the idea of modernity), it influenced all areas of design, from jewelry and household goods to cars, trains, and ocean liners.

Art Deco buildings are characterized by a linear, hard edge or an angular composition, often with a vertical emphasis and highlighted with stylized decoration. The Chicago zoning ordinance of 1923, which required setbacks in buildings above a certain height to ensure that light and air could reach the street, gave Art Deco skyscrapers their distinctive profile. Other important features include:

- An emphasis on geometric form

- Strips of windows with decorated spandrels, adding to the sense of verticality

- Use of hard-edged, low-relief ornamentation around doors and windows

- Frequent use of marble and black and silver tones

- Decorative motifs of parallel straight lines, zigzags, chevrons (see illustration at left), and stylized florals

Chicago Board of Trade.

Prime examples of this period include the **Chicago Board of Trade,** 141 W. Jackson Blvd. (1930), with its dramatic facade and pyramidal roof; and **135 S. LaSalle St.** (1934), which has a magnificent Art Deco lobby.

International Style (1932–45)

The International Style was popularized in the United States after 1932 through the teachings and designs of Ludwig Mies van der Rohe (1886–1969), a German émigré who taught and practiced architecture in Chicago after leaving the progressive Bauhaus school of design. Structures all shared a stark simplicity and vigorous functionalism, a definite break from historically based, decorative styles. Interpretations of the "Miesian" International Style were built in most U.S. cities as late as 1980. In the 1950s, erecting an office building in this mode made companies appear progressive. In later decades, after the International Style was a corporate mainstay, the style took on conservative connotations.

Features of the International Style as popularized by Mies van der Rohe include:

- A rectangular shape

- Frequent use of glass

- Balance and regularity, but not symmetry

- Horizontal bands of windows

- Windows meeting at corners

- Absence of ornamentation

- Clear expression of the building's form and function (the interior structure of stacked office floors is clearly visible, as are the locations of mechanical systems, such as elevator shafts and air-conditioning units)

- Placement, or cantilevering, of building on tall piers

Some famous Mies van der Rohe designs are the **Langham Hotel** (p. 140); 330 N. Wabash, once known as the IBM Building and now AMA Plaza (1972); **Chicago Federal Center,** Dearborn Street between Adams Street and Jackson Boulevard (1959–74); and **860–880 N. Lake Shore Dr.** (1949–51). Interesting interpretations of the style by Skidmore, Owings & Merrill, a Chicago firm that helped make the International Style a corporate staple, are the **Sears Tower** (1968–74), now begrudgingly (sometimes) called Willis Tower, and the **John Hancock Center** (1969; p 36, **4**)—two impressive engineering feats rising to 110 and 100 stories, respectively.

Postmodern (1975–90)

Postmodernism burst on the scene in the 1970s with the reintroduction of historical precedents in architecture. With many feeling that the office towers of the previous style were too cold, postmodernists began to incorporate classical details and recognizable forms into their designs—often applied in outrageous proportions.

Postmodern skyscrapers tend to include:

- An overall shape (or incorporation) of a recognizable object not necessarily associated with architecture

- Classical details, such as columns, domes, or vaults, often oversize and used in inventive ways

- A distinctive profile in the skyline

- Use of stone rather than glass

190 S. LaSalle St. (1987) brings the shape of a famous Chicago building back to the skyline. The overall design is that of the 1892 Masonic Temple (now razed), complete with the tripartite divisions of the Chicago school. An extremely modern interpretation of a three-part skyscraper—but you have to look for the divisions to find them—is **333 W. Wacker Dr.** (1979–83;

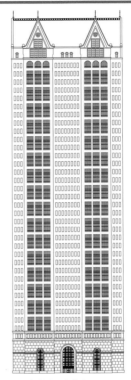

190 S. LaSalle Street.

p 30, ❸), an elegant, green-glass structure that curves along a bend in the Chicago River.

Toll-Free Numbers & Websites

Airlines

AER LINGUS
☎ 800/474-7424 in the U.S.
☎ 01/800-600 in Ireland
www.aerlingus.com

AIR CANADA
☎ 888/247-2262
www.aircanada.ca

AIR NEW ZEALAND
☎ 0800/737-000 in New Zealand
www.airnewzealand.com

AMERICAN AIRLINES
☎ 800/433-7300
www.aa.com

BRITISH AIRWAYS
☎ 800/247-9297
☎ 0844/493-0787 in Britain
www.britishairways.com

DELTA AIR LINES
☎ 888/750-3284
www.delta.com

FRONTIER AIRLINES
☎ 801/401-9000
(note: not toll-free)
www.flyfrontier.com

QANTAS
☎ 800/227-4500 in
the U.S.
☎ 13 13 13 in Australia
www.qantas.com

SOUTHWEST AIRLINES
☎ 800/435-9792
www.southwest.com

UNITED AIRLINES
☎ 800/864-8331
www.united.com

Car-Rental Agencies

ALAMO
☎ 844/354-6962
www.alamo.com

AVIS
☎ 800/633-3469 in the
continental U.S.
☎ 800/TRY-AVIS
(879-2847) in Canada
www.avis.com

BUDGET
☎ 800/218-7992
www.budget.com

DOLLAR
☎ 800/800-4000
www.dollar.com

ENTERPRISE
☎ 855/266-9289
www.enterprise.com

HERTZ
☎ 800/654-3131
www.hertz.com

NATIONAL
☎ 844/382-6875
www.nationalcar.com

THRIFTY
☎ 800/THRIFTY
(847-4389)
www.thrifty.com

Major Hotel & Motel Chains

BEST WESTERN INTERNATIONAL
☎ 800/780-7234
www.bestwestern.com

COMFORT INNS
☎ 877/424-6423
www.choicehotels.com

CROWNE PLAZA HOTELS
☎ 877/2CROWNE
(227-6963)
www.crowneplaza.com

EMBASSY SUITES
☎ 800/EMBASSY
(362-2779)
www.embassysuites.com

FOUR SEASONS
☎ 800/819-5053
www.fourseasons.com

HILTON HOTELS
☎ 800/HILTONS
(445-8667)
www.hilton.com

HOLIDAY INN
☎ 800/HOLIDAY
(465-4329)
www.ichotelsgroup.com

HOWARD JOHNSON
☎ 800/221-5801
www.hojo.com

HYATT HOTELS & RESORTS
☎ 800/233-1234
www.hyatt.com

INTERCONTINENTAL HOTELS & RESORTS
☎ 877/424-2449
www.ichotelsgroup.com

LOEWS HOTELS
☎ 855/401-8122
www.loewshotels.com

MARRIOTT HOTELS
☎ 888/236-2427
www.marriott.com

OMNI
☎ 888/444-OMNI (6664)
www.omnihotels.com

RADISSON HOTELS INTERNATIONAL
☎ 800/967-9033
www.radisson.com

RITZ-CARLTON
☎ 800/542-8680
www.ritzcarlton.com

SHERATON HOTELS & RESORTS
☎ 800/325-3535
www.sheraton.com

WESTIN HOTELS & RESORTS
☎ 800/937-8461
www.westin.com

Index

See also Accommodations and Restaurant indexes, below.

Photo **Credits**

p i, left: Rudy Balasko; p i, middle: DiegoMariottini / Shutterstock.com; p i, right: John Gress Media Inc / Shutterstock.com; p ii, top: Tinnaporn Sathapornnanont / Shutterstock.com; p ii, second-from-top: Tahaa / Shutterstock.com; p ii, middle: Courtesy of EnjoyIllinois.com; p ii, second-from-bottom: Courtesy of Merz Apothecary; p ii, bottom: Artesia Wells/ Shutterstock.com; p iii, top: Courtesy of Heaven on Seven; p iii, second-from-top: Courtesy of Old Town School of Folk; p iii, middle: Mike Liu / Shutterstock.com; p iii, second-from-bottom: Courtesy of The Ritz; p iii, bottom: EQRoy / Shutterstock.com; pp viii—pp 1: Peter James Sampson / Shutterstock.com; p 4, top: Steve Broer / Shutterstock.com; p 4, bottom: f11photo; p 5, top: MaxyM / Shutterstock.com; p 5, bottom: Felix Mizioznikov; p 6, top: Sean Pavone; p 6, bottom: Tupungato / Shutterstock.com; p 7, top: Thomas Barrat; p 7, bottom: Michel Curi; p 8, top: amslerPIX; p 8, bottom: elesi / Shutterstock.com; p 9: Tinnaporn Sathapornnanont / Shutterstock.com; p 11, top: VICTOR TORRES; p 11, bottom: Capture Light / Shutterstock.com; p 12, top: AnjelikaGr / Shutterstock.com; p 12, bottom: Nathalia Segato Tomaz / Shutterstock.com; p 14, top: Peter James Sampson / Shutterstock.com; p 14, bottom: MaxyM / Shutterstock.com; p 15: Brad Hagan; p 17: f11photo; p 21: Vlad G; p 24: YaromirM; p 25: Lou Stejskal; p 26: Felix Lipov / Shutterstock.com; p 27: Tahaa / Shutterstock.com; p 29: ssuaphotos; p 30, top: FeyginFoto; p 30, bottom: Manuel Hurtado / Shutterstock.com; p 31: R Scapinello / Shutterstock.com; p 32: Tinnaporn Sathapornnanont / Shutterstock.com; p 35: James Kirkikis / Shutterstock.com; p 36: Sorbis / Shutterstock.com; p 37, top: Michael Rosebrock / Shutterstock.com; p 37, bottom: Kristopher Kettner / Shutterstock.com; p 39: Sergei Gussev; p 40: anjanettew; p 41, top: Mike Liu / Shutterstock.com; p 41, bottom: Mustafa and Aziza; p 43: Mark B. Schlemmer; p 44: Allan Henderson; p 45: Benny Mazur; p 47, top: Mr.TinDC; p 47, bottom: ocean yamaha; p 49: Courtesy of EnjoyIllinois.com; p 51: Banalities; p 53, top: Marlin Keesler; p 53, bottom: Lou Stejskal; p 55, top: stephen boisvert; p 55, bottom: David Wilson; p 56: Deatonphotos / Shutterstock.com; p 57, top: maggiejp; p 57, bottom: Courtesy of Chicago History Museum; p 59: Courtesy of EnjoyIllinois.com; p 61, top: Zagalejo ; p 61, bottom: Victor Grigas; p 62, top: Courtesy of the Robey/ Adrian Gaut; p 62, bottom: Nate Burgos; p 63, top: Edsel Little; p 63, bottom: Jeremy Atherton; p 65, top: Danita Delimont Creative / Alamy Stock Photo; p 65, bottom: Adam Alexander/ Enjoyillinois.com; p 66, top: Hrag Vartanian; p 66, bottom: Manuel Hurtado; p 67, top: Zol87; p 67, bottom: EQRoy / Shutterstock.com; p 69: Courtesy of Merz Apothecary; p 70: Courtesy of French Market/Lana Neiman; p 75, top: Courtesy of Antique Resources; p 75, bottom: Lou Stejskal; p 77, top: Courtesy of Unadbridged/ Shane Khosropour; p 77, bottom: Courtesy of Women and Children First/ Mike Rivera; p 79: Courtesy of Stock Mfg; p 82: Courtesy of Galleria Andersonville/ Elliot Ferris Foley; p 84: Courtesy of Lego; p 85: Artesia Wells/ Shutterstock.com; p 87: Big Joe / Shutterstock.com; p 89: Amy Tseng / Shutterstock.com; p 90: alisafarov / Shutterstock.com; p 92: JW_PNW / Shutterstock.com; p 93: David Wilson; p 95: Courtesy of Heaven on Seven; p 96: Courtesy of Bistro Campagne; p 100, top: Courtesy of Avec/ John Philp; p 100, bottom: Courtesy of Bistronomic/ Kailley Lindman; p 101: Courtesy of Chicago q; p 102: StockPhotoAstur / Shutterstock.com; p 105: Courtesy of Piccolo Sogno/ Eugene (Huge) Galdones; p 107: Courtesy of Old Town School of Folk; p 108: Courtesy of Three Dots/ Melissa_Hom; p 113: Courtesy of Ace Bounce; p 114: Courtesy of Big Star/ Cassie Stadnicki; p 115: Courtesy of Parson's/ Clayton Hauck; p 116: Courtesy of Andy's Jazz Club; p 117: Courtesy of House of Blues; p 119: Mike Liu / Shutterstock.com; p 125, top: Seth Tisue; p 125, bottom: jphilipg; p 126: Chicago's North Shore Conventions & Visitors Burea; p 127: elesi / Shutterstock.com; p 130: Pamela Brick / Shutterstock.com; p 131: Courtesy of The Ritz; p 136: Courtesy of ACME/Leigh Loftus; p 137, top: Courtesy of Athelitic Hotel/ Thomas Hart Shelby; p 137, bottom: Courtesy of Conrad/ Neil Burger; p 138: Courtesy of The Four Seasons; p 139: Courtesy of The InterContenintal; p 140, top: Courtesy of JW Marriott; p 140, bottom: Courtesy of Lowes/ Nathan Kirkman; p 141: Courtesy of Robey/ Adrian Gaut; p 142, top: Courtesy of The Talbott/ Zach Dobson; p 142, bottom: Courtesy of St. Jane/Emilie1980; p 143, top: Courtesy of The Wit/ Maxim Cantiru; p 143, bottom: Courtesy of Viceroy/ CHRISTIAN HORAN PHOTOGRAPHY; p 144: Courtesy of Waldorf Astoria/ John Muggenborg; p 145: EQRoy / Shutterstock.com; p 147: Jennifer Morrow; p 148: Nagel Photography / Shutterstock.com; p 149: Brian Crawford; p 151: Eugene Moerman; p 152: Teemu008; p 153: David Prahl; back cover: Felix Mizioznikov.

Before, During, or After your use of a Frommer's guidebook... you'll want to consult

FROMMERS.COM

FROMMERS.COM IS KEPT UP-TO-DATE, WITH:

NEWS
The latest events (and deals) to affect your next vacation

BLOGS
Opinionated comments by our outspoken staff

FORUMS
Post your travel questions, get answers from other readers

SLIDESHOWS
On weekly-changing, practical but inspiring topics of travel

CONTESTS
Enabling you to win free trips

PODCASTS
Of our weekly, nationwide radio show

###
Hundreds of citie

Valuable, offbea

Smart trav